MORE THAN THEY BARGAINED FOR

Books by Isadore Barmash

The Chief Executives
For the Good of the Company
Great Business Disasters
More Than They Bargained For
Net-Net
The Self-Made Man
Welcome to Our Conglomerate—You're Fired
The World Is Full of It

More than They Bargained For

The Rise and Fall of Korvettes

Isadore Barmash

Lebhar-Friedman Books/Chain Store Publishing Corp.

With gratitude to Barbara Miller, Executive Editor, Thea Beckwith, Senior Editor, and Joseph Morse, Director of Marketing, all of Lebhar-Friedman Books, for their forbearance with the author and their great skills on behalf of this book. And to Arnold D. Friedman, the late founder of Lebhar-Friedman, Inc., who was enthusiastic about this project—the first book telling the entire story of Korvettes—but unhappily did not live to see it published.

Copyright © 1981, Chain Store Publishing Corp.,
425 Park Avenue, New York, N.Y. 10022

Printed in the United States of America.

Library of Congress Cataloging in Publication Data:
Barmash, Isadore.
    More than they bargained for.
    Includes index.
    1. Korvettes—History.   I. Title.
HF5465.U6K673   381'.45'000974   81-17124
ISBN 0-86730-553-9   AACR2

Book Design: D. Beckwith

5   4   3   2   1

*To all those who labored
to make the dream come alive*

Contents

Introduction

On Christmas Eve 1980, the lights went out in the few remaining Korvettes stores of a once proud and powerful fifty-eight-store chain. It was a pathetic end to one of the brightest, most exciting chapters of American enterprise since World War II.

Few business sagas, few examples of American initiative from humble beginnings, have been as impressive or as inspiring as that of Korvettes in its first two decades. And few have been as dismaying, even as shocking, as that pioneer discounter's decline in its latter years. What seemed incomprehensible to so many was the hard-to-swallow fact that the astonishing success and the equally astonishing failure had all been compressed to the time span of one generation.

After World War II, like Ford Motors, Singer sewing machines, A.&P., and the Levitt houses, Korvettes helped spawn a new way of life for Americans. The retail chain brought appliances to hungry consumers at prices they could afford more easily than at department or appliance stores. It opened the first giant suburban stores in the East which led to the immense air-controlled complexes of today. It greased the way for the eventual demise of the Fair Trade laws, end-running the nationally branded, price-maintaining producers, demurring when slapped by a summons and repeating the process with others. Court hearings became a comic, hand-slapping affair by sheepish judges, a page out of Gilbert and Sullivan's boisterous "Trial by Jury." And by its willingness to flout the rules, to try new things (perhaps because its executives didn't know that it couldn't be done), Korvettes became a seminal force. It showed the way to even larger discounters and traditional department-store operators who nowadays admit they owe some of their expertise and survival tactics to the *shtick* and the gaffes of the company which began in 1948 as a second-floor luggage shop with three inexperienced employees.

It's not too hard to imagine some hundred thousands of families in the fifties and sixties on Long Island, the 100-mile-long peninsula sometimes called "Fertile Acres" (for people, not agriculture) in this manner: A Ford or Chevrolet on the driveway outside of their Levitt home, a Singer sewing machine in the den, frozen and packaged foods from A.&P. in the kitchen, and a houseful of appliances bought from Korvettes. That's not to say that lots of household durables weren't bought from Sears, Macy's, Abraham & Straus, and Friendly Frost. But, somehow, because of its youthful verve, its spirit and willingness to joust with the giant windmills, Korvettes became identified with the burgeoning young families which exploded from the return of the war veterans from Europe and the Pacific. Later, too, as it grew into a major retail chain, senior citizens took to it as Korvettes became one of the first retailers to give shoppers sixty-five years and older a 10 percent discount one day a week.

Despite its great success—hailed by Harvard University, *Time* and *Business Week* magazines, every major newspaper in the East, and the most flattering compliment of all—imitation or adaptation—Korvettes fell into decline, attrition, and, at this stage, demise.

What happened?

Was it, as Eugene Ferkauf, Korvettes' founder, told this writer, the hazards of being first? "You know what happened to the pioneers, don't you?" he asked me.

"What?"

"They were shot down by the Indians," Ferkauf said with a wry smile.

Maybe.

But his remark, like many newspaper and magazine pieces that have attended the startling turn in Korvettes' fortunes, is simplistic. The widespread coverage has uniformly asserted that the company failed to keep up with changing public tastes and changing economics. This charge might have been true if Korvettes had had a consistent ownership and a consistent management, providing a straight line of supervisory responsibility that could be directly blamed for either not enough flexibility or too much. As at least five mergers attest, that was hardly the case.

The real story behind Korvettes' amazing success and dramatic decline is a people story. The company's life force rose and ebbed, as the protagonists and antagonists moved on and off the stage. They were alternately geniuses and fools, hedonists and ascetics, skilled merchants and nincompoop merchants, prodigies and dunces, quite often all in the same person. They lucked in and they lucked out. And there was something else, too, a truism that frequently dogs American business—when the founder goes, so does the momentum, unless by sheer good judgment or sheer luck new skilled professional managers are brought in at the top by the new owners. That was one of Korvettes' biggest obstacles. While Ferkauf, peripatetic, endlessly mobile, an odd combination of an ideas man and a hands-on man, created lots of his own problems, no one who succeeded him had either the talent or the freedom—or the opportunity—to function, to swing as he did.

Over its more than thirty years, Korvettes reverberated like a spinning top to one merger after another and to the new faces that were brought into the top suite. It was like a super ocean-liner that charts five different courses under as many captains and arrives nowhere. But meanwhile, even the sharpest critics must admit, it hit some great ports.

Accordingly, this book will tell the Korvettes' story through the people who swaggered across its stage. It will use two time frames, the past and the present, in an attempt to give both the story as it happened and the hindsight observations of some of its main actors. Interspersed will be the remarks of other retailers who lived through it all as competitors or mere observers, so that the reader will also be able to get the reaction of outsiders as well as insiders.

There are many figures who will appear prominently in our story:

Eugene Ferkauf, of course. The handsome, complex New Yorker, both introspective and garrulous, founded Korvettes on the basis that if he made $1 profit on a refrigerator he would make millions of dollars if he sold millions of refrigerators. And he did, too.

Eve Nelson, who for a while became the most famous woman in American retailing after Dorothy Shaver at Lord & Taylor. She was Korvettes' first sales promotion expert, founded its Eve Nelson cosmetics departments as well as a house-to-house cosmetics business that for a short time appeared would rival Avon's success. She was the first woman to join the Korvettes team.

William Willensky, one of the original "Gene's boys," an expert at smelling out the most likely sites for new stores. As such, he was directly responsible for finding the locations which turned Korvettes into such a growth company and diverting it to such exotic out-of-town markets as Detroit, Chicago, and St. Louis, where it bombed. But then who's perfect?

David Rothfeld, generally considered the most skillful merchant of phonograph records, tapes, and audio equipment in the country. Shy and introspective, he became a Korvettes' vice president and gave the company its greatest contribution of profits because he sensed early how technology would change the musical scene and the way people relaxed at home. Ferkauf called him "the absolutely greatest merchant I ever met." But for the first fifteen years Rothfeld never earned more than $20,000 a year because Ferkauf never boosted his own $25,000 salary. Ditto for the other "Gene's boys."

Charles C. Bassine, a brilliant, domineering, apparel-company owner who became a father figure to Ferkauf. Tired physically and emotionally, Ferkauf was convinced to sell out to Bassine's Spartans Industries. A great pleasure-seeker but a tough businessman with an effulgent manner, Bassine insisted when he assumed ownership in 1967 that Korvettes had to raise its markups to make more money and he did.

Leonard Blackman, who became Korvettes' president under Bassine and caused some of Ferkauf's stalwarts, including Eve Nelson, to depart. Some devoutly claimed that Blackman, who lasted only briefly, was one of the worst presidents of a retail company in history. On the other hand, the compact, dapper Blackman with the trim mustache unquestionably had been put in an untenable position be-

cause he had little administrative talent and insufficient
background for the job.

Arthur Cohen, Bassine's son-in-law. A quiet, keen,
smooth guy long considered one of the nation's sharpest real-
estate entrepreneurs, he built his company, Arlen Realty &
Development Corporation, into the largest developer and
owner of shopping centers in America. Bassine stiff-armed
the board into approving the sale of Spartans-Korvettes to
Arlen Realty, weathering a storm of protest on nepotism with
a verbal thumbing of the nose.

David Brous, a charismatic Macy's merchant whom
Cohen tapped as Korvettes' upteenth president. But Brous
also got the title of chief executive officer, a prime badge of
authority which inspired him to drag in a bunch of department store types to help him upgrade Korvettes. It would,
he proclaimed, "fill the gap between discount and department stores." Only no such gap developed. Discounters
were all trading up and department stores were trading
down. So it was probably true that you can take the man out
of Macy's but not Macy's out of the man. Nonetheless, the
fast-talking Brous was a good motivator although not such a
hot administrator and was probably the most dynamic figure
at Korvettes since Ferkauf. Only, as circumstances showed,
it didn't work out.

Joseph A. Ris, who became chairman of Korvettes in
May 1980, perhaps the month and the year of the company's
final ignominy. The bluff, straightforward Ris, a Frenchman
who became an American citizen in the early sixties, nonetheless bears some of the complex traits developed in the
Byzantine politics of Europe where he was an international
vice president for Chrysler Motors. The new French owners
of Korvettes tapped him to head their first American subsidiary but he had an impossible job. How can you try to
recapture the clout of a rapidly fading company while you

have to close more than forty stores, fire 8,000 people, and fend off over 600 hopping-mad creditors?

An excellent "people's" man who quickly achieved credibility, Ris confused people when he often said "no" when he meant "yes" and "maybe" when he meant "practically never." Yet, he staved off bankruptcy and even at the twilight said he hoped to eke out a surviving nucleus of ten to twelve stores. It's ironic that the two most dominant, complex personalities in an entire gallery of such people came at the very beginning and very end of the Korvettes' saga.

Those are some of the people who will march across our word-stage but there are others, too.

How important are people, individuals in business? After all, don't the fortunes of companies resound to changes in the economy, both local and national, the automobile business being a prime example?

People are unquestionably the difference between success and failure in business, as in politics, the arts, and education. The right man or woman in the right situation is capable of working wonders. Observes Carl Menk, chairman of Boyden Associates, "Four, five, or six guys set policy for a company and the company reflects their style. But one guy, it's usually the chief executive, sets the style for the rest of them. And the company goes or doesn't go based on that." But the proper support, environment, chemical rapport must come from the owning management. In most cases of company failure, the backup falters late in the game. In Korvettes' case, the momentum slipped right after the founder left, appeared later to revive, and then completely vanished.

Yet for years executives have pointed to national economic downturns as the reasons for waffles in their company's fortunes. True? Not for everyone. Edward S. Finkelstein, chairman and chief executive of R. H. Macy &

Co., declares, "We don't figure the national economy into our marketing plan. We decide what we want to stress, mostly those things we do best and that perform best for us. Within the plan, regardless of the economy, are upside and downside alternatives." Joseph E. Brooks, chairman and chief executive officer of Lord & Taylor, adds: "Every retail management has to take a position, a marketing stance based on its perception of the market and the company's place in it. You stick with that position for several years, and make sure that you and your people do everything possible to make that position strong. You don't worry about competition—your competition is what you did yesterday and the day before. If it doesn't work, then you study it and find out why and adjust it. And then work like hell to make that succeed."

Early in 1981, Caldor Inc., the Connecticut-based discounter, was acquired by the Associated Dry Goods Corporation, for the stunning sum of $313 million. What made Caldor so attractive and successful? its chairman and founder, Carl Bennett, was asked. "I'm often asked why is Caldor so successful when so many others have failed," he said. "Two things come to mind immediately. One, we remained a regional chain and as our controls succeeded we expanded our territory gradually into other areas. And two, we were fortunate in being able to pick people who feel about the company the same as I have felt. All these people have grown with the company—and I think that's the answer. People. Loyal, dedicated people—and we are fanning out. We have the two basic ingredients—money and people—to do it."

Perhaps the reason behind Korvettes' decline and demise is ultimately a subjective judgment. However it is inescapably true that, in its two decades of great success— many freely predicted that it would become another Sears

Roebuck—Korvettes spawned not only the discount revolution which now accounts for almost half of the country's general merchandise sales, but taught many traditional department store and specialty store managements what do do and what not to do. In its heyday, Korvettes' drive, innovativeness, and esprit were the talk of the town, the industry, and much of the country. In the post middle years of the twentieth century, Korvettes was a shining hour in American enterprise.

Here is the Korvettes story.

PART ONE

The Great Early Years
(1948-1956)

1.
Simple Is Beautiful

A warm, sunny day in June 1948. It is scarcely three years since the two-ocean war has ended. But in mid-Manhattan, a few blocks from Grand Central Terminal, many people on the busy streets still bear the look of relief, of happy anticipation. Peacetime is sweet, even if things are a bit grinding. If many of the basics and luxuries that make life pleasant are still lacking, there's always hope.

A scrappy little man in the White House battles Congress. He demands price ceilings on housing and authority to channel more of the nation's building materials into houses priced at $10,000 or less. But the construction lobby blocks him, preferring industrial construction despite the urgent need for at least five million new homes. Then prefabricated developers spring up. William J. Levitt's purchase of a 1,500-acre Long Island potato farm on which to build his basic, prototypical $6,990 houses will soon be greeted by a flood of customers. One thousand young couples will wait outside his tiny sales office, many for several days, some subsisting only on coffee and doughnuts.

If housing is the biggest need, there are still many others: appliances, furniture, housewares, not to mention cars and clothes. Slowly, massively, industry gears up, shifting from its wartime production, to meet the demand. It even issues new products: electric knife sharpeners; lighter, more efficient vacuum cleaners; and the first, seven-inch Dumont television sets. Industry begins to supply not just what the war veterans and their brides need, but what the almost one million babies a year that the war veterans have enthusiastically produced need now and will need soon. Disposable diapers may still be two decades away but for that, at least, mothers can be patient. Life, it's clear, is moving ahead at a fast clip, but right now, consumers' desires greatly exceed supply.

At 6 East 46th Street, three anxious faces glance at the open second-floor doorway in the dilapidated building.

Only the sounds of the busy street come up. They stare at each other, swallowing uncertainly. A photo taken a bit later in the tiny, 400-square-foot store shows them in typical storekeeper stances, eyes extended hopefully into space, with two of them wearing sheepish smiles. They look as if they were thinking, *What the hell are we doing here? What do we know?*

But it's not as though they haven't prepared, prepared their heads off. And prayed.

Eugene Ferkauf is a tall, athletic-looking man of twenty-seven with blondish hair, blue eyes, and ceaseless energy. His father, Harry, successfully operates two luggage shops nearby and has wanted Gene to run one of them. Gene did, too, after a year of studying accounting at City College; he spent some five years in the store before enlisting in the

Army in 1942 at age twenty-two. Five years later when he returned from the Philippines, Harry kept after him, reminding the young man that he has responsibilities, after all—a wife, Estelle, whom he met while canoeing in Prospect Park in Brooklyn and married in 1945, and a baby daughter, Barbara. And, insisted Harry, how many young men who are discharged from the Army can walk right back into a job with entrepreneurial opportunity?

Gene doesn't deny any of it. But for months after his return, his head has been working out some very specific but different plans. He had discussed his ideas with Joe Zwillenberg, a childhood friend from Brooklyn. Meeting again by chance in the Philippines, they had watched a baseball game one day in Rizal Stadium and pledged to go into business together when the war ended. It was not an unusual promise. Many young men, away from home and lonely but warmed by the friendship with another guy in similar circumstances, are convinced that they want the relationship to continue afterward. Few carry it out.

Home again, Gene's eye is on discounting. He likes the excitement of its competitive edge. Not that there's anything new about discounting. Plenty of small jewelry stores around Manhattan had successfully carried on sideline operations by placing on their counters catalogs from which shoppers could order well-known brands of appliances and housewares at cut prices. But Gene was more interested in the practice of another retailer he had heard about.

Operating in lower Manhattan before the first World War, that legendary merchant had sold luggage, too, but in an unusual manner. He would solicit the purchasing agents of companies in the neighborhood and sell them all manner of leather goods at "keystoned" prices, that is, for double an initial 10 percent for overhead and double his cost price. He did very well that way because he maintained a good inventory, gave personal service, and still underpriced his competition. But it is another technique the merchant used that fired Ferkauf and reverberated in his imagination.

As he circulated around the offices nearby, the ingenious retailer left stacks of business cards; whoever picked one up would receive, as the card promised, a 25 percent discount. The idea, of course, was to lure not just executives and buyers but secretaries, salesmen, clerks, janitors, *et al,* to the tiny store in the neighborhood. It was "membership" discounting in its infancy; it made the merchant rich, as well as those others who were alert enough to imitate him.

As he waits impatiently this first morning, Gene Ferkauf has more than one qualm. Why discounting instead of traditional selling? Why didn't he keep Harry happy by going into the family business? Maybe he should have stayed in accounting? But he has already answered those questions a hundred times to himself and his family. He wants to make it on his own, not latch on to Harry's success. He loves business, even though Harry had urged him for years to consider some other endeavor and convinced Gene to spend lots of time in museums and at concerts to enrich his mind. As for discounting, he sees it as the best way to get a fast start and to sustain a business that will please many customers.

He stirs. The other two, just an elbow length away in the crowded quarters, stare at him. Gene shrugs. They have done everything they could think of to prepare. With his own savings of $4,000—he hasn't asked Harry for a dime—he has ordered leather goods from the same suppliers that he has dealt with in his father's store. He cut the markup to price them at a one-third discount. And Gene's inventory is not just leather items—he has displayed and stocked housewares, such as mixers, juicers, and steam irons; jewelry, such as pins, earrings; and clocks, shavers, lighters. And luggage, of course. Almost everything bears brand names that the public wants. Will there be trouble because of it? Maybe. Will the public grab them? They'd better. To ensure it, Gene and the two others have taken the cue, a few in fact, from that other retailer of almost half a century ago.

In the past month, Gene and his associates have deposited discount cards in the offices of many large companies in the area. Poring through the telephone books, they had extracted more than a hundred company names that seemed right. Each man took his share of names and visited the offices, leaving the cards that announced their opening and offered the 33⅓ percent price reduction on fair-traded, branded goods. In addition, each left sheets listing specific branded products with the discounted prices, preferring, when possible, to post them on the office bulletin boards. And they have talked, bragged, boasted to friends, acquaintances, and other businessmen about their venture.

Joseph Zwillenberg smiles back at Gene. He is tall, too, and athletic. They have been friends since childhood and Joe has helped Gene as friends should. Ferkauf, more intuitive than skilled in such things as math, would never have passed them in high school without Joe's help. Even though Joe was Brooklyn College's boxing champion somehow he has always deferred to Gene whom he had decided long ago had the instincts of a leader. Joe, who will be responsible for accounting and just about anything else he is called upon to do, appreciates Ferkauf's gracious gesture in naming the new business. It will be "E. J. Korvette," "E" for Eugene, "J" for Joe, and Korvette for the Canadian sub-chaser whose trim lines Gene has always liked. Joe fervently wishes for success if for Ferkauf's sake alone. He has put everything into it, not the least of it the first, vast hope of a young man with nothing but the future in sight.

Murray Beilenson, in turn, stares at the two of them. A chunky, smiling man, he is impressed by the others, Ferkauf's drive and energy, Zwillenberg's figure-sense and devotion. As the first "employee," Murray has his inner doubts. He knows something about retailing, having worked in his father's stationery and luncheonette business before enrolling in New York University. He also knows something about moving merchandise from managing warehouses during the war in Europe for the Quartermaster Corps. But he senses—or is it only wishful thinking?—that he and they may be on the ground floor of something important. But where, where are the customers?

There is a sound of footsteps on the stairway. A man enters. A customer. As he glances curiously around and the three wait with bated breath, there are some more footsteps. Then a group comes in. Then individuals. The proprietors, eager to please, have set up a bar in a corner from which they will offer a drink after a sale is made. This is done, repeatedly. But soon the three are so busy there's no time for any more amenities. During the noon hour, the tiny store is crowded shoulder to shoulder. People are waiting to get in. Once Ferkauf laughs out loud in sheer joy and disbelief. Joe and Murray can't help it. They join in. All day long the place is jammed. By the end of the first week, they have sold out to the last piece of merchandise.

Everything was simple. Maybe too simple. But it worked in the first flush of success and even for quite a few years after that. What Ferkauf-Zwillenberg-Beilenson did—and those friends and others who soon joined them—was to cut through all the frills and red tape that bound up all the other retailers. They didn't know any better. They were prodigies who were precocious beyond all the small merchants because they were supercharged with energy and ambition and didn't know enough to become complicated.

After the first week's business cleaned them out, Ferkauf

drove in every day from his home in Queens to a distributor, loaded up his car, and unloaded it outside the store. If one brand sold out, it was promptly replaced by another at the same reduced price. Everyone had to have strong back muscles. Who handled the daily deliveries? Ferkauf, Zwillenberg and Beilenson, and George Yellen, the newest employee. Up the flight of stairs, down the flight of stairs. Even customers, caught up in the excitement of those days, helped to carry up the merchandise so that they could buy what they wanted. It was a sort of family party, with even the wives helping out.

It was all bare-bones simple. Forget warehouse, reserve storage area, free deliveries, layaways, credit. In a small 20 by 20-foot loft, they did about $1 million in sales that first year. That works out to about—what?—*$2,500 per square foot?* Impossible. But true. Inventory was turned over more than thirty times that first year and a few years after that, at least five times faster than other retailers. Small was good, simple was better. There was the beauty of economy, of miniature scale. That first Christmas in 1948, they rang up $13,000 daily. They were stunned, almost falling over one another in unbelieving joy. Had they—had they discovered the pot of gold that everyone had just overlooked?

Yes, they had, but it was exhausting success. Simple could be tough, too. That Christmas, they closed every evening at six and then worked through most of the night bringing up merchandise, lining it up, getting things arranged to open at eight the next morning. When they did open, it was a delight. Most days, shoppers had already lined up all the way around the block waiting to get in. And Korvettes wasn't even advertising yet! The day sped along in a flurry of movement, talk, and excitement. They were so busy in the tiny, crowded space that often there wasn't enough time or room to get to the cash register so that the four of them crammed the money into their pockets until they could ring it up.

Not all the faces that showed up were those of customers. Here and there through the montage they saw some hard, skeptical, professional faces. Jack Straus of Macy's or Bruce Gimbel of you-know-what-store sent "shoppers." Or even Sidney Solomon of Abraham & Straus, that wiliest of merchants. This new pimple on the butt of New York retailing couldn't, after all, be entirely overlooked. Maybe if ignored it would just subside. But how could you ignore a hole-in-the-wall that brought a block-long line every morning? It was like the promotion of S. Klein-on-the-Square on Washington's Birthday with its $9 TV sets to the first three, hardy customers. Only this was every day.

The manufacturers' salesmen came too. They were drawn to 46th Street like giddy moths to a fiery bulb. Sticking their heads through the door, they received a snarling, harassed welcome and a shouted order. A merchandise-ordering system? Who had the time or the know-how for it? Every housewares salesman in the vicinity showed up. Should he be lucky enough to appear in the midst of a particular shortage—and there were plenty of them—he could get an immediate verbal order for a gross or two or three. But it had to be shipped almost instantly. So the rep dashed back down the steps, found the nearest telephone, and shouted in his order. There was never even any discussion, any haggling over price, at least in those days. The boys would just hustle up the merchandise from the truck and sell it at their usual low markup.

But that cumbersome, laborious system taught them a lesson. In the next few Korvettes stores, Ferkauf and his team ensured that there would be sidewalk chutes permitting shipments to be unloaded into the basement from which merchandise would be trundled up as needed. But the pavement chutes produced some unexpected moments. Sometimes, a cat, a dog, and once a woman pedestrian came shooting down into the basement. Simple was good but sometimes hazardous.

Manufacturers didn't take the heavy discounting of their goods without complaining. Almost from the beginning, the fledgling merchants were slapped with summonses and injunctions. The regular department and appliance stores were complaining and the fair-trade laws were enforced in the courts. When that happened, the brand involved was dropped and replaced by another, similar brand. The press began to enjoy the game of hit-and-run. One day, there would be sober stories of Korvettes being hauled into court. The next day or two, there would be a feature story about the excitement consumers felt about buying a GE refrigerator or Thor or Bendix appliance at $25 to $75 less than the department stores charged. Advertise? Korvettes didn't need it. The publicity and the resulting word of mouth was more than enough.

Simple continued even when things got a bit more complex. Intrigued by what Ferkauf and his boys were doing, some appliance suppliers opened up their lines to Korvettes. It proved a windfall, and not only for the added volume. Until that point, Korvettes had been primarily a luggage discounter; appliances were sold as a convenience to shoppers. Now, with the opening of the pipelines for major appliances, new horizons unfolded for Gene and his boys.

But the addition of the appliance line necessitated change. Can you put a refrigerator on your back and carry it up from the basement? No. But the Korvettes' people soon met the challenge and kept the simplicity. They placed an order for a carload to get the quantity discount but stocked the shipment in the distributor's warehouse. As one was sold, the distributor would ship the appliance directly to the consumer. The first year's servicing would be the distributor's responsibility and Ferkauf absorbed the delivery and full servicing charges in the selling price. He claimed that he sold Thor washing machines at only $3 above cost. The shoppers loved it. A carload, or about sixty Thor machines, walked out of the tiny store every week.

Whether by naiveté or design, the budding business maintained its competitive thrust by holding to a principle that the other retailers in town would have choked on. Korvettes' team operated strictly on the estimated dollar profits it could make on a sale. The other merchants had a percentage markup. That meant that they were restricted to a profit level arbitrarily foisted on the cost of merchandise. Korvettes had no set markup but adhered simply to a formula of some dollars in profit on top of the cost of goods and the store's overhead. That gave Korvettes not only great flexibility but also the opportunity to "deal" with any salesman who popped in. Money flowed into the store which Korvettes rented at only $550 a month. Titles meant little and job descriptions meant nothing. Everyone did everything whenever something needed doing and whatever it was.

The lure to the public was simple—the one-third reduction off everyone else's prices. But the approach was wildly free-wheeling. For every person who came in with his or her "membership card," two cards were given out. Catalogs were distributed in the thousands and taken back to company offices and examined hand-to-hand for the best buys. The proximity of Grand Central Terminal was fortuitous. Ferkauf had become friendly with many people who worked at the ticket windows and on the trains; they patronized *his* store and brought in their friends. An informality existed between customers and those who waited on them. Was it because those who flocked in saw ordinary guys, just like themselves, eagerly hustling and smilingly breaking their backs to make a success of it? No doubt about it.

Through all, Ferkauf kept hiring his old friends and friends of friends to staff the ever-growing business. Within a few years, Korvettes' personnel resembled a picture of Ferkauf's graduating class of Brooklyn's Tilden High School. But in those early months and years, it was one at a time, until by 1950, a year before the second store was opened, there were twelve of them working, jostling, kibitzing in that second-floor hole-in-the-wall.

"I was the thirteenth man to work for Korvettes but I almost didn't join them," said Mel Friedman, who eventually became the company's executive vice president and later its vice chairman of the board. "I knew Gene from Brooklyn. He lived at Rockaway Parkway and Church Avenue and I lived at Rockaway Parkway and Willmohr. I didn't know him as well as Joe Zwillenberg, though.

"Joe and I were supposed to have a double-date with a couple of girls but he was late that night. I waited and soon he came along with Ferkauf. I knew him just vaguely. I was a jewelry salesman for a New York retail chain at that time but, of course, I heard what he and Zwillenberg were doing. Joe introduced me and Ferkauf said, right off the bat:

" 'How'd you like to come and work with me?'

"I said, 'I heard all about your store. I don't know. I'm making $125 a week. Can you match it?'

" 'I'll give you $60 a week.'

" 'You're kidding.'

"Ferkauf shrugged. 'I'm not kidding,' he said. 'I can't pay any more right now. You'll work your ass off—but you'll never have so much fun again in your life. You'll be so goddam excited you'll run to work every day. We're on to something, maybe something real big. Later on, you'll make a lot of money. Look, don't be a schmo. Come in and learn the business.'

"I said, 'I need a couple of weeks. I've been thinking of starting my own discount business. But now I don't know. Give me some time—'

"Gene stared me straight in the eye and said, 'I need guys right now, not later. If you can't start on Monday, forget it.'

"So I started that Monday in June 1950. But I wanted to quit after a week. You could go nuts in that place. It was dark, painted a funny green, and the floor creaked. Everybody was banging into everyone else. At night, after the store closed, we used to hang around and nail back the floor boards. There wasn't a single college graduate in the crowd. They say that Ferkauf hired the first fifty guys who showed up for jobs but he didn't. He had to have a sense of rapport with everybody he hired, like he could see it in their eyes. So what he got was a bunch with the greatest work ethic I've ever met. Yet every item of expense was watched closely. I never worked in such a place. But it was too much. I kept hanging on until Christmas Eve when I was going to tell Gene that I was quitting to open my own store with a friend.

"But he surprised me. When I went to pick up my paycheck that night, I got it plus three bottles of whisky and a separate envelope. Inside was a bonus—a check for $1,500. That wasn't bad for 1950. So I decided to stay. I couldn't leave a man like that."

The simple way continued even when Ferkauf, inevitably, decided that the momentum of the store was so explosive that a second store was essential. A former cafeteria, at 42nd Street and Third Avenue, perhaps seven city blocks away, turned up in 1951. The new site held 3,000 square feet, seven times as much space as the original store, and its

$15,000-a-year rental was more than double. But the second Korvettes took off like a rocket. That same year, Ferkauf moved the first store downstairs so that there were two street-level stores.

But, while there was one coordinated office to handle invoices, each store bought goods separately to ensure that it would be in stock to keep up with the huge demand that just seemed to keep mounting. In 1951, Korvettes had total sales of $5 million and an enviable pre-tax profit—for a discount operation—of 10 percent on its sales. The business was a smash success, without having taken a single line of advertising. Everyone was impressed, even the detractors. Not just by the volume of business but by the great spirit of the thirty employees on the payroll as of 1952, even though the critics liked to poke fun at them as "the corner boys," or "those stickball players."

But, by the end of four years in business, Ferkauf seriously began thinking of some big expansion plans. And that was when the "simple" days ended.

2.
The Unbelievable Luck

E very once in a while, they slow down. Catching their breath, or puffing on a cigarette, or grabbing a chocolate seltzer from the sidewalk peddler outside, they stare at each other and exchange sheepish grins of delight. "Do you believe this?" they ask one another. No, it is not to be believed.

It is, in fact, astonishing.

There they are. Gene, Joe, Murray, George, Mel, Dave, Bill, Leo, and all the rest. Running, jumping, darting, yelling, exhorting, schlepping but somehow sustaining two of the busiest, most profitable stores in the metropolitan area and now, the boys' newest venture, the first suburban store in White Plains, New York, on Mamaroneck Avenue facing Alexander's. Three stores in four years. Each one knocking out 10 percent profits before the tax collector gets his.

But that's not what staggers the mind. What does is how fortune smiles on them, like a protective angel.

Whatever they do wrong comes out right. Whatever they forget turns out better forgotten. Whatever they neglect someone does for them. Every misjudgment becomes self-correcting. Every unfortunate development manages to right itself. And just when they get to feeling they don't know anything, they turn around and find the pros studying them like they know plenty.

Who could believe it? Take, for instance:

Each store bought for its own needs, defying the principle of the economics of bulk buying. Yet inventories hewed closely to sales long before the advent of computerized point-of-sale systems.

While it was scarcely true that Ferkauf had "emptied the poolrooms" of Brooklyn and the Lower East Side to staff his stores, as carpers insisted, his personnel policy was more visceral than cerebral. Yet everyone seemed to find his own level. Those with the genes to be executives became executives. Those happy to remain salesmen graciously did so. Ferkauf gave everyone a chance by letting them all work their tails off but no harder than he worked himself.

Shoplifters should have walked away with the stores. But in spite of the loose security they didn't. The boys developed a sixth sense about theft. But even they were amazed when they apprehended a bulky young woman who almost, just almost, walked out with an expensive portable typewriter strapped around her thighs.

Take White Plains. Who ever heard of signing a lease for a store with four feet of water in the basement? They did. The landlord promised to remove the water and have a sump pump on hand if it returned. Still if the water returned it might have ruined a lot of inventory. But the water never came back.

White Plains again. The local merchants raised lots of complaints about the appearance of a shabby, dark, discount store in their handsome, bucolic area. But aside from the fact that the store did well after a slow start, White Plains merchants themselves began coming in to buy goods from Korvettes. The chain's big orders allowed the small competitors to buy more cheaply than they could from their own jobbers.

Take the fourth store. Late in 1952, Ferkauf sits fuming in his "office." Ferkauf never had a real office; he is too busy for one. When he needs a place to sit and think, he uses a tiny chamber normally occupied by the controller. At that particular moment, he is unhappy and frustrated. The Brenninkmeyers, a tough bunch of Dutch merchants who later bought the Ohrbach's chain, had been trying to sell their unprofitable Manhattan store to Gene but had been abrasive and haughty. He had broken off the discussion and walked out. Now, the phone rings. "Yah?" he snarls into it. It is a broker with a little store available on 48th Street between Fifth and Sixth Avenues. Can he come right over? He does and finds it is opposite the Rockefeller Center skating rink. He grabs it, the Dutchmen forgotten.

Or the fifth store. Which led to the sixth store.

Would anyone in his right mind take a store facing a cemetery? They did. It was another small site, a rundown former Grand Union supermarket in Hempstead, Long Island. Even those who thought Ferkauf was a genius and the rest of his guys near-geniuses had their doubts. Would people ignore the forlorn sight across the street to come in for bargains? But they did—and how. The first year, the drab little Long Island store rang up $5 million in sales and $500,000 in pre-tax profits. All that despite the nearby presence of the mammoth Abraham & Straus store in Hempstead, a hundred times as big as Korvettes and the second largest suburban store in the United States.

And the sixth store. One day, Ferkauf is on the way to the Hempstead store and passes a huge potato field in the Carle Place section of Westbury, Long Island. It is flat, accessible to the main roads, and has enough acreage for a large, really large store and lots of parking space. Are they big enough, smart enough, lucky enough for the big venture? Everyone discusses it together and the decision is yes they are! Certainly they are already doing very well. Five holes-in-the-wall racking up sales of $20 million with a pre-tax net of 10 percent. Are they actually ready for a real department store of three floors and a staggering 90,000 square feet? If anyone had any qualms, he swallowed them. Momentum, after all, was momentum. Who could deny it?

And now the benign presence that always seemed to smile on them broke out in a big grin.

As fate would have it, the boys happened to meet a couple of eager, hungry developers much in their own mode. Kane and Schwartz had been building houses on Long Island just like Levitt, but on a smaller scale. They were anxious to expand. Could they build a store of that awesome size in the potato field, with carpets, the latest in store fixtures, escalators yet, top illumination and parking for 500 cars? Of course they could! But once they heard that, the boys decided that it would be just great to open in time for Christmas that year.

Was it possible? Normally, it took at least a year and often two to open the doors of a new store of that size once the lease was signed. But Kane and Schwartz, swept up in Korvettes' enthusiasm, did it all in five months. It was a stunning coup. But what was stunning, too, was the response the Carle Place store received from the moment it opened. Shoppers surged in like a dammed river let loose. They clustered five- and six-deep around the cash registers and there was some rough jostling which required the assistance of the security people. Employees could only cope automatically with the customers who surged around them. Matters got out of hand many times. Ferkauf, Zwillenberg, and Beilenson manned registers, helping the 115 employees. When the day ended, they counted the receipts and found that they had transacted a remarkable $138,000 that first day. If that were to continue all year, they would ring up $385 per square foot of gross space, three times what the giant A.&S. store did not far away. Between December 2, the day the store opened, and Christmas Day, more than $2 million in sales were recorded. It was, again, not to be believed.

It was time now to take some stock, not of merchandise but of what had been accomplished, why, and what to do next.

Six stores and not a failure in the lot. Five were tiny, of course, ranging from 3,000 to 10,000 square feet. The newest, 90,000 square feet, was a giant and for the first time allowed Korvettes to carry apparel. They were a smashing success, a bunch of untrained merchants who while learning on the job had taught the pros a few things. But their real advantage lay not so much in their ability to learn, which was good enough at least in those days, but in their cohesiveness, their motivation, their devotion. They were like spokes in a wheel that turned readily enough, groaning, sputtering, shooting sparks but moving, *moving*. They were all in their mid- and late twenties or early thirties, with eager, young wives willing to let them put in long hours at not-the-greatest pay.

Ferkauf ran the show. He had occasional staff meetings at which everyone was invited to express his opinions, but mostly his contacts were one to one and about as informal as possible. He would drop in on one of his store managers without warning, sometimes pre-studying the store and its competition. "So how are we doing?" he would ask. "And how are we going to do better?" Often he would stand by the cash registers with Joe or Murray or Bill and carefully observe who bought what. Sometimes, he would even ask the customer why. All in all, though, as the company grew, it became more difficult to contact the peripatetic founder. He was always on the move. He owned all the stock in the first two stores outright. The White Plains ownership was shared, with Ferkauf the main principal. But, with the fourth store, the one facing Rockefeller Center in Manhattan, he altered his procedure. He announced that it would be a cooperative, capitalized at $350,000 and he invited everyone to participate. He himself contributed $25,000 which would be the voting stock with the others having non-voting but profit-earning right. About 100 employees, suppliers, and friends came up with $150,000 which was sufficient to get the store going. Within a year, they had earned 30 percent on their investment.

Later, Ferkauf claimed that he paid "extremely generous" salaries. But some of the boys didn't recall it that way. Yet they spoke with enthusiasm about the bonuses he paid. And that was probably what he meant by the big "salaries." He decided quite early in the game that by limiting salaries, he could keep the operation tight and functioning properly; instead of high regular salaries he paid generous bonuses. By the end of 1963 when the then five-store chain had sales of $20 million and a pre-tax net of $2 million, Korvettes paid out bonuses to all employees ranging from $1,000 to $60,000.

Some middle executives would get bonuses ranging from $5,000 to $10,000. It was not unusual for Ferkauf, his face reddening as he listened, to take calls from grateful wives thanking him for "your generosity."

Yet, despite the great success that drew raves from everyone, he had a conservative streak, perhaps inherited from some ancestor whose instinct was to worry if things go too well. That caution was one factor in his decision to make the 48th Street store a cooperative. It didn't need outside funds, he knew. But he didn't want the Rockefeller Center unit to siphon off any of the other stores' assets. He wanted each to stand on its own foundation. That conservatism, too, was the reason they maintained a shabby, nondescript loft in Manhattan that served as Korvettes' headquarters. The bare, tasteless surroundings testified loudly to an apparent desire not to capitalize upon or glorify the success. What that unwittingly also did was to support the lingering sense of ridicule in which Korvettes was held by its conventional competitors, even much later when it became considerably bigger and more prominent. The antidote to that probably would have been a display of greater self-respect on the principle that no one values you as highly as you seem to value yourself.

At any rate, there they were, six years after their start, a muscular little chain of six stores. The discussion got hot and heavy around the stores, with or without Ferkauf. Should they go for the big type of store and drop the five small ones? Should they, in the face of the continuing summonses and subpoenas, shift to non-branded goods, or goods with their own label? Should they expand to the surrounding states? Go public? Merge? All of them? Or what?

William Willensky was a lieutenant in the New York City fire department when he became the fifteenth man to join Korvettes.

In 1950, he ran into Mel Friedman, the thirteenth man, who raved about the new discount store even though he had almost quit after a month. "Mel," Bill Willensky recalled thirty years later, "was a very enthusiastic guy. Besides, I wasn't crazy about staying in the fire department. He induced me to join Ferkauf and I did the same year. What did I do when I got there? Everything was very informal so I became head of the camera department because photography was my hobby."

Willensky, who later became president of Korvettes and at the same time one of the most aggressive real-estate experts in retailing, found those early years "very exciting. The public was just beating a path to our door and we did lots of business. The huge volume covered a lot of mistakes. The mistakes, at least in those years, were in diversification. We went into the furniture business and we weren't right for it. We were a cash-and-carry house with great turnover. With furniture, our fine inventory turnover disappeared and it ate up our capital and our profits went down. That was later, of course, but it was our first mistake.

"All the same," he went on, "people responded enthusiastically to our main appeal—price. We also had a free advertising umbrella, our fight against the fair trade laws. A lot of people followed it sympathetically. The publicity made us white knights and we got a lot of good-will out of it. We hired a bunch of lawyers who carried the fight for us. I think it is a statement of fact that we were the forerunners in getting fair trade kicked out. But then we lost our umbrella although by then we were doing our own advertising."

Real estate, he found, was his real forte, perhaps because of his fire-department background or because he realized, as Ferkauf did, that the company's potential had to be realized by opening more stores. "But, then," he recalled, "we all seemed to fall into our own niches. Gene was the merchant prince. Mel was the operations guy. George was labor relations. Joe was in economics and the accounting end. Murray was in hard lines. A lot of the original fifteen to twenty guys didn't move into top executive spots but stayed as department managers.

"We were doing great, writing like $1,000 a square foot. But we had an ongoing problem. Our merchandise mix was very limited and some were very vulnerable. The conventional stores could easily have knocked us off on our limited assortment. We had no ready-to-wear up until Carle Place. But they didn't. I guess they just thought some kind of wind would just knock us out and blow us away.

"But that was one main reason we went into the Carle Place store," he went on, with a fond smile of recollection. "We had to get that store open in a hurry to latch on to the holiday business. We almost didn't make it, at that. I was the store manager and I still recall that my people were putting merchandise on the shelves with plaster coming down on their heads. Out on the parking lot, there was a tow truck pulling cars out of the mud. And in the midst of it, there were all the regulars, working their cans off and kibitzing like it was one big family working together.

"Well, the crowd that waited outside that Carle Place store when it opened was something to shout about. People drove twenty-five miles to buy a giant size of washing-machine powder at fifty or seventy-five cents below everybody else. That was just a symbol, though. We were really synonymous with value at that time. That day or in the days after, we had visits from all the local retailers, not just A.&S. but even from the May Company in St. Louis. We were creating big waves and it wasn't just on account of price. Don't underestimate the great feeling we all had, the feeling of working like hell for something we believed in and especially for one that was clicking so well. There were no frills, either. We shared each other's offices. Ferkauf didn't need any, he was always traveling to the stores. In those formative years, especially during the holidays, none of us got home before one to two in the morning. I don't think any bunch of guys worked so hard for such a long period of time. But we did it all by ourselves."

Willensky paused to take a breath or two and then resumed. "Later, when I was concentrating on real estate, I would collar Gene and show him some pro-forma break-downs of the site, the costs, the rents, the estimated sales and then if he would agree he would take it before the board. He and I had a real fight later on over my idea to open a series of drug stores. We were doing very well with pharma-ceuticals but he wanted to keep them as departments in the stores to draw traffic. I saw them as the basis for a bunch of drug stores that would sell a lot of other stuff. But he dis-agreed and I almost left."

He shook his head with something of a smile as he recalled the incident. "But it was the Carle Place store that did it," he said. "The great success we had in that first, big store opened our heads. That's when we began to see our real potential."

In many ways, the Carle Place store was the real eye-opener, or, "head-opener," as Willensky put it. It was a classic case of enthusiasm garnering more enthusiasm, of success breeding more success. Again, Ferkauf, wanting to keep each store a separate entity, sent out a call for investors with a target of $500,000. The participants in the 48th Street store project voted to invest $100,000 into Carle Place and Ferkauf put in a like amount. Kane and Schwartz, the land-lord, after being given advance rent of $100,000, also be-came a stockholder to that extent. Suppliers, friends, and opportunity-seeking strangers plowed in the rest of the $500,000. The first year, the store had sales of $20 million, as much as all the other five stores combined. And by the end of that year, the entire investment was repaid. It was a rare feat, possibly unique in retailing for that size of store.

It was something else, too. For the first time, the operators of five small discount houses had a successful department store on their hands. It was a legitimate one, too. It had not only household durables but some sort of soft lines and an apparel operation. It was large, spread across three spacious floors, and had a parking lot. "E.J." had gone big time, at last, and it literally turned the boys' heads. Especially Ferkauf's.

Hope and ambition—and quick action—merged in blindingly sudden decisions.

Badgered by apparel producers angered by the discounting of their lines, Korvettes moved into its own line of unbranded apparel, hoping customers sold on name-brand hard lines would extend their faith to no-name clothing, sportswear, and accessories.

The first diversification moves were taken. A sort of franchised carpet and furniture showroom was opened by a pair of eager young hot-shots across the street from the Carle Place store, using the Korvettes name and the big store's shopper overflow. It proved successful and paid Korvettes a handsome percentage fee. And on the parking lot, Ferkauf opened an adjacent luncheonette. This paid off well, too. And so did a pretzel vendor who prevailed on Korvettes to allow him to open his stand in the back of the parking lot.

For more than two years, the company's founder had been having increasingly hot discussions with Bernard Waltzer, an outside accountant, on the subject of Korvettes' becoming a public company. Now, the subject really heated up. The company was a not insignificant factor in Eastern retailing and those were the early go-go years on Wall Street. But the desire was hardly enough. A plan was needed that would both show an important need for new equity and excite investors. Later, Ferkauf was to quail and even writhe under investors' demands. But in 1954 when he began consulting with Lehman Brothers, the investment bankers, Eisner & Lubin, the certified public accountants, and Richard M. Dicke, of the law firm of Simpson, Thacher and Bartlett, Ferkauf followed all the rules laid out for a company about to invite new investors in.

His earlier talks with Waltzer and Edward Friedman, Korvettes' in-house counsel, and with a number of his boys, had led to the formulation of a plan that was sweeping, courageous, and quite possibly risky. Korvettes would close all of its five small stores, concentrate on the big Carle Place store, and use it as a prototype for other department stores on the same or even larger scale. Underlying all of that would be a program to build Korvettes into a national retailing chain. Lehman Brothers finally bowed out of the plan, not because it was skeptical but because it already represented conventional retailers who would complain if it supported the expansion of a mortal enemy, the discounter. Lehman recommended another investment banker, Loeb Rhoades & Company, and Ferkauf scooted over there.

He had, in the meantime, been having some exciting, if aimless talks with several of the other soft-goods merchant princes in New York about a possible merger. They were Joe Weinstein of J.W. Mays; George Farkas of Alexander's; and Nathan Ohrbach of Ohrbach's—all pioneering company founders and builders, although differing somewhat in personal styles. More than the conventional department store operators, they recognized the auspicious arrival of a new boy in town and came forth to extend their hands. And seeing that Korvettes was weak in soft lines, which was their strength, merger was a natural possibility even though it might strain against the flinty individuality of all their personalities.

Yet, it's possible that Ferkauf's relative youth—he was hardly in his mid-thirties in 1954—made him seem appealing and acceptable to these men in their fifties and sixties. But the four-way merger—Korvettes-Mays-Alexander's-Ohrbach's—was not to be. Weinstein bickered with Farkas about "jurisdictional" rights when the latter invaded the former's Queens turf with a big store in Rego Park. And Farkas had signed a paper obligating himself that in case of a merger Alexander's ownership passed automatically to his four sons. But Ferkauf most admired Alexander's, not for its comparatively low profits, but for its excellent soft lines business. And he wondered if somehow he couldn't buy into that business.

At Loeb Rhoades, Ferkauf met Richard Weil, Jr., a former president of Macy's and before that of Bamberger's, who had later become a consultant to the investment bankers. Weil had an unusual history. As Macy's president, he had decided that the discounters were deliberately sending customers to Herald Square to see what they would like to buy—then customers would buy it cheaper in their own stores. He decided he ought to retaliate by launching some price discounting within Macy's. When other department stores quickly joined the fray, Macy's board, led by Jack Straus, the chairman and large shareholder, ousted Weil for damaging Macy's "image."

At Loeb Rhoades' behest, Ferkauf took Weil around the Korvettes stores so that an independent appraisal could be made of the potential public company. As he proudly showed Weil around, Ferkauf got the feeling that the ex-Macy's man looked down his nose at what he saw. Shortly after the tour, however, Loeb Rhoades reported back to Ferkauf that Weil's opinion was that Korvettes would be another Sears, Roebuck & Company.

In 1955, Korvettes' stock was offered to the public at $10 a

share and quickly was sold out. The company derived about
$2 million in proceeds, with Korvettes and its people retain-
ing about half while the investment banker got warrants on
the stock at $10 a share. A year later, the stock had risen to
$28 a share. It was a double coup. Korvettes now had plenty
of cash to mount its new, ambitious campaign and it also had
scored an important victory that marked authentic recognition from both Wall Street and the public.

That same year, Ferkauf balmed his frustration over the
aborted four-way merger by acquiring 42 percent of Alexander's privately held stock for $9.7 million. That stock had
tremendous appreciation potential, everyone knew, if Alexander's were ever to go public. And Ferkauf, the merchant
and non-financier, knew it too. In 1965, Alexander's went
public and in 1968 Korvettes sold its Alexander's stock for
$23.5 million.

And that was how 1955 ended. Two major strokes.

It was luck—or genius—or something.

3.
Stretching Outward and Inward

W as 1956 *the* pivotal year? At the time, of course, it didn't seem so. Every year seemed to be pivotal. Each seemed reluctant to take its place, to disappear into the kaleidoscope that whirls around them all. But 1956 . . .

In Carle Place, Gene Ferkauf, Murray Beilenson, and Bill Willensky look on with awe as shoppers flutter on the main floor. Women surround several garment pipe racks, select a style or two or three and, clutching their purchases, march excitedly to a cash register. The incident repeats itself again and again. What is it? A simple $4.60 dress has caught the fancy of economy-minded housewives. Ferkauf shakes his lean head in happy disbelief, briefly turning away from his colleagues. He senses that they consider him too emotional at such times.

He can't help it. When he sees what is happening, a warmth moves through him that makes him feel proud and yet inadequate. So many women from so many different homes and backgrounds buying something that *his* company has selected for them. If moving merchandise were music or art, he thinks, the happy clamor should make him feel like Beethoven or Rembrandt. But it also sinks in on him that what he has done in dresses, appliances, and lawn mowers means that he understands what people have in their hearts and heads, right? And that, being above and beyond mere retailing, makes him feel humble. There are moments as he stands there watching them with bulging eyes when he could have kissed them one and all.

And it is hardly the money or the fact that the simple dress was selling, well, like so many hot bagels on the Lower East Side. About every ten days, he figures, 2,500 dresses are carried out of the store. This adds up to a turnover of more than twenty-six times a year, five or six times as rapid as dresses in conventional department and apparel stores.

The pragmatist in him thrills to the simple equation. *Price* plus *need* plus *depth* equals *energy*. But the budding connoisseur in him, which later is to cost him dearly, can't be denied, either. The equation is framed and enhanced, he knows, by its flashy new mounting—the now prototypical Carle Place store.

But the bounding enthusiasm wasn't created only by the flashy mounting. The emotional mounting counted, too, as well as the successful flowering of a new concept. For they had, in those early months of 1956, broken through several barriers at once.

- They had built their first, honest-to-goodness department store.
- They had ventured for the first time into soft lines—40

percent of the merchandise offered at Carle Place was apparel, linens, and domestics—a major commitment.

• They had established the viability of a freestanding store, a self-sustaining business that did not need to feed off others in an expensive rental situation in a shopping center.

• Perhaps most gratifying of all, they had entered the fray of big-time competition for the first time, butting head to head with A.&S., the most profitable, most respected department store in America.

And one thing more. Awed as they all were by the great Macy's, they had, deliberately or inadvertently, opened a big store only a couple of miles from the Roosevelt Field Shopping Center, the giant complex in Garden City, L.I., where Macy's had been planning to open the largest store. As it turned out, Korvettes was in Carle Place two years before Macy's appeared in Roosevelt Field, enough time for Korvettes to develop a sharp competitive edge.

In a phrase, Carle Place exploded their horizons. Never before had they been so excited, so sure of themselves, so full of imaginative plans of what they could do. Suddenly, just as if it had not happened before, they were riding a star and there was no telling how far it would carry them.

Ferkauf began spending most of his time seeking new sites. Before he would concentrate on watching the logistics of store operations, of studying what shoppers bought, what prices they paid. Now he was shooting across the countryside in a big, expensive car searching for the most likely potato farms on Long Island, or cow pastures in Westchester County, New Jersey, and Pennsylvania. As quickly as they could that year, they closed the five small stores and geared up to replace them with the large new prototype.

Inevitably, it dawned on Ferkauf, and on Willensky and

Beilenson, that there were immense advantages in a multi-store umbrella. The concept—which later became standard procedure for almost every ambitious retail management—was that it was more economical, synergistic, and even efficient to open clusters of stores in a major metropolitan area than to jump from one such area to another with only one or two stores. The multi-openings provided the benefits of size—less waste and better utilization of capital—in management, advertising, promotion, warehousing, and servicing than the occasional store permitted. Most important, it made a greater impact on customers. It ensured them an important, vital retailing force had arrived on the scene with all its concomitant clout of big inventories, better pricing from "power" buying, more salespeople, and ability to service merchandise. Simple may be beautiful but complexity could be bountiful.

And so, in 1956, the expansion program leaped ahead. That year, three new stores of the Carle Place size or larger were opened in Harrisburg, Pa., in New Jersey on Route 22, and in Northeast Philadelphia. They would be the nucleus of eventual clusters. All three store openings were successful enough to stoke the fire under their seats and led within a few years to the fastest expansion program in modern retailing history: Ferkauf and his team were to open a new 150,000 to 250,000 square foot store every six weeks. This would amount to a startling twenty-five new department stores in a brief three years.

But what about the people needed to staff and operate the expansion, and the *"in-*spansion"?

Despite the growing number of discount operations, everyone still scoffed at Korvettes. *What* were they anyway? Ferkauf, an untrained luggage merchant, who seemed to hire only people who assured him of complete loyalty, and were preferably relatives or old pals. And *who* were they?

Joe Zwillenberg, his boyhood buddy. David Thorne, Ferkauf's brother-in-law. George Yellen, Zwillenberg's brother-in-law. Mel Friedman, Zwillenberg's old friend. Murray Beilenson, also Zwillenberg's friend. Bill Willensky, Mel Friedman's friend. And another Mel Friedman friend, Leo Cohen . . .

"I was in the men's clothing business for three years," recalled Leo Cohen, "and had no thought of joining Korvettes. My father was in the clothing business, too, and I was comfortable in it. Then I met Mel Friedman, whom I had known from the old neighborhood. I knew Ferkauf, too, but vaguely. Mel brought me to meet Ferkauf and he painted a great picture. I joined. I had a variety of jobs the first few years, selling jewelry, managing the photography department, and then I became an assistant manager of the small Hempstead store where Bill Willensky was the manager.

"He became the manager of the Carle Place store. I was the manager of the Hempstead store and then the manager of Carle Place. I seemed to be dogging Willensky's steps. But I was happy, working my can off but caught up in all the excitement of a proliferating, successful business.

"We all worked very hard; it was like a religion and we were very honest about it. In fact, we were very honest in everything. Ferkauf set the pattern there, both in dedication to the business and in moral behavior. In the beginning, I could easily see what kind of work schedule I was getting into. In fact, when I joined the company in September 1951 I kissed my wife goodbye for four months. And that's not much of an exaggeration, either.

"But we lacked centralization and everyone could see it. I noticed it especially when I managed the Carle Place store. The decentralization was costing us an arm and a leg. In the half-dozen stores we had after Carle Place opened, everyone and anyone was buying merchandise. And we weren't buying it right because we were individually in the hands of a salesman who could quote us any prices; we had no continuity or knowledge of what was going on in the marketplace. Something had to be done, we saw that a year after Carle Place opened and the following year, 1957, the company decided to centralize all hard goods buying. Although I had a soft goods background, I had been in hard goods those years at Korvettes and so I became, at Ferkauf's request, a hard goods merchandise manager. It determined the rest of my time at Korvettes until I finally left in October 1979."

That's how it went. Unlike most of American industry in which there is a general horror about putting square pegs in round holes, or vice versa, Korvettes was willing to install unschooled or untrained executives in key positions. At least, that was true of the early years when speed was vital and the tiny chain felt like the bad boy on the block who didn't have any friends. It's likely, too, that the policy of putting square pegs in round holes permitted the company to expand so rapidly. It's also just as possible that the same policy gave Korvettes practices and routines that eventually hurt it.

All of that, of course, was academic in 1956. The proof was the results: when a business can convert within eighteen months or so from five tiny stores into four giant ones, it's a reasonable conclusion that it was blessed with the right people to do it. What did they have? As Beilenson put it much later, "The main thing our people had was their love of *merchandising* instead of just buying and selling. The second most important thing they had was their honesty in putting in a full day's work plus. Nowadays, I think, the biggest problem in retailing is that there aren't enough people in the business who enjoy it."

To which Bill Willensky adds, "As the company got bigger and bigger, we grew, too, from a base of ignorance, to become very knowledgeable and build a dynasty. It was all through on-the-job training, of course. But the very fact that we had to perform while learning turned us into experts in such things as suburbanization, discounting, merchandising, and so on. Probably never before in retailing did so many people have to learn so much in such a short time. And did it, too."

Later, of course, Korvettes was able to entice trained managers and executives. Bright young people also were brought in for a minimal training program. Once placed in departmental jobs in the new stores, they later became the cadre for yet newer stores. And many of them stayed with the company virtually their entire working lives. Though Korvettes continued to be laughed at for its unorthodox methods and "amateur" executives, its success after only eight years drew professionals to join its ranks from competing retailers.

Everyone seemed to be watching the new public company with a hushed sense of observing a star exploding. But other companies, too, in 1956, were bidding for fame or misfortune.

In Port Chester, New York, a liquor salesman, Carl Bennett, operated a single store named Caldor, much in the manner of Korvettes, after having started in business in 1951 with $8,000 in savings. In New Jersey, another proliferating discount chain, "Two Guys from Harrison," was being aggressively run by Herbert and Sidney Hubschman. Later, they bought the O. A. Sutton Company, a Kansas appliance producer and adopted the corporate name of Vornado, Inc. They had started by operating a diner in Harrison, N.J., near the plant of the Radio Corporation of America. They began to sell RCA products obtained through friends in the company at less than the producer's list prices. The word was passed along to those interested in saving money that "you ought to see those two guys over in Harrison." The Hubschmans responded to their immediate success by opening a small store adjacent to their diner, then more than forty giant-sized stores.

In New England, the seat of the discount industry, there was an entire series of low-margin operators, many of which had started as lofts in mills deserted by the fleeing textiles industry. Arlan's Department Stores, in New Bedford, Mass. Ann and Hope, Cumberland, R.I. Atlantic Mills, New Bedford. J. M. Field Stores, Salem, Mass. Mammoth Mart, Framingham, Mass. King's Department Stores, Springfield, Mass. Coatsfield Shoppers World, Pawtucket, R.I. Lechmere Sales, Boston. Some were to go, like Arlan's, J. M. Field's, Atlantic Mills. Others were to prosper like Ann and Hope, King's, and Lechmere.

They all watched Korvettes, the New York phenomenon. The two companies which seemed most like Ferkauf's were Two Guys and Masters, perhaps because they were headed by similarly endowed entrepreneurs. Stephen Masters, founder of the Masters stores, was as dynamic and self-motivating as Korvettes' founder. But Masters didn't have the same scope of vision, willingness to take risks or, for that matter, the same number of years. He died prematurely and his company went bankrupt, although it was later resurrected on a reduced scale. Herbert Hubschman, co-founder of Two Guys, also died prematurely. Neither lived to see the full flower of their enterprise.

So, all around the rapidly growing Korvettes, there were others, too. It wasn't quite a vacuum for Gene-Joe-Murray-and-Bill, but they had almost no time to look around at their contemporaries. They were too busy trying to control the world within a world that they themselves had created. And it seemed at times as though they had a tiger by the tail.

What used to be so simple, so beautiful, was complex and untidy and the disarray hurt since the early momentum just kept growing.

The centralization showed growing pains, even though Beilenson spent lots of time grappling with the proliferating hard goods business and Ferkauf assigned Leo Cohen to assist him in running the merchandising staff. Costs began to run out of control. Startup expenses were higher than expected. Home office costs also shot up. Total expenses, in fact, almost doubled over the levels of a year and two before. The effect on the bottom line was expectedly harsh. In 1954, Korvettes enjoyed a net income of $1.4 million, but the next year it fell to about $900,000.

Undoubtedly, Ferkauf himself created part of the problem. He was constantly running, spending too little time in the office and spending too much looking for the right potato patch. But he became alarmed when the profit decline created concern in the financial community and the stock dropped to $9 a share.

Looking back on that year of 1956 twenty-five years later in 1981, Ferkauf said with a shrug, "In those early days, we were on too fast a track, so hell-bent for expansion that we didn't see the panorama. Day after day I watched the stores because I felt at that stage it was incumbent on me, on other executives, to live in the store. I'm not condemning anyone for that, including myself, or for what happened later. We might have lost some of our perspective but the stores benefitted."

But the problems weren't so difficult that some greater attention to costs, to inventory control, couldn't alleviate them. There were hurried meetings flavored by friendly recriminations, much kibitzing, but some hard planning. Ferkauf cautioned everyone "to watch the nuts and bolts—

we're on our way but we can't keep our heads in the clouds."
If everyone silently snickered at the advice coming from the
greatest sinner, they took pains to keep their faces expres-
sionless. He demanded strict loyalty and despite his informality (Ferkauf rarely wore a tie or suit), he maintained a
certain dignity that demanded its own recognition.

In the meantime, the public continued to love Korvettes
and what it stood for. The stores were busier than ever. The
shoppers knew that the ongoing price wars involving Macy's,
Gimbel's, A.&S., Alexander's and, of course, Korvettes, were
good for consumers. And Ferkauf and his boys remained the
heroes. In that pivotal year of 1956, there were thirty-five
fair-trade lawsuits against Korvettes on the court dockets.
But the company received a strong legal endorsement that
year when a New York judge denied a suit by the Parker Pen
Company against Korvettes on the ground that the producer
hadn't made a case that it was properly enforcing its fair-
trade program. The publicity didn't hurt Korvettes one bit.

So everything was pulling together. The stock began to
appreciate and head from the previous year's low of $9
toward its eventual astronomical height of $160 a share.

So well did the tightening up of costs and operations
work, in addition to strong openings in the new stores, that
profits returned to their former, cheerful level and went even
beyond. By the end of 1956, net profits had catapulted to a
record $3.9 million.

But the boys were beginning to feel like paper millionaires. Ferkauf frowned on co-workers selling any of the
stock, no matter how badly they needed funds. They could
always borrow from him, he said. But a few sold a portion of
their holdings surreptitiously, although in the main the original group and many of those who followed them loyally held
on to the stock. But they felt disappointed though paper
rich.

Thus, the pivotal year ended. They had four giant new stores accounting for about $75 million in sales that year, the best profits in the discounting field, and the intangible but infectious good-will of literally millions of customers. They felt they were poised for a big breakout in the next decade and there was simply no telling how far they could go.

PART TWO

The Growth Decade
(1957-1966)

4.
The Un-Merger Splurge

The heavy old man with the flat, bald head spat across the room at the spittoon that he had posed there as a target. He missed by a foot. "Dammit," he said. "They must've moved it."

He tried again and, plunk, it hit dead center. He looked over with satisfaction at the tall, youngish man in the tan corduroy jacket and baby-blue turtleneck sweater who had been observing the target practice with amazement.

"Son," the old man confided, "I hear good things about you up in New York. You're just the kind of man with the kind of company I'm looking for."

The younger man shrugged. He still could not quite accept the other's crude behavior in the midst of the staid, conservative investment-banking environment, the dark, paneled walls, the vast high rooms. What must the old guy's secretary, a very proper, cold-eyed matron, think of such behavior? What would his own secretary think of his own odd behavior?—that is, if he had a secretary.

"Ferkauf, right? You know about me? The media are full of stories about me—but most of them are wrong. They call me lots of nasty names. But look at the tremendous empire I'm building, keeping lots of companies alive. Franklin Simon. Oppenheim Collins. McCrory. The Loft Candy Company. The Yellow Cab Company. The Bellevue-Stratford Hotel. Lots and lots of real estate. You know what the chamber of commerce calls me, don't you? 'Mister Philadelphia.' "

All he elicited was another shrug. Mister Philadelphia, straightening up in his imposing, chief-executive chair, scowled and it made him look menacing. "Look, young fellow," he said in a high-pitched voice. "I'll offer you $8 a share for control. I'll let you continue to run your company and I'll put you on our board."

The other man got up. "Our stock is trading at $16," he said calmly. "I drove all the way down here from New York and get this ridiculous offer, Mr. Greenfield. Now I'm gonna drive all the way back and forget I ever heard it."

"You will be part of a great company, one of the fastest growing in the United States," the old man promised. "You'll never have to worry about finances. Naturally, we'll have the final say. But we've got experts in every field here. And great influence in the highest places, especially Washington. Think it over."

Ferkauf walked to the door and the demanding words trailed after him. "Maybe you think I'm trying to buy you cheap but you'll never get a better offer than Albert M. Greenfield makes. That's why we got all these great companies. The men who owned them were just as smart as you, believe me. Don't make me wait too long. I'm not known for my patience. I can always make a tender offer."

As Ferkauf went sullenly out the door, he heard another

"plunk" behind him. Mister Philadelphia talked just like he spat, dead center. Only sometimes he missed, like today, just as he had with Gene Ferkauf.

All the way back to New York as he wheeled the big car from lane to lane, he felt frustration rising in his throat. The old shark! Greenfield was a wheeler-dealer from the old school who had pulled himself up by the bootstraps by always looking for bargains, for old companies on the downgrade and young companies hungry for the funds to become big. He already owned all of Philadelphia, part of New York, and pieces of several Southern cities. But he was an opportunist who always went for the jugular.

I'll let you continue to run your company and I'll put you on our board. The soothing words with their hypocritical underlay picked at him with their patent putdown of his intelligence and wordliness. Did Greenfield and the others think that just because he dressed in his casual, almost careless manner, had built his company with a bunch of old buddies from the neighborhood, and still operated largely without systems, he was a schnook, a lamb who could be led to slaughter? Greenfield, who on one hand did keep companies alive, on the other hand beat their founders into the ground, applying the insult of personal denigration to the injury of buying them for a song.

But then, Gene thought, replying with a never mind wave to the angry blasts of motorists when he wound in and around them, wasn't he asking for trouble? There was the conflict in him, he knew. He just couldn't be satisfied with the success of Korvettes; he kept listening with excitement to the blandishments of others who wanted to absorb him. Yet each discussion with would-be merger partners quickly raised alarm signals within him. They were all scavengers at heart. Greenfield may have been the biggest of all but all the others had that same instinct in the soul. Like alligators, they ate or were eaten.

Veering off the turnpike to a bluff overlooking Route 22, he stopped the car and stared over at the unfolding construction of his new store on the highway. The scene was an open beehive of activity, with bulldozers, other earthmovers, trucks, and men swarming over the site. His pride swelled. *He* was a builder of things. The others were acquirers of what others had built. But, as he pondered, an unwilling laugh rumbled up in his throat. The problem, the problem was that now apparently he wanted to be one of them, too! If he didn't exactly want to acquire what someone else had built—or did he?—he craved to be part of something bigger, much bigger. What caused those feelings? His impatience? His fear that perhaps he had had too much success? The gnawing insecurity that he and his boys had built a house of cards that would tumble down all around them? Or that he and they had grown immeasurably in the decade since they had started out together?

Whatever it was, he assured himself as he started the car and hurtled it down to the construction site, the real spur for the merger hunt came from outside him and the boys. It came from the most famous empire builders on the American landscape, mostly much older men who were excited and intrigued by what he and a bunch of other young guys had created right under the astonished noses of major retailers who had been asleep at the switch. Grinning, he braked practically on the toes of a group of hard-hats, jumped out with a "How we doing, guys?" and strode toward them. In a moment or two, in front of their surprised foreman, he would be grabbing a shovel himself or even manning a bulldozer. What the hell could be so hard running one of those?

"They used to say that Ferkauf was a womanizer, a guy who had to take advantage of all the glory he fell into, with women falling all over him," recalled a close colleague. "But that was just plain wrong. He was first of all a happily married man with a growing family. He got his kicks from the business. There never was a merchant who got so excited when people would buy what he sold. He used to run from store to store and stand by the cash register and practically cry with joy when people would come through the checkouts with loaded carts. If he saw a shopper buying the wrong thing, a not-such-hot value, he would tell her. He'd take her by the arm and show her the shelf where she could do better. And she couldn't thank him enough."

Some of the rival merchants, and some of Gene's own boys, concluded that the Korvettes' founder was "a bit of a *shlemiel*," Ferkauf's longtime colleague continued. "He was so damned honest and he kept all of us that way that you couldn't help feeling that he was naive, a guy who never grew up," he said. "But the real story is, I figure, that he saw everything through fresh eyes, maybe like a kid does. But what it allowed him to do was to try things that everyone else knew couldn't be done and do them. Remember that guy who ran the wrong way on the football field, who almost made a touchdown on his own goal line, then reversed himself when everyone else was laughing and made an easy touchdown on the right goal line? That was Ferkauf. He did it a thousand times. And all the rest of us, the guys he worked with, learned how to help him do it."

Those days, the pre-John F. Kennedy years when Eisenhower was President "and everybody was running with the ball because there was a let-them-do-it guy in the White House, there were a lot of men doing great things in American business. There was Harold Geneen at I.T.T. building the world's greatest conglomerate. Larry and Bob Tisch putting together a giant hotel-movie-resorts empire. Jimmy Ling knocking them dead in Texas with his aircraft building business. Charley Bluhdorn welding his auto-parts and zinc business. Meshulam Riklis and Albert M. Greenfield wheeling and dealing in retailing and real estate. And Gene Ferkauf building the biggest American discount chain. . . .

"When Kennedy got in, we all sat there, including Ferkauf, and watched the inauguration on the tube," he went on, "and we were all excited. Here was another young guy, like we were, the youngest President of all time, a Catholic yet, telling everybody to move their ass and do things for the country instead of just for themselves, just like we were. We were doing something for the public that no one had ever done before or since. And getting lots of flak for it, too. . . .

"But we were creating excitement and all the hot-shots came after Gene to acquire him," he said. "Not only Greenfield but Joe Weinstein, Nathan Ohrbach, George Farkas, Louis Stein, Isaac Wolfson, and Montgomery Ward. They were old guys and old companies but they were smart enough to sense something that was new and hot and promising as all-hell. . . ."

Greenfield, Joe Weinstein, Nathan Ohrbach, George Farkas, Louis Stein, Isaac Wolfson and Montgomery Ward. All famous names in the world of American merchandising. And in "Sir Isaac's" case—the fabulous success of a titled British merchant whose aggrandizing style wasn't unlike Greenfield's —international merchandising. All of them came close to either a merger or a joint venture with Korvettes. Yet each deal foundered at the last moment.

Why? How could at least seven corporate nuptials fail virtually at the altar, especially when in each case all principals were really so eager for the match, at least inwardly? All of those instances occurred within a tight time frame of about five years, from about 1955 to 1960 or so. And, in most cases the meetings, feints, and forays between the heads of each company and Ferkauf recurred several times during the period.

Why indeed?

Most mergers fail not because assets, facilities, finances, or even purposes fail to mesh. They fail because of the lack of respect, or the expression of respect, between the principals.

Perhaps it is exaggerating a bit to liken the exercise to a meeting of mafia chiefs. Assuming that there are questions of jurisdiction, of affiliation, or of subservience to be discussed or whether it's merely an exchange of "market" information, the sensitivities of all in the room are close to the surface.

They are surrounded, even insulated, by captains, lieutenants, and foot-soldiers, not to mention lawyers and accountants if the situation demands them. Phalanx confronting phalanx, the capos face each other warily for any signs of denigration of their professional or personal standing. They might give up authority, turf, armed force more or less willingly as long as they can maintain respect. That's absolutely vital in confrontations, business or otherwise, where surrendering one's rights is involved. The phalanxes also watch one another's words and faces. Power has many levels. It can be secured on any of them, providing there are no damaging innuendoes. In the world of the mafia where the complexity of human relations in the midst of vast aggressiveness has age-old nuances, everything will go as long as personal feelings are preserved. The wrong word, the harsh inflection, the streetwise muttering, the rolling of the eyes—forget it.

In business mergers, where fortunately there is no capo-di-capo to arbitrate the dispute, the same human principle prevails. And it kills many mergers practically in conception.

The callousness of Albert M. Greenfield's approach to Ferkauf was merely more open and candid than the attitude of most of the others who approached him for merger purposes. It's likely that the lack of respect toward Korvettes arose from several causes. Despite its great success, the company still had little reputation for professional performance. Ferkauf himself was an unlikely chief. He was still alternately self-effacing and extremely aggressive. He rarely wore a business suit but a sport or golf jacket, turtleneck or open shirt. In the early 1960's, recalls Peter J. Solomon, managing director of Lehman Brothers Kuhn Loeb Inc., his father, Sidney Solomon, then the much respected chairman of the board of Abraham and Straus, invited Ferkauf to lunch at a restaurant of his own choice. The Korvettes' chief selected one in the Herald Square area which he often frequented. The restaurant owner quickly recognized Solomon and engaged him in conversation but ignored Ferkauf. Amused, Sidney Solomon told the restaurateur, "Don't you know who this man is? He's Eugene Ferkauf, the founder of Korvettes, one of the most important retailers in America." "I've never had the pleasure," the host said. "That's strange," Solomon said, with a smile. "He eats here every day, right, Gene?" But, unlike Solomon, many of the important, traditional merchants continued to disparage Ferkauf and Korvettes, which was another reason, no doubt, why the merger-mavens sought out the discounter and his company but did so condescendingly, as though they were doing Ferkauf a favor.

Another reason was probably that most of the merger-partners were older, almost old enough to be Ferkauf's father. To bridge the age gap, it would have been necessary for them to give full consideration to the younger man's needs and demands. But, lacking any sort of blood relationship, most of them behaved typically—they always wanted to get the best of the bargain—and they showed it.

Once, Ferkauf himself was greatly disrespectful of an older man, Nathan Orbach, thereby killing, at least at that time, any chance of a consolidation between their companies.

Ferkauf was brash, no question about it, when he met Ohrbach. The fashion-store entrepreneur, a gentle, soft-spoken man vastly different from the tempestuous Joe Weinstein or the craftily introverted but sagacious George Farkas, listened carefully to Ferkauf's commentary of Korvettes' achievements. When he did not respond with the enthusiasm that Gene expected, Ferkauf got up and walked out. It was one of his most inconsiderate moments, he later admitted.

Several years later, he approached Ohrbach through his son, Jerry Ohrbach, and much more respectfully sought an attentive ear. Spurred by Lehman Brothers, Ferkauf offered to acquire Ohrbach's for $15 million in stock. It was woefully too little and probably too late. Shortly after, the Brenninkmeyer retailing interests of the Netherlands sweetened its offer to acquire an important American retailer and walked off with Ohrbach's for $25 million in cash.

The incident—now no more than a footnote in the history of American enterprise—might have been more productive if the reverse had happened for all three parties. Korvettes kept seeking a way to improve its never quite successful fashion apparel business and might well have triumphed with the addition of Ohrbach's. The Dutch company for years afterward never seemed to quite know what to do with Ohrbach's, shifting its thrust first one way and then the other and limiting its expansion. And Ohrbach's, one of the pioneers in off-price fashion apparel, continued to wallow under an ultra-conservative ownership when the off-price trend boomed in the 1970's and early 1980's.

Weinstein, the founder of J. W. Mays, seemed willing enough to merge with Korvettes, even though he and Ferkauf would probably not have gotten along. The chemistry would have been explosive, Weinstein's tough veneer and shouting manner and Ferkauf's complex soft-hard approach scarcely being complementary. Perhaps the Korvettes' chief sensed potential conflict, although he took pains not to say so to the Mays owner. But Ferkauf's real desire was for Alexander's, where the fashion apparel approach most impressed him. He felt that a potential Korvettes-Mays-Alexander's merger, with perhaps Ohrbach's thrown in, would present a formidable enterprise.

But Farkas, while using the restrictions of his will as the stumbling block, was not a merger-oriented businessman. He was essentially a builder of an ever-growing business, a sharply-honed merchant with a flair for accumulating valuable real estate in store sites and shopping centers. At his core, he was a fiercely independent man. Ferkauf soon sensed the real problem—Farkas's clear, shrewd eyes sent different messages than his warm greetings. And Gene realized that the older man really didn't respect him for what he had done or, for that matter, could do.

Other potential merger candidates also gave him that impression. Louis Stein, the president of Food Fair, told him that the big supermarket chain had decided to go into the business of discounting general merchandise. He liked Korvettes but offered much less than the company's stock was selling for in the open market.

As Ferkauf recalled in an interview much later, "I told Lou Stein that my wife, Estelle and I, were convinced that the food business would help the company. We both owned about one-third of the stock, and though it was selling for $16 share we would sell ours to Food Fair for $10 each if they would offer $20 to the other shareholders. I told Stein that we wanted to do this to help the shareholders cash in on their investment with us. We were grateful to them; maybe it was time for me to get out, with strength and goodwill.

"Stein said that that was fine and let's go ahead with the deal. He would take the Ferkaufs' shares at $10 and offer the other shareholders $16 a share. When I protested and told him that the reason Estelle and I were selling our shares cheap was so that the other shareholders would get a premium on their stock, Stein blew his top. He said that that was the deal or nothing. And then he walked out."

The aftermath of that story is that a few years afterward Food Fair acquired another discount chain, J. M. Fields, which had been involved in a Chapter XI bankruptcy. Food Fair was not only unable to benefit from that acquisition, which continued to worsen, but when Food Fair itself went into Chapter XI in the late 1970's the first thing it dumped was the entire Fields chain.

Contacts with the Penn Fruit Company, also a large food chain, proved unavailing. But the near-miss with Food Fair turned out to be a stunning stimulus to Korvettes' stock.

It shouldn't have been so surprising. In any merger announcement, investors, especially the institutional ones such as insurance companies and big investment portfolios, react characteristically. The stock of the "surviving" company drops, usually because its outstanding stock is diluted by the transfer of a chunk to the company being sold. Another, equally important reason is the uncertainty whether the merger will inure to the benefit of the acquiring company. But the stock of the company being acquired invariably advances, sometimes dramatically. Reason: its securities must be a great value if another company, supposedly wise and opportunistic, shells out for them.

At the root of it all, of course, is that basic, human drive: cashing in on an opportunity. Proponents call it enterprise. Opponents call it greed. But arbitrageurs, who accumulate stock in advance of a portended development that will drastically change its value, call it great.

In the case of the aborted Food Fair-Korvettes merger talks, the shifts in the two stocks were typical in direction but unexpected in degree. Within days, Korvettes' stock rose from $16 to $20, then to $22, $26, $30, and to $40. Food Fair's common, which had been double that of Korvettes at $32, began slipping to $25, then $20, then $10, and then $8. By 1961, the momentum behind Korvettes' stock had catapulted it to an unbelievable $160 a share. Korvettes became one of the hot stocks of the time. It was one of those ironic twists that later brought exciting changes in the course of other companies which almost but not quite made mergers.

For Estelle and Gene Ferkauf, the explosion in the value of their holdings was a great windfall. The value jumped from $6.4 million to $64 million. For Beilenson, Zwillenberg, Willensky, Mel Friedman, and the others, it was also a tremendous boon. They were more "paper millionaires" than they had ever been. But they couldn't cash in. Ferkauf insisted that doing so was a sign of disloyalty. Some did it, though, circuitously, by transferring shares to relatives. But the amount involved was infinitesimal.

Aside from the personal benefits, the stunning advance in Korvettes' stock gave the company an aura of vast success and significance, a public imprimatur. It raised a halo of enthusiastic acceptance over the controversial company that was painful for the persistent hard core of critics to swallow. Inevitably, it brought down some of the barriers among suppliers, bankers, and Wall Street that had been directed against Korvettes in the previous dozen years.

Louis Stein, tempestuous and disrespectful of Ferkauf as he had been, couldn't have done him a better favor by making the offer.

On the other hand, while his satisfaction over the investors' enthusiasm for his stock was deep, the incident and the previous ones involving mergers only whetted Ferkauf's

desire for a merger. He wanted a food company to complement his stores with attractive, adjacent, or nearby supermarkets to draw bigger traffic for Korvettes. And there were
other reasons, some of which he wasn't eager to define for
himself. One was the simple fact, some of his closest colleagues said later, that the constant charge that he wasn't a
good manager or administrator, that the company was getting to be too big for him, were beginning to reach him and
become part of the inner doubt that never quite left him,
success or no. And it's likely that that insecurity, expressed
or not, was what spurred him to seek out mergers. Now, at
last, he knew it for what it was. The old pirates were intrigued by what he had done with Korvettes and did come
after him—and the bug had infected him. The initiative was
now coming from him. Defensively, or otherwise.

Yet, in that incomprehensible way in which he sometimes did things, he behaved perversely when he received
an approach that could have resulted in an actual merger.
Isaac Wolfson, the founder-owner of Great Universal Stores
Ltd., of England, prevailed on Louis Stein to introduce him
to Ferkauf. Wolfson, peppery and full of power from a most
successful business in the United Kingdom, behaved in a
condescending manner at the meeting. Ferkauf found himself in quick time announcing that Korvettes wasn't for sale,
now or ever.

But the canny Wolfson realized that he had made a
tactical mistake. He had two nephews in New York who kept
him abreast of what was happening. They were Howard
Suslak, president of McDonald & Company, a merger-
specialist consulting firm, and Victor Barnett, who was a top
executive at Revlon Inc. And he had his own people who
provided intelligence. On subsequent visits to New York,
Wolfson decided to romance Ferkauf and Estelle. They went
out to dinner and visited with Barnett. Gene took the stout

old man for a tour of some of the Korvettes' stores and the response was promising.

Still, no merger resulted as Wolfson and Ferkauf kept feinting with one another. The Briton's manner kept irritating the Korvettes' chief, annoying Ferkauf with its kidding, condescending manner. In a word or two, he felt that Wolfson was showing a lack of respect.

Finally, at Ferkauf's suggestion, they decided to open the first of a projected Korvettes' chain in London which would offer American-made merchandise at discount prices. The two signed papers, a site was located, which was one of the smaller G.U.S. stores, and everything seemed to be set for the start of a combined effort. Seemed to be, that is, until Leonard Wolfson, the heir-apparent to Isaac's fortune and empire, objected to the entire project.

Ferkauf never again saw Isaac Wolfson, who was later knighted. Their relationship, which had come so close to fruition in a joint business, was ended permanently.

As to Montgomery Ward, its overtures tended more to put Ferkauf off from seriously talking to them. The big Chicago retailer and catalogue chain, which was obviously heading into severe problems of its own, had an alien form; Ferkauf wasn't comfortable thinking about a possible combination. Several years later, however, when Korvettes opened several stores in Chicago, he was more willing to listen to Montgomery Ward but he found its management intractable on several key matters.

Was he the kind of person who would never really give in to a merger, much as he wanted one? he wondered. And was Korvettes so odd, so one-of-a-kind, that it would never fit with any other company? Or was Korvettes destined to go it alone?

He wanted to believe, almost desperately, that none of those was true.

5.
More Geniuses and
a Geniuess

The vivacious blonde with the big hat glances around the table and tries to hide her amusement.

The ten men speak in dribs and drabs, staring uncertainly at her, their occasional smiles resembling painted grimaces of friendship. Their faces perspire visibly in the warm room. All are wearing jackets. She is a woman, right? So they must keep them on, seems to be the attitude. One man stops in the middle of a tirade about something, the imprecation abruptly stuck in his teeth as he glances nervously at her. Someone else starts breathing loudly as though in pain. The air hangs heavy, inert.

Suddenly, even without being immediately aware of it, she is standing, leaning over the big, round table and speaking directly into their faces.

"Listen, guys," she says, "I, woman, you, man—or men. Okay, now that we've resolved that, let's act like human beings. For an hour, you've been afraid to talk and this meeting seems to be going nowhere. Please forget that I wear a skirt and let's get at it. Use four-letter words, whatever you want. I'll match you two for one. Look, I was raised with eleven brothers. I know what little boys are made of and big boys, too. You guys have no secrets from me. So let's relax with each other. And take those damn jackets off."

At the head of the table, the heavy-set man with the square, pragmatic jaw chuckles. "Thanks, Eve, for straightening us out," he says. "Now," he adds, his chin jutting out, "does any guy here have any objection to getting on with our business?" Smiling, everyone shakes his head and Bill Willensky, the president, grunts gratefully and proceeds.

Eve Nelson sits down and listens to the renewed discussion. She is the first woman executive to be hired by the company and one of the first important professionals to be brought in from another company. She is impressed by the fact that Korvettes decided that it needed a skilled sales promotion director with established credentials. It was too important and successful a company to go on handing out major, specialized jobs to men who had come up through the ranks and had little expertise in those specialties. Recognizing the problem was one thing. But doing something about it was even more important, she realizes. Definitely a sign of burgeoning maturity. So these, she can't help asking herself curiously, are Ferkauf's "boys"? She is tempted to laugh. They all seem so stolid, successful, wealthy men, not "boys." They seem more like garment tycoons who started out pushing the racks or trucking-company owners who made it up from the trucks. But, of course, time has changed them. It is, after all, 1958, a decade since they all started out.

She remembered, years later, that she was impressed by the discussion, the solid content of the ideas, and the perceptive analysis which came across the table. She was also gratified that once she had cleared the air, "They accepted me. Men are like that. They were very nice and decent people to work with. Men were always a cinch to me and people in general, for that matter. I had those eleven brothers and I was the youngest of seventeen children. After that, working with people at Korvettes was easy—until things changed, but that was years later."

Born Eve Amigone in Buffalo, she attended the University of Buffalo and came to New York to work at Macy's. Having had some retailing experience in her home town, Eve moved up fairly quickly at Macy's and eventually became a divisional merchandise manager. But she had always had a flair for fashion promotion that had helped her at Macy's. When Ferkauf hired her to be Korvettes' first sales promotion chief, she soon found that "they didn't even know what sales promotion was but they let me do whatever I wanted. They were a great, innately talented group. Ferkauf didn't come to many of the plans board meetings but, of course, they all reported back to him."

The Korvettes' founder had an indefinable quality of inspiring people, she found, and "of exciting them to stretch their ability." It could have been simply that the great demands he made upon everyone forced them to rise to the challenge. But she concluded that it was a bit more subtle. Somehow, all the co-workers responded to him because his feats were truly exciting. In one sense, he was a sort of Don Quixote sparring with windmills. In another, he was a sort of Robin Hood, stealing booty from the other merchants by under-pricing them. But whatever it was, his imagination and *chutzpah* motivated her. She developed the prototype Korvettes' advertisements with good graphics and come-buy-quick copy. Working with Ferkauf and the fashion merchants, she maneuvered Korvettes onto the major fashion pages and even got the discounter mentions on television talk shows.

Brassy, pugnacious, but imbued with a sixth sense about what makes people stop and stare, Eve Nelson helped to make the public even more aware of Korvettes than it had been. Having to make herself heard in a big family helped her stand out and to gain the company much more mass-media attention. "She was great in promotion and advertising," Bill Willensky said of her. "She had a way of using names, celebrities, entertainers, anyone, that brought a new dimension to Korvettes." If Gene Ferkauf was a sort of recluse from notoriety, Eve Nelson was drawn to it; she created it. If purists and those of conservative tastes didn't quite take to her, it couldn't have mattered less. She became a New York personality and a well-known trade figure. And the big, showy hats she wore didn't hurt.

As it soon emerged, the combination of the restless Ferkauf and her own promotional instincts eventually transformed the Italian girl from Buffalo into one of the most famous women in American retailing after Dorothy Shaver at Lord & Taylor, Mildred Custin at Bonwit Teller, and Geraldine Stutz at Henri Bendel.

Ferkauf "got crushes on companies and people," Eve Nelson recalled. It was reflected in his contacts with Food Fair and Louis Stein, Alexander's and George Farkas, Great Universal Stores and Isaac Wolfson.

One of Ferkauf's hottest crushes developed one day in the office when he was getting off the elevator and Eve Nelson was getting on. He seemed very excited, she recalled, and asked her, "Where are you going?"

"I've got a lunch date."

"Cancel it," he declared. "Come with me. I gotta hot idea."

As she reconstructed it years later, "He was all excited about Avon Products, the big house-to-house cosmetics company. He had been reading Avon's profit-and-loss statement. He just couldn't believe that they could do so much business going from house to house and building up millions of loyal women who seemed to have nothing to do but wait for the Avon Lady. 'Eve, let's get into that goddam business and make millions,' he told me. There was no holding him back. I, too, thought we could make a go of it and add to Korvettes' business."

She went to Lee Arlett, the cosmetics buyer, and told him, "Look, Gene wants to go into the house-to-house cosmetics business. Talk to the suppliers. See what we can do in a hurry." There was one company in particular that she urged Arlett to see. This house could take any health or beauty-aid product, break down its components, and duplicate it. The supplier had already done it with such products as mouthwash and shampoo, reproducing with new packaging as part of the company's Kor-Val private brands group.

"Lee arranged for me to meet those people," she said. "I told them that we had to put together a full cosmetics line under our name, including nail polish, makeup, foundation, and so on. 'I'll pick out the best products of the most famous lines and you reproduce them,' I told the knock-off company. They worked very fast for me. Gene put us on a very tight deadline. He wanted to introduce the line when the Fifth Avenue store opened. Our art director wanted to take his time with the graphics but I kept pushing him. He worked several nights through. We wouldn't even *let* him go home. I got him a fresh shirt from one of the stores and he kept working. So did I. And it was all in addition to my regular work."

And, as Mel Friedman, the "Thirteenth Man," related it, "Our managers hired girls to go out with the line and make the rounds of the residential areas. They would write up the orders and come back to the stores to pick up the inventory. The concept was a good one. We had problems with some of the inventory because it had a bad shelf-life but it created another new concept for the company."

In all, one hundred products were developed and the brand was named "The Eve Nelson Line." Eve took her married name as a professional one after marrying oil-executive Warren Nelson. Eve Nelson cosmetics departments were also established in almost all the Korvettes' stores. The entire project lasted only two years, achieving sales of $1 million the first year and somewhat more the second year. The in-store departments were largely promotional, however, building impact for the house-to-house line. Korvettes' shoppers saw the counters and were ripe for the Eve Nelson "Lady." And it made Eve Nelson's name into a household word.

Looking back, she observed, "Gene Ferkauf never had a bad idea : . . . but he did have one impossible one."

Stopping in at her cubicle one evening, Ferkauf told her with typical excitement, "I've been reading *Good House-keeping* Magazine. We ought to put out our own magazine! It won't cost us anything. You could write the fashion features. Jack, Leo, Murray could write regular features on their departments. We could get our printer to put it out for us. The vendors will take ads! It will be terrific, Eve, a real money machine!"

Then his flushed face vanished from the doorway of the cubicle. She felt a bit dazed. His last words came after him as he walked away. "Terrific! Everybody's got talent! All you gotta do is stick 'em and let it come out!" She wondered, is it possible that he could be on to something, that they could put out a major magazine from the bowels of Korvettes? She sighed deeply. Of course, she did nothing about it and

Ferkauf, ever true to himself, never brought up the subject again.

The same year that Eve joined, a slight, stammering man named David Rothfeld phoned Gene Ferkauf. Since the latter had neither a secretary or office, the switchboard operator at the shabby, crowded offices on Sixth Avenue took his calls. Finally, he answered, "Yeah, who is this?"

"This is Dave Rothfeld. I'm a vice president for Urania Records. I've got an idea for you."

"So what is it?"

"I have to talk to you in person."

"I don't have an office."

"You don't need an office. Just a place for the two of—of us to stand and talk. I'll tell you what. Give me five minutes—of your time—and I'll pay you $250."

"You'll pay me—? Listen, I'm busy."

"I'm busy, too."

Ferkauf laughed, There was something about this guy with the strange, stammering, furry voice that he liked. "All right," he said. "Come in—and bring a check."

The five minutes turned into an hour and a half. Ferkauf pushed Rothfeld's check back at him. He was fascinated. Not only did he sense that the wispy, intense merchandiser could sell lots of long-playing records for Korvettes but Rothfeld had an idea that caused Ferkauf's sensitive antennae to jangle. The first stereophonic records had just come out and created quite a stir. Stereo equipment was already remarkably good but obviously in a transition stage. The demand would surely compel technology to forge ahead. That meant, Rothfeld insisted in his calm but measured manner, that the flow of new products would be great, sales of equipment and records would boom, and a retailer which pushed its way to the forefront in the field would make lots of money and attract considerable attention to itself.

Soon after he was hired as the company's records buyer, the first hard-goods buyer brought in from outside, Rothfeld came up with the bones to structure his idea. The blend of common sense and daring made Ferkauf weak in the knees but eager to jump into it.

"Let's go into the audio business, not just with the famous brands but with our own brand," Rothfeld proposed. "Right now, the industry is nervous. New products are coming out every day and there's a lot—a lot of competition. And prices—prices are high. But with our own brand, we can offer our own prices—and—and great values. It's a real opportunity—"

Within two years, promoting its own house brand of audio equipment, "XAM," Korvettes became one of the country's largest sellers of those products. XAM? What else but Max spelled backwards. And who was Max? Max was the cat owned by Harold Weinberg, the audio buyer under Rothfeld. In a few years, falling into the wide-open pricing track among the name-brand stereo components and sets, the XAM line became one of the best-known in the field and one of Korvettes' top money-making departments.

Not that the pricing situation was an easy one. The majors were fierce competition, advertising heavily but able to maintain their suggested prices. Equipment in general was expensive. But there was some "give" in speakers, Rothfeld recalled, "and we got around the pricing problem by packaging the stereo components with the XAM speakers and absorbing the price differential on the speakers."

It was in records, though, that Rothfeld and his associates scored best. For one thing, Rothfeld knew the business well, having worked in it for years. For another, he was a music-lover, not only of classical but of Broadway musicals and popular music, too. Korvettes took on an ever-increasing inventory of all the major and minor labels, discounting them by one third, and supporting it all with strong, consistent advertising. And grabbing their opportunities.

In the 1960's when Pope John visited New York and spoke at the United Nations, then at Yankee Stadium, Rothfeld and his team were ready. They had arranged at a record-pressing local in the city to record the Pope's main talks, all of them in the public domain, and put the master recording through production. The process went on all night. The next morning, all the Korvettes stores had the record backed by a full-page advertisement in *The New York Times*. Rothfeld's men had picked up the pressings at 8 a.m., then distributed them to the stores. It took both RCA and CBS several days to come out with their versions of the Pope's visit. By then, Korvettes had sold 3,000 records at $5 each. It was no great windfall, Rothfeld said, "but it was an exclusive and we got some very good public relations out of it."

After a few years, Korvettes had become the largest retailer of records and tapes in the metropolitan New York area and one of the two or three biggest in the country. At its height, the chain's record department accounted for about $60 million, running number one or two in sales volume in the company and among the top four best profit-makers.

The same techniques were applied to books. Placed under Rothfeld's domain, the book department was beefed up in inventory along two lines—discounted best-sellers and a constant flow of "remainders," wholesale lots sold by publishers at large price reductions. Korvettes vied with the specialty book stores, Macy's, and Gimbels to stage famous author book-signing parties. Rothfeld would study the book industry trade press for forthcoming titles that appeared headed for the big lists. "We used to jump on a new book and sometimes race the clock to have it first on our counters," Rothfeld said.

As the company expanded and the book business soared in stores, Korvettes bought a controlling interest in a book wholesaling company and supplied other retailers.

Taking in Rothfeld's amazing prowess, Ferkauf gave the shy, soft-spoken merchant his head. For fourteen years, David Rothfeld appeared on the "Korvettes Music Hour" on The Times radio stations, WQXR-AM and FM, commenting on new releases and playing them. "I wanted to attract the classical music consumer," Rothfeld said, "and hoped that his record purchases would overflow to the photography and camera departments, audio and soft goods, too. And it did."

As he later admitted, the aggressive merchandising of audio, records, tapes, and books brought Korvettes considerable cooperative advertising allowances. The heavy advertising that resulted gave the company unquestioned leadership in those fields for years.

Ferkauf credited Rothfeld publicly with recognizing very early in the process the massive effect new technology would have on the musical scene and on how people relaxed at home. "He's the greatest merchant I ever met," the Korvettes founder would say and sometimes look up at the ceiling as if waiting for something. "Next to you, Gene?" was implied perhaps but never actually said. It didn't have to be.

A major move was on the way. For the first time, the founder was actually considering bringing in someone else from another company at the very top of the corporate edifice. Korvettes was performing very well, with sales of $157.5 million in 1960, twelve stores in New York, Connecticut, New Jersey, and Pennsylvania, and was enjoying a strong earnings trend. It was poised for a big expansion program. But there were frequent times when all the top executives and many of those under them felt that they were stretched too thin, that they needed outside help, a sort of blood transfusion. None felt that need as deeply as Ferkauf.

An important solution came about almost inadvertently, all because he had never actually lost his interest in Alexander's, the successful promotional fashion chain run by the wiry, canny George Farkas.

If he merged with Alexander's, Ferkauf figured he would get not only the fashion merchandising expertise he still lacked but a profitable apparel business with major press clout and even the extra management infusion from Farkas himself. But that wasn't to be. The word was out, though. Ferkauf's interest in the chain which was getting massive media play on its quasi-haute couture promotions was deeply visceral and he never stopped talking about it. Inevitably, the opportunity developed but from an unexpected, non-Farkas source.

In 1928, George Farkas had opened his first store in the Bronx, subsequently expanding it thirty times. During that time and the later expansion, he had a strong right arm in Louis Schwadron, his brother-in-law. Besides his own four sons who took an increasing role in the growing business, Farkas also promoted Schwadron's two sons, Jack and Arthur, and gave them an increasing responsibility in his business. But, as in many family companies, Farkas and Schwadron and their respective offspring didn't always get along. The Schwadrons often felt that they were relegated to a sort of second-class citizenry in the company. And besides, though the company's founder often talked of going public, he always tip-toed away from it in fear that his paternal control would be reduced. Thus, the Schwadrons' approximate 20 percent holdings in the business lay fallow, a source of additional irritation.

The hunter and the frustrated were brought together in 1961. The Schwadrons and other members of their family agreed to sell their 124,176 shares, or 20 percent of Alexander's common stock, to Korvettes for 83,800 shares of its stock—closely held stock for a widely dispersed public equity—and $1.24 million in cash. Jack Schwadron, an Alexander's vice president and director of its merchandising operations, was elected a Korvettes' vice president. His brother, Arthur, who had been an Alexander's executive, joined Korvettes as a merchandise manager.

George Farkas was stunned and angry. He felt betrayed by Louis, who had married Farkas's sister, and by the two Schwadron sons. But his fury was to be further fanned. Within weeks, he learned that his three sisters, who owned 22 percent of Alexander's stock, had been approached by Ferkauf's lawyers and had granted Korvettes an option, later exercised, to sell it their holdings, too. Ferkauf now had 42 percent of Alexander's, not exactly control because the Farkas family owned 55 percent, but enough to make the Alexander's chairman feel he wasn't his own man. Yet, he insisted he would not permit a merger with Korvettes and posted $200,000 with Korvettes' law firm as a down payment to buy back the stock.

But the more he fumed over it the more Farkas was convinced that he had been stabbed in the back. In July 1961, he filed a suit for $10.5 million against Korvettes and the Schwadrons, charging violations of the Clayton Antitrust Act, which seeks to prevent businesses against unlawful restraints, monopoly, and combinations. The suit said that Korvettes' efforts to merge with Alexander's would lessen competition, that the Schwadron's sale of their stock and the purchase of the sisters' stock were moves aimed by Korvettes to acquire Alexander's.

The Farkas suit also charged that Korvettes had enticed away "many" of its key employees and also accused that company of issuing false and defamatory statements concerning Alexander's and urging suppliers to stop doing business with it.

The suit, however, was thrown out. Farkas licked his wounds and fumed some more. But he was an entrepreneur at heart—i.e., he never let a disappointment throw him too hard because there was always another opportunity—and decided to forfeit his $200,000 option to repurchase the stock that Korvettes had grabbed. "I propose," he said stonily at the time, "to use our funds to expand our own business, not someone else's." And expand he did, a few years later building a vast new store in Manhattan on Lexington Avenue opposite Bloomingdale's. It cost him $21 million to construct the most expensive store in New York; it was Manhattan's first major new one in forty years.

Well, if Ferkauf couldn't have Alexander's to satisfy his ever-deepening desire to merge with another company, he did have a potentially highly profitable investment in Alexander's. Most important, he had Jack Schwadron who had effectively managed Alexander's most important entity, its fashion operation.

A slim, doe-eyed, articulate man of thirty-four years old, Schwadron seemed almost too boyish and undynamic to be responsible for Korvettes' merchandising. But, besides his expertise gained at Alexander's, he had two qualities that quickly gained him respect among the Korvettes' old-timers. He had an easy, pleasant personality that ruffled few feathers and invited a warm response toward him. He also had a flair for sensing what clothes and accessories women wanted and, if he had any weakness in that regard, it was that he was inclined more to higher than lower fashion. That made some of the company veterans stand back and pause. But Ferkauf, though he never really said it in so many words, was intrigued by it since that was what he had admired most about Alexander's under Farkas.

Jack Schwadron had another endearing quality. He was there. His presence at the top—he was instantly more than just a vice president because he bore the mantle of potential heir-apparent partly because of his heavy stock holdings in the company—allowed the founder to worry less about the business and to devote himself to carrying on his expansion program and unyielding desire to merge. A week after Schwadron was appointed, he was elected a director, later named general merchandise manager, and in 1964 he was appointed president and chief operating officer, the first outsider to be given those titles.

Willensky willingly gave up the presidency, becoming vice chairman. Now he had the opportunity to carry on what he did best—finding the best sites for Korvettes' ambitious expansion. Between 1961 and 1964, Korvettes opened twenty more stores on top of the twelve it already had, filling in the metropolitan New York area and venturing about 1,000 miles from home base into Chicago and Detroit. The outward foray was one of the company's most controversial, yet strategic moves.

But the headlong expansion sapped the company's earnings. In a June 1965 interview with Leonard Sloane of *The New York Times*, Schwadron declared that "Our major task is to see that our profit margins move along with our volume. Our profitability has been hampered by the rapidity with which we have opened new stores. But we have finally been able to build the kind of base from which we can develop profitably into a nationwide company."

He conceded that the profit improvement would be a big undertaking for a company that had just completed a year with a 44 percent rise in sales after successive yearly increases of 40 percent and 31 percent. Korvettes, after an early, successful venture into food retailing, had opened a number of supermarkets adjacent to its regular stores; they were proving to be an especial drain on earnings. The turn-around approach will be to make them "less promotional but we'll still remain competitive," he said.

Yet, in the midst of its earnings difficulties, Korvettes was plunging ahead with more store openings. These would be seven new stores to be opened by that Christmas, including four in the metropolitan area in Staten Island, Port Chester, N.Y., Cedarhurst, Long Island, and Douglaston, Queens. And the following year, 1966, the company planned five more stores in New York City and its suburbs, Chicago, and Baltimore.

Other talented executives joined in those last years of the 1950's and early 1960's. Herbert Ricklin, industrial relations director; Joseph Lamm, a financial man who later became executive vice president; George Schwartz, whom Schwadron tapped from the McCrory Corporation to become his successor as Korvettes' vice president for merchandising. They were among the first top pros from other companies to join an increasing flow of starry-eyed executives attracted by the glowing magnetism of Korvettes' triumphs.

If there was any indication that Ferkauf hadn't quite found his man in Jack Schwadron, it was not openly hinted in those days. But based on this writer's contacts with the principals from 1962 onward, the vagrant thought came through that Schwadron might be too easy a man, too genial, to be Ferkauf's number-two executive. Was someone needed to occasionally say "No" to Ferkauf's unbridled enthusiasm and acquisitive drive? Probably. But whoever it might be, Schwadron for that matter, it was a difficult if not impossible task. The founder of what was already the country's largest discount department store chain, Ferkauf had already been bestowed the accolade of a cover article in *Time* Magazine and had been hailed by Professor Malcolm McNair as one of the six greatest merchants in U.S. history. Altogether, he was in the early 1960's the most visible merchant in America, a prize-winning stallion who wouldn't be reined in or beaten to the starting gun.

6.
The Glory of Fifth Avenue—and of Herald Square

O n May 25, 1962, Korvettes invaded the Gold Coast of international retailing, the turf of the mighty, by opening a seven-level, crystal chandeliered, stylish store on Fifth Avenue and 47th Street in Manhattan.

The opening, even the advance reports of it, created consternation. The traditional Fifth Avenue merchants immediately envisioned a drab store with pipe racks, pretzel vendors and peddlers outside, and a ragtag populace flowing in and out. But when they entered the store for a surreptitious look, they found that it was attractive, dignified, and tasteful. They were surprised at some of the high fashion merchandise, high-priced fur stoles and coats, designer-name men's suits. Obviously, the energetic new team of Ferkauf-Schwadron had done plenty of scouring in the markets. And, even more surprising, perhaps, over the ensuing months, was that the shoppers were obviously affluent, some even arriving in chauffered limousines.

One can imagine Ferkauf's reaction when he came upon the limos idling outside the new store. Or the tide of customers coming in and out, on Fifth Avenue yet. Only fourteen years up from the bootstraps! The other big stores nearby— Sloane's, Lord & Taylor, B. Altman—were at least a hundred years old each, entrenched by time, place, and convenience. Korvettes . . .

Yet, as the months came and went after the opening, and as the store obviously prospered, the chiefs of the prestigious stores continued to look down their aristocratic noses. Perhaps the likes of Walter Hoving at Tiffany & Company, Melvin E. Dawley at Lord & Taylor, and Adam Gimbel at Saks Fifth Avenue were even laughing now, quoting bits and pieces of a *Time* Magazine piece that had appeared only three months after the opening of the Fifth Avenue store:

"Cy, please, so why is it so schmootzig *(dirty) around the soft-drink machine? I told you that should never happen. Cy, do me a favor. Clean it up. I mean go get a boy and clean it up right now. . . . So Dave. I was downstairs and there was a line at the cash register and only a part-timer to handle the traffic. Dave, tell me, so what happened to the other girl? Dave, you know it will hurt the store. So why do you let it happen? . . . Irving, so why doesn't someone pick up this shirt? It looks like a* schmuttie *(rag). And Irving . . ."*

This excerpt of the typical, gently needling monologue with which Ferkauf often prodded his colleagues was part of *Time* Magazine's cover story on Eugene Ferkauf and Korvettes—an unusual and coveted recognition of the man and the company. But the *terms* of the recognition? If he knew people were laughing at him, Ferkauf must have shrugged a dozen times. He claimed later that he didn't know that *Time* planned to publish such an ambitious article, to single him out to such an extent. But why did they have to show him washing dishes in his home to dramatize what a homebody he was in the midst of his vast success? But then he'd said the same thing about the first article about him in *Women's Wear Daily* in 1956. He didn't know about that, either. The trouble with publicity was that you couldn't control how it came out. And who the hell, he kept telling the boys, needed it anyway?

But, having established a prominent part of Fifth Avenue as his turf, he personally also became part of its scene. The casual pedestrian might have had difficulty recognizing Hoving, Dawley, or Gimbel but many of them seemed to know Gene Ferkauf. His corduroy jacket and turtleneck shirt, his closely-cropped, blondish hair and his fast, often running gait made him easily identifiable. What was it that Joe Weinstein had called him? "The Fluke." He was that, all right. He would buy that.

In the meantime, the Fifth Avenue store did well, extraordinarily well. Schwadron, who was sharp and made people like him, knew lots of suppliers. He and Ferkauf had to engage in some fast footwork to get desirable soft goods. The result was a sometimes dazzlingly circuitous route to merchandise which ultimately resulted in great bargains for shoppers. Like fur-trimmed, cashmere cardigans at $26 which were normally sold by the branded producer for $60. The supplier, who carefully kept his sweaters away from discounters, was stunned by Korvettes' ability to get his goods with the name labels still sewn in. So he checked the route of the goods to Korvettes and discovered that there had been two side-roads to that particular flow—a producer of sweater linings who sold them to a producer of fur collars who sold them to the Avenue upstarts. The Fifth Avenue stores complained bitterly. But Ferkauf, Schwadron, and their merchandisers and buyers wouldn't be put down. Well-known branded women's slacks appeared without the label at a good price cut below the tags on the same goods up and down the street. Jantzen and Catalina swimsuits, 10 to 15 percent below regular retail. Hand-knit, Italian men's sweaters at $9. French alligator handbags for $50. Men's Dacron-and-wool summer suits for $25.50.

That was in soft lines. In hard lines, Dave Rothfeld, Murray Beilenson, and Leo Cohen were simultaneously performing a deft tap-dance on records, books, stereo hi-fi, television, and housewares. The traffic into the new store seemed endless that first year. Korvettes was delivering a lesson on retailing, on Fifth Avenue, to some of the most skilled merchants in the world.

What lesson? The economics of lower costs. The synergism of high sales productivity. The beauty of simplicity—still.

First, there was self-service with its lower costs, fewer employees, less duplication of effort. Second, there was a lower standard or average markup, about 22 percent against the conventional merchants' which started at about 38 and went up quickly. Third, there was the high sales per employee, about $37,500 a year against about $20,000 in the other large stores. And fourth, and most important, the impact of discount prices which gave the store an inventory turnover rate of seven times a year, almost twice that of the competition. This yielded an enviable sales per square foot of $300—against Macy's $150, Saks Fifth Avenue's $190, and Abraham & Straus's $175.

Retailing as successful as this breeds excitement. Abe Goldstein, the store manager—and one of Gene's boys from Brooklyn whom Gene had met at Camp Crowder, Missouri—was enjoying every minute of it, racing around the seven floors and trying to anticipate every whim of the company founder's.

Visits by this writer to Korvettes' Fifth Avenue usually included a stop in the basement where Goldstein had his tiny office. Abe would always insist on conducting the visitor on a tour in which he would proudly and excitedly present some new department, counter, or corner. "We're keeping up, you know," as Goldstein put it. "We're not standing still."

These comments by the slight, genial Goldstein came to mind in 1981 when a former top executive of Korvettes discussed the company's decline and the Fifth Avenue store in particular. "It was opened in 1962 but they didn't touch it for about eleven years," he said. "It was the flagship store and it's axiomatic that any major store should get a general overhaul every seven years and touch-ups every three or four years. But they didn't put any real money into it until 1973. And it had been a gold mine, too . . ."

A gold mine it was. The first year, 1962, the store had sales of $30 million, considerable for a retailing structure with only 100,000 square feet. The annual rent was $1 million. It needed only $14 million in sales to break even. Total costs, not including home-office contributions, came to about $13 million, including costs of merchandise. Thus, it had a 10 percent pre-tax net income. Its real secret was its customer draw—it was unique on the Gold Coast and even the top-drawer merchants realized it.

"Korvettes is an individual kind of operation," said Melvin Dawley, president of Lord & Taylor, several years after the store's opening. Dawley, who was also president of the Fifth Avenue Association at the time, added, "They're not typical and one cannot say that they have enhanced the prestige of Fifth Avenue. But they haven't hurt it, either. And they have stimulated customer traffic to the area."

With the initial success of the Fifth Avenue store, Schwadron was able to take an increasing burden off Ferkauf's shoulders. Feeling the urgent need to keep expanding (he had already publicly made the statement: "All I want for this company is that it should do all the merchandising business in the United States"), Ferkauf turned to other matters. Two of them were high on his mental agenda. One was to improve his lagging retail food business. The other was to merge with another company which would boost his company's price-earnings multiple, substantially increase its sales, and even bring him additional top management.

All those desires finally combined in a merger—a merger at last—with another company. It was to give him everything he wanted, except peace of mind.

Hilliard J. Coan was a tall, disciplined man with a slightly dour personality. He had a piercing look at times which together with his somewhat skeptical nature made command easy for him. But he also had a fine sense of dimension and form. He knew how to obtain volume, squeeze the processing cost out of it, and come up with a viable profit. He was, in short, an excellent food merchant.

He was to become much more.

His first meetings with Gene Ferkauf, after the Wall Street investment bankers brought them together, went well. He was a great admirer of what Korvettes had done and, though its founder struck him as unlikely, he realized that the man had a touch of genius about him. Korvettes' volume in 1965 was awesome, some $500 million. Pre-tax profits were $17 million. And a good reason for the lowered profits was Korvettes' deficit-ridden food business. Coan decided to make the plunge. In February 1965, Hill's Supermarkets, Inc., of Long Island, became a subsidiary of Korvettes. Three months later, as Ferkauf stepped aside to become chairman of the executive committee and to remain chief executive, Coan became Korvettes' chairman, and Jack Schwadron was renamed president.

It seemed like a good marriage and a good set of partners, even if there were three of them. For the first time, Korvettes had three top men at the helm, two of them professional, outside merchants. And, if anyone began to wonder whether the ship was beginning to slip away from its moorings, Ferkauf was still there, as ubiquitous or as invisible as ever.

It was a powerful company, too. Korvettes was the largest discounter in the country. With Hill's, it had forty discount stores and sixty-three supermarkets. It had inherited in the merger a 330,000 square foot warehouse in Long Island which was big enough for both food and non-food. In New York, Korvettes was pushing Macy's hard as the largest-volume retailer and there were hints that it had already succeeded to that role.

But big and powerful as it was, it had big problems.

Even though the merger with Hill's had hiked Korvettes' food volume to more than $200 million a year, food profits remained elusive. Price wars cut the margins and yet tonnage and sales had to be maintained, which meant giving business away. In addition, as with the distant Korvettes stores themselves, the out-of-town food markets were not productive. And an unexpected problem developed when the furniture lessee, the H. L. Klion Company, ran into severe difficulties. It became overextended and subject to so many late deliveries that customers cancelled orders totaling about $2 million. Ferkauf had gone heavily into furniture, allowing Klion to serve many of his stores. Now he had to either allow the furniture firm to sink or bail it out. He bought out Klion. Now Korvettes was in the furniture business on its own hook. To go a step further as his own hard goods operator, Ferkauf bought the Federal Carpet Company, its carpet lessee. Norman Rothman, head of Federal, joined Korvettes as head of its carpet business.

And then, of course, there was the still unsatisfactory performance of the stores in Chicago, Detroit, and the newest, St. Louis. There weren't enough of them in each market and somehow the locals didn't seem as impressed with Korvettes as the public was in the East. Yet, possibly it was only a question of time. After all, it never took less than three years and as long as six for a store to click, didn't it? And in a completely new market?

Coan began functioning quickly and the results were soon apparent. If he was more of a tactician than a strategist, what was wrong with that? They had plenty of strategy but not the methods or the systems to capitalize on it. He defined executive responsibilities, reassigned jobs leaning heavily on performance history, hired additional buyers, laid down rules and procedures in clear statements. Studying the various outside data processing systems that Korvettes had gone into, he brought the company into modern times by installing its own E.D.P. It was one of the early instances of a widespread use of data processing by a retailer. An additional distribution center was erected in New Jersey. And the food division, under Coan's piercing eye, commenced to show new strength.

As he observed what was going on, Ferkauf felt he had been luckier than he deserved. Long an admirer of Sears Roebuck and of its chairman, Gen. Robert E. Wood, whom he considered instrumental in its success, Ferkauf went around to everyone, exclaiming, "Hilly Coan has got to be the greatest executive since Gen. Wood."

But history has never been kind to triumvirates, and the trio at the top began to show hints of friction. Coan took his role as chairman of the board very seriously. He *was* the top man; Ferkauf was only . . . well . . . the "gray" eminence. Yet Coan felt that Ferkauf subtly stood in his way on changing things that had been done in a certain way—Ferkauf's way—for years. And Schwadron was maneuvered awkwardly between the two, attuned more to Ferkauf's style and merchandising genius, but, in the organizational hierarchy, fully subservient to Coan.

And, just as inevitably, alliances were formed, cutting across the layers of command. It was Coan, Norman Rothman, the carpet man, George Schwartz, the merchandiser who had been hired to succeed Schwadron in that role, and Alan L. Haberman, Coan's nephew whom he had brought with him to run the food business. And on the other side it was Ferkauf, Schwadron, and all the remaining boys, of which there were many.

"The problem was Coan was a professional businessman," said a top executive who was thick in the shadowy melee. "He understood business and he was all business. He wanted things organized. But that could never, never be as long as Ferkauf was around. Gene brought Hilly in for food and management. But what Ferkauf didn't figure on was that Coan would be playing with his toy. Some people didn't like Hilly because at times he behaved like a martinet. Personally, I liked him and respected him.

"Look at it this way. Here's a guy who merges his company with another one and becomes chairman of the board. But the other guy, who founded the big business and is still the largest stockholder, doesn't really change. He keeps coming in with a new idea twenty times a day and he drives the new chairman off his nut," he continued. "And all of us were caught in the middle. That's the story of our time—the guy who more-or-less sells out but doesn't bow out. The second thing is that nobody is all hero and all villain. All of what happened then and later proved it."

As far as the outside world was concerned, there was no indication of the internal tension. At that point it was all a matter of controlled differences, muttered words, glints in the eye, and covert discussions within each alliance. Gene's "boys," of course, continued to consult with and take orders from Ferkauf. But it became clear to many inside the company that the spark was inching closer to the explosion.

On June 4, 1965, Korvettes announced to a packed press conference that it would open a store directly opposite Macy's Herald Square. It would take over the site of Saks-34th Street, a specialty store owned by Gimbel Brothers which had the dubious distinction of being one of the few large specialty stores not yet having any escalators. With this stunning expansion coup, the general perception was that there was simply no end to the height that Korvettes could attain.

A bit nervous but outwardly confident, Jack Schwadron told the press that Korvettes would remodel the sixty-three-year-old building and open a $12 million neoclassic structure of fifteen floors. The first eight were to be used for selling, and the upper seven, to be known as the Korvettes Tower, would house the company's executive offices.

Schwadron said that Korvettes had taken a thirty-year lease with options on the building. After extensive renovations, it would be the chain's third unit in Manhattan, the seventh in New York City, and with its 240,000 square feet the largest of Korvettes' thirty-nine stores.

Gimbels had leased the store for almost fifty years from several landlords and had another ten months to decide if it wanted to continue the lease. Several months earlier, however, as Schwadron informed the reporters, Arlen Properties Inc., a rapidly growing developer, had purchased the building and had signed a contract for Korvettes to take over the site conditional on Gimbels' decision not to renew its option.

Only the day before, Bruce A. Gimbel, the president of Gimbel Brothers Inc., had given the decision. "After much consideration," he had announced, "the decision has been made to close Saks-34th Street because it was unprofitable and there is no indication that this situation could be reversed." The three other Saks-34th Street branches on Long Island and in Stamford, Conn., would be turned into Gimbel stores, no doubt continuing their profitable performance.

At the Korvettes press conference, Schwadron, flanked by Hilliard Coan, stern but paternal looking, noted that the new store would face immediate competition from two long-entrenched stores, the powerful Macy's Herald Square and Gimbels' flagship store on Broadway. But on the basis that one company's reverses are another's opportunity, Schwadron, his voice warming and his fingers resting on a model of the neoclassic building, declared, "We are confident that we can do what Saks-34th couldn't—operate profitably. Why? Because we represent jet-age retailing. By that, I mean that we, as promotional department stores, will offer department-store merchandising and discount prices. We'll continue to keep our prices below our competitors and yet give good service. And we hope to bring Fifth Avenue high style to 34th Street. And we aren't at all"—he added after a reporter's query—"worried about competing with 'the world's largest store.'" His thumb motioned over his shoulder at Macy's.

Bruce Gimbel and David L. Yunich, chairman of the Macy's New York group, issued statements that day welcoming Korvettes, saying that their presence would add further shopper stimulus to the area.

The architectural plans for the new store were striking and lavish. The curved front was a modernized replica of a

Grecian temple with twenty-six recessed, six-story high, white marble pillars. These, each separated by fourteen feet and topped by arches, were to be illuminated at night, "accenting Korvettes' Herald Square as a new city landmark," Schwadron said. On top of all that, the seven-story tower would be recessed from the understructure, allowing the installation of a restaurant in a terraced area at the foot of the tower. This area, he declared proudly, will be shielded by a plastic "bubble" for all-weather dining.

The grandiose design scheme, perhaps too esoteric for Herald Square and possibly even Fifth Avenue, was impressive nonetheless. It spoke of much internal confidence and a dynamic outlook. Obviously, Korvettes had some problems, declined earnings, low return on the food business, the distant stores. But who didn't? Three years after its stunning opening on Fifth Avenue, here was Korvettes with a new store to open on Herald Square! The press meeting broke up on a solid, warm note. Schwadron, Coan, and a bunch of other Korvettes' executives shook hands all around and invited everyone to partake of drinks and hors d'oeuvres.

The story ran on the front page of every New York newspaper and was featured prominently on all the television night newscasts. Everyone, friend and foe and in between, called it Korvettes' most dramatic coup, an inspired move.

But where was Ferkauf? He hadn't been at the press conference. He was being seen less and less at the Avenue of the Americas headquarters. But the Herald Square coup and especially the artistic design of the proposed store smacked of the Ferkauf style. Where was he? And what was he doing?

Ferkauf at that time was greatly emotionally stressed, torn between his constant need to pounce on opportunities and the constraints on him acquired in the merger. He saw opportunities out there but was unable to act quickly enough or adequately enough to seize them.

For instance, Estelle and he were avid movie-goers. (In fact, Gene would not infrequently go to the movies in the afternoon while things were hectic and decisions had to be made in the main office. His excuse was, how else could people rise to the challenge unless they were confronted with decisions?) He was a particular fan of Japanese movies. He found two properties of great artistic and commercial potential for conversion into movies with American appeal. But he didn't buy them; instead he pondered the project for months and months, knowing that people would say that Ferkauf was only taking another flyer.

Finally, he broached the matter to the Korvettes board. Admitting that the idea was remote from discount retailing, he offered to take on any losses that might accrue from the project if it were accepted as a company activity. Oddly, the board accepted it. Ferkauf hadn't lost his genius at salesmanship. But, as he prepared to act, it was too late. Two other producers got there first, each making a fortune by exploiting the projects they had acquired.

Then there was the big flurry in original art. A collector of art, sculpture, and first editions, Ferkauf had some years earlier convinced his people that the stores in the more affluent areas would cash in from having in-store art galleries. The main showcase was the Douglaston, Queens, store. It did very well for a while—but there were problems. First, indulging a personal love, Ferkauf spent too much time in the Douglaston and other stores helping to sell the paintings, etchings, and lithographs and ignored more important matters. Then, there was the scandal about the fake art that he purchased. Although he was lured in only to the extent of two fake Picassos, for a total of $7,000, the publicity and the ridicule stung him badly. David Stein, the indicted art dealer who painted the counterfeits himself, softened up prospective customers by first showing and selling them genuine Picassos, Chagalls, and Matisses. Ferkauf was one of many customers who were fooled, including Victor J. Hammer, one of the world's best-known collectors, but Ferkauf felt personally ashamed for not having studied the situation thoroughly enough.

But he wasn't always off-base. The Eve Nelson beauty salons, controversial though they were for being a too specialized offshoot of the Korvettes stores, continued for awhile and gave the company, especially its Fifth Avenue store, a cachet it might not have otherwise had. And there were the snack bars. Ferkauf was always looking for or open to subsidiary ventures that could be tied in to his stores like barnacles. First, there was furniture, then toys, pretzels, carpets, cosmetics—and then there were the snack bars. It was an odd, perhaps prescient concept. The idea was to have snack bars as part of the store proper, but with their own doors so that they could be entered without the need to go into the store itself. Opened in all the stores in the New York area and in some of the major out-of-town units such as Chicago, Washington, and Detroit, the snack bars served truck drivers or any other motorists with breakfast. And they also produced a profit.

One of the biggest disappointments was the venture, much of it dictated by necessity but also by entrepreneurial drive, into private label or store-branded merchandise. "Spring" was such a Korvettes private label, used on many housewares items. If conceived and followed through properly, the private-label effort could have blossomed, much as Sears, Penney, Montgomery Ward, and major department store chains have profited from "house brands." But the move became diffused, suffering from a lack of direction, cohesiveness, and delegation of responsibility. It was perhaps another example of Ferkauf's failure as a manager, and that, of course, led in a straight line to the other conflict. In terms of the job he had given Coan on their merger and the behind-the-scenes role he has assumed as chairman of the executive committee, his conservatism had deeply wanted someone else to take care of the major administrative problems with a cool head, but his aggressiveness resented being pushed aside. So he had hired new management, but couldn't seem to take the back seat that the situation demanded. Of course, mergers always led to that sort of thing, but why was it happening this way? "Within weeks after Coan got there," one of Gene's boys recalled, "Hilly already wasn't listening to Gene."

But wasn't he, after all, still the founder, still the largest stockholder, and still the personification of the company?

Thinking in that vein, Ferkauf came to suspect that he may well have backed into the marriage with Hill's and Hilly Coan while he was on the rebound. Eager for a merger and also for some new strength in the lagging food business, he had some years earlier approached Shoprite Stores, the food cooperative, for a merger. The answer was a flat no and it sent Ferkauf off to find a new potential partner. Hill's and Hilly. The thought left a bad taste in his mouth, despite the respect he had for Coan's abilities.

To all this was added another disturbing element. Jack Schwadron, whom he genuinely liked and respected, had from the first urged a trading-up effort in apparel and soft lines. Ferkauf had developed a gnawing feeling that Jack might be unrealistic. Was it his own basic merchandising conservatism or was Schwadron on to something potentially important? Ferkauf's experience told him *no*. Didn't he know the Korvettes' customer best? Or was Jack right in sensing it was time for a change? Opportunity or protective caution? His own instincts were out of sync on this one.

And, as he moved around in an ever-widening circle from company headquarters, avoiding such matters as appearing at the press conference, Ferkauf was in an obvious stew. Caught in his own conflicts.

Four days after Korvettes' press conference, this writer was assigned a pleasant task. He was asked to write an analytical feature about Korvettes tied to its big expansion move and reviewing some of its problems. An initial contact indicated that the spokesman would be Jack Schwadron, the president. Coan was available but busy. Ferkauf was, as usual, unavailable.

Everyone was very friendly and welcoming. Executives were affable, secretaries beaming, Schwadron the epitome of cooperation. As in the previous meetings, I was intrigued by Jack's candidness, his ability to talk nuts and bolts and his lack of pretension which many retailers have. There is, after all, a certain core of mystique or deep expertise that they will not allow you to penetrate. The implication is that if you did you might find that there are lots of things they don't know and thus you will lose respect for them. It had, I learned, no relationship to age. A young man can be just a stiff as an old one. But the Korvettes' president was neither stiff nor old, a delight to interview. He answered even the tough questions with all the depth that he gave the easy ones. I walked out with him to the outer offices, feeling that I had one of those easy-come, easy-go assignments that wouldn't give me any heartaches. In retrospect, I found one thing that surprised me a bit. Everyone had his or her head bent to the task, busy at the desk. I thought it a trifle odd—or maybe I was just odd?—that no one thought it worthy of their attention that the president of their company had just had a two-hour interview with *The New York Times*. But I shrugged. I was probably imagining things.

As I said goodbye to Schwadron and turned to leave, a woman approached me. She identified herself as Coan's secretary and said that he would like to see me if I could spare a few more minutes.

I had met Hilliard Coan before and had considered him friendly, if remote. As I approached him at his desk, he arose, tall and austere, and motioned me to a chair. He hesitated just the briefest time and said:

"I understand that you have just interviewed Jack Schwadron?"

"Yes."

"You spent two hours with him?"

"Yes. We had a good interview."

His face tightened and he seemed almost angry. "Would you," he said, "tell me what he told you?"

"Sure," I said. "I'll be happy to give you a rundown." But I hesitated for a bit. Why didn't he ask Schwadron himself? That's what most top men do when the number-two is interviewed, that is, if they consider that necessary. It was strange, I thought, as I proceeded to give him a 10-minute review.

Walking back to the office just a few blocks away, my mind was in a whirl. What was going on? Obviously, something was. But what? Only four days earlier, Schwadron had capably handled a press conference with a happy Coan looking on. But, as an experienced newspaperman, I had to conclude that there was something not quite right between them. Distrust, jealousy, certainly lack of communication. But there I was, with only two or three days to go before I turned in a purported responsible and knowledgeable piece about the great Korvettes. And suddenly, for the first time that day, I realized that I was on the griddle. What had appeared to be an assignment on which I could lavish as much time on style as on substance had turned into a reporting nightmare.

The next two-and-a-half days were a blur of hurried phone calls, hurried pleas for information, hurried visits to suppliers, analysts, and some Korvettes' employees. Suddenly, Schwadron and Coan became inaccessible—let's not even mention Ferkauf—but I kept phoning. A little after 7 p.m. the third day, I reached Coan, told him what I planned to write. He became irate. He asked if he could come over to *The Times* and meet with me. A half-hour later, he appeared in the building with Paul Gould, his public relations man.

For the next half-hour we exchanged information. Coan more-or-less confirmed exactly what I had obtained from other sources. Very heatedly, he also told me some things that were on-the-record and some things that were off-the-record. But his main message was that I would be much wiser if I held up on the story until everything was more conclusive. I told him and Gould that I could not do that and Coan left, quite angry. In any case, he icily said, he would "not be available for comment." The next morning, Friday, June 11, 1965, the first financial page of *The Times* carried the following story, headlined over four columns, with photos of Schwadron and Ferkauf, in excerpt:

PRESIDENT OF KORVETTE'S MAY RESIGN TODAY

Jack Schwadron, president of E. J. Korvette, is expected to resign today, and Eugene Ferkauf, founder of Korvette, will take a more active role in the dramatically-growing discount store chain, according to Wall Street sources.

Mr. Ferkauf is expected to continue to hold his present titles of chairman of the executive committee and chief executive officer.

Reports from the financial community of impending changes in Korvette's management came, paradoxically, only a few days after the discount chain announced its most dramatic expansion move. . . . Hilliard J. Coan, chairman of the board, could not be reached for comment. Mr. Schwadron declined comment and Mr. Ferkauf was not available.

A source close to the company indicated that Mr. Schwadron's resignation was caused by policy differences with other members of management.

It is understood that Korvette's board will hold a special meeting this morning to take up Mr. Schwadron's resignation. If his resignation is accepted, as it is expected to be, Mr. Schwadron will become a retail consultant, it was indicated

. . .

Of Korvette's 4,802,064 common shares outstanding as of last October, Mr. Ferkauf held 502,937 shares, Mr. Coan held 167,185 and Mr. Schwadron held 95,551.

According to financial sources, Mr. Schwadron, who continued as president during the management changes in May, has had differences of policy with both Mr. Ferkauf and Mr. Coan.

Among these differences were opposing philosophies on merchandising of goods and certain administrative matters, as well as on methods of advertising and public relations.

An apparent breach also developed when George Schwartz, a long-time executive of the McCrory Corporation who joined Korvette last year as vice president and general merchandise manager, resigned when he and Mr. Schwadron found their merchandising philosophies incompatible. There are reports that Mr. Schwartz may soon rejoin Korvette in roughly the same capacity he held before.

Similarly, trade sources conjecture that Mr. Ferkauf, who has operated as a catalyst and "idea" man rather than as a direct administrator, will assume either the presidency or be elected chairman of the board. In any event, Mr. Coan will either remain as board chairman or become president and he and Mr. Ferkauf will head Korvette jointly.

The next day, Korvettes abruptly called another press conference. The early afternoon meeting at the company's offices at 1180 Avenue of the Americas was stormy almost from the very outset. The crowded room contained representatives from all the newspapers, the wire services, most of the television and radio stations, and members of the trade press. One of the latter, an aggressive, independent older man, immediately insisted that Coan answer all the questions raised by *The Times'* article. The reporter's manner was pugnacious. He was obviously angry, as were some of the other press people that *The Times* had snagged an exclusive. But pugnaciousness was the last thing that Coan wanted from the press at that time. Sparks flew between them; there was a growing murmur that Korvettes probably had deliberately leaked the story to *The Times*. The mood of the thirty or so press people put Coan on the defensive, even though Paul Gould had spoken individually to some of them in an effort to soothe their feelings. Coan read a prepared statement in a hoarse voice confirming just about everything in *The Times* story, occasionally darting a grim glance at the offending writer who tried vainly to blend into the wall behind him.

Eugene Ferkauf assumes the company's presidency that day, Coan read, but also continues in his prior posts. And in a prepared separate statement included in the general one, Ferkauf and Schwadron said that the latter had resigned "so that he could establish his own retail and merchandising consulting firm." Korvettes, the statement said, will be the new consultant's principal client, although, as a query determined, it already had a dozen consultants. But Ferkauf and Schwadron said that the departure stemmed from policy differences between them. And George Schwartz had been elected senior vice president for mercantile operations and a director at a Korvettes' board meeting that morning.

The newspaper's disclosure of top management changes at the highly visible discount chain also brought a sharp reaction in the stock market. By the end of the day, 96,800 shares of Korvettes common shares had moved on the New York Stock Exchange, making it the second most actively traded stock on that exchange. But the reaction was apparently disapproving, as the stock closed down two points to 38⅜.

In a telephone interview after the press session, Schwadron declared, "My decision to retire from the Korvettes organization arose as a result of an honest difference between Mr. Ferkauf and myself as to the timetable which should be followed in the evolution of our merchandising philosophy. Our basic difference was the trading-up policy which we were carrying on. Mr. Ferkauf felt we had come too far too quickly and we should slow down."

Schwadron's thrust in merchandising increasingly had moved away from other discount chains toward emphasizing higher-priced, higher-quality goods. And, in fact, only a few days earlier at the press conference that he had hosted, he had stated that Korvettes intended to bring the "high style" of Fifth Avenue merchandise to 34th Street.

Neither he or Ferkauf were present at the press conference. But their names continued to be referred to throughout the discussion. In answer to a question, Coan asserted that Schwadron's resignation "will not lead to any changes in our operations." And, as to the elusive Ferkauf, Coan also responded to a question by saying that he "suspected that Mr. Ferkauf would continue to avoid publicity in his new role as president."

And with that came—is it only a nasty newspaperman's needling recall?—Hilliard Coan's only smile of the entire meeting.

7.
The Big Merger, At Last

A nd so it was business as usual. Coan ran the plans board meetings with the same confidence and dispatch. It was almost the same as before except that there was no bright-eyed Schwadron to sit in with him nor any Gene Ferkauf who was supposed to replace him. The tall, restless Hilly Coan was obviously more in charge, yet there was something else there at those long, rambling meetings. A presence, not quite palpable, a ghost.

As they sat and shifted and listened, the dozen or so men and the two women executives, Eve Nelson and Pat Astor, the personnel director, wondered what was wrong. Some—those with penetrating eyes and hypersensitive ears—soon identified the ghost. It was Coan's frustration. He may have been running the meetings with more authority, but the *real* boss was out there in the hustings. The lean, blondish, youngish man was out there badgering the managers, massaging them with the old Brooklyn patois, sweet-talking the customers and, late in the day, checking in with a rash of crazy ideas.

It was that cloud of Coan's frustration—not Ferkauf's absence—that hovered over the meetings and convinced the smart ones that things were not quite what they seemed.

Schwadron had not quit because of Ferkauf. *Coan* had wanted the young, amiable president out. And because Coan had insisted, Ferkauf took it on himself to make it appear that he and Jack were on an irreversible collision course. In all the flurry and attendant publicity surrounding the ouster, the only thing that hadn't rung true was the Ferkauf-Schwadron tiff. Yet there was always the possibility that Ferkauf and Schwadron had really quarreled, given Ferkauf's difficult, chameleon personality.

"Hilly pushed Schwadron out," Eve Nelson recalled. "Why would Gene want Jack out? He brought him in to trade up our fashion image. But Jack was in Hilly's way. And Jack called a spade a spade. Coan didn't like that."

To most of the original-originals, it all became very obvious. Coan had never liked Schwadron coming between him and Gene. And assuming that, the next step was easily foreseen, in the view of Mel Friedman, Bill Willensky, and some of the others.

If the company didn't quite realize it, Schwadron's unexpected "resignation" right after a dramatic and positive press conference on the new Herald Square store stirred the business and trade press. And Coan himself hadn't bought any bouquets at the raucous press meeting on Friday, June 11. The media now were on the prowl. Perhaps the sacrifice of Schwadron didn't quite sit right. Coan's vocal resentment and self-righteousness also annoyed. And everyone was puzzled over Ferkauf's continuing lack of visibility.

The New York Times, the *Wall Street Journal, Women's*

Wear Daily, and *Discount Store News* were particularly irksome to Coan. They continued to stutter about Korvettes, to putter in its problems, and generally to stir the pot. So Coan threw a veil over the operations at 1180 Avenue of the Americas. It was difficult to know what was going on there, but the word drifted out from unhappy, troubled employees who were being torn between Coan's growing anger and frustration and Ferkauf's off-the-scene activity.

Soon, the Korvettes' chairman ordered that no one in the organization was to talk to the press. Every query, however trivial or innocent, was to go through Paul Gould, the public relations man. Under no circumstances was anyone to accept calls from Barmash at *The Times,* Dan Dorfman on the *New York Herald-Tribune* and later on the *Wall Street Journal,* or Fred Eichelbaum of *Women's Wear Daily.* The reason behind these orders was unknown at the time.

Early in 1981, I interviewed Raymond Blank, a management consultant in Baltimore where he heads a firm under his own name. He was administrative vice president of Korvettes in the mid-1960's. He and his brother, Alvin, had founded a consumer finance company in Baltimore, the Northern Acceptance Company, which also sponsored a credit card. In 1963, the firm was purchased by Korvettes and operated as the NAC subsidiary, handling its credit and accounts receivables.

In a discussion of Korvettes' "watersheds," he delivered himself of this unexpected and unsettling disclosure:

"We are talking about watersheds. *You* were one of the watersheds. You came out booming in *The Times* with the full details of the shenanigans that were taking place. Coan became frightened. He would read what you wrote and he became convinced that people were betraying him."

But that wasn't enough, Blank recalled. Coan convinced

himself that the board room was "bugged"—or was the leak in Baltimore where the credit business was based? "What scared the heck out of him and his closest associates," Blank said, "was that there were no secrets anymore. If the press could wire into the board room, no discussions were private. An aura of fear was growing in the main office and no one was sure that he or she wouldn't be accused of consorting with the press."

Coan had the board room swept for evidence of a wiretap or similar device. Nothing turned up, and the press continued to jab away.

Then, as always seems to happen when a bogeyman is sought, a negative event spilled fire on Coan's suspicions. Without warning or apparent reason, the First Pennsylvania Bank, Philadelphia, decided that it didn't care to renew a loan to Korvettes for $1 million. It was not a major disappointment since the company had plenty of credit line left with other banks. But the unexpected turndown convinced Coan that the bank had been influenced by the negative stories in the media and that the media were truly plugged into his board room and his people. He raved.

But he had the command seat. Coan looked like a chairman of the board. The decisions, the bankers, the visitors came to him and he handled them well. Ferkauf, having fulfilled the fiduciary role of accepting the presidency, preferred to stick it out in the hustings. The fulcrum of the business may have been divided between them but Coan's presence at headquarters clearly gave him the edge, even though the company's profits were still waffling.

A minor irritation was the Schwadrons' liquidation of their stock holdings in Korvettes in November of that year. Jack and his brother, Arthur, sold their combined 150,000 shares for about $4.3 million in the open market. The stock was still a hot one, though sharply down from its high, and when the Schwadrons' shares were snapped up Coan and Ferkauf reacted with the shock of opposing messages. Obviously, investors were closely watching the company, willing to increase their stake in it. At the same time, it was just as obvious that they, Coan and Ferkauf, were on the griddle to firm up the company's profits.

There was little doubt, however, among Ferkauf's boys, now increasingly infiltrated by Coan's cohorts, that power was slipping away from the Korvettes' founder. The food merchant was ultimately practical; the discounter still an idealist. Now, Coan was running not just a retail food business but a general merchandising business with a substantial food arm. Technically, Ferkauf should have been present at the plans board meetings to give the discussion the benefit of his vast experience. Sometimes, he showed. Most times, he didn't. So Coan's voice carried in all spheres.

Eve Nelson recalled that she listened with growing unhappiness to the misguided decisions, but she could only shrug at the time. She remembers thinking, "A dress ain't a can of beans," and she spoke up about it, vainly, of course. She was, after all, thoroughly identified with the Ferkauf rather than the emergent Coan group, and the tension was growing between them.

The tug-of-war was telling on Coan, too. Every so often, Coan would completely reverse what he had said at a previous meeting, or schizophrenically cancel a policy decision he had issued in a company-wide memorandum, keeping the company in a constant state of indecision. Added to that, his rather arrogant, ascetic manner held back any critical comments from his own people. "Follow me, don't question me," was clearly his attitude.

Beyond that, however, the alliance was growing stronger all the time between himself, Norman Rothman, Korvettes' carpet chief, Alan Haberman, the food supervisor, and

George Schwartz, the general merchandiser. Between them, Coan and Rothman, who had received Korvettes' shares when he had sold his own carpet company, owned a formidable amount of Korvettes' common. Arrayed on the other side, of course, were Ferkauf and his own in-house associates, Willensky, Mel Friedman, Eve Nelson, Dave Rothfeld, Leo Cohen, and Murray Beilenson. Each group had lots of stock. But there was one difference in the tightening power struggle. Sitting in his command seat, Coan could pull the strings to further his own team's moves more easily and effectively than could the field commander. By 1966, as many members of Korvettes' board of directors were loyal to Coan as were loyal to Ferkauf. Now the teams were even, and they were squaring off.

In the latter half of 1965 and the early months of 1966, Gene Ferkauf often felt that he was leading a charmed life. Traveling from store to store, indulging himself in art galleries, buying first editions, enjoying the increasing beauty and charm of his three growing daughters, finding the companionship of Estelle an ever-growing satisfaction, and with it all basking in the great repute of having founded the nation's largest discount chain, he was often quite happy. The unpleasant Schwadron incident was behind him. And if Coan represented a cloud in his sunny horizon, Ferkauf consoled himself with the realization that when you give up part of the act, you simply have to let the other guy strut on the stage.

On the other side of the ledger, of course, his pipelines remained firm inside the company and he took calls at night from his resentful, unhappy loyalists. Characteristically, he helped them to rationalize that things couldn't be the same as they were when the company had become so huge, with sales of almost $750 million. "When a business is small, you can put your arms around it," he'd say. "When it gets big, it needs other arms, too." One thing that they could all be sure of. They could all count on him, big or not, and he would never let them down.

He made new friends or warmed up relationships with old ones. John Loeb of the important investment-banking house of Loeb, Rhoades. Two of Loeb's close associates, Thomas Kempner and Sandy Weil. Herbert Brody of Supermarkets General. Some important suppliers became close friends. Richard M. Dicke, Korvettes' outside counsel, was almost like a brother. And one of the most important new relationships came in 1966, when Ferkauf met Charles C. Bassine, a dynamic, charismatic apparel manufacturer and operator of the Spartans discount stores, who operated the diversified Spartans Industries.

The Bassine friendship had three roots. First, Bassine was an apparel supplier to Korvettes. Second, his son-in-law, Arthur Cohen, chairman of Arlen Realty & Development, was a landlord of Korvettes and a major developer for their other stores. And soon there was an even stronger root. As the families met and socialized, Bassine's twenty-six-year-old son, David, was attracted to Ferkauf's oldest daughter, Barbara, nineteen, and they became engaged to the great joy of both families.

Tied by business and personal relationships, the Bassines and the Ferkaufs decided to travel abroad together. For several weeks, the two men and their wives spent an idyllic time in Greece and the Grecian isles. They even visited a store in Italy that Ferkauf had invested in and the men decided that it had been an interesting but unproductive tangent for him. During the trip, Ferkauf unburdened himself to the older Bassine, discussing the matters of Korvettes, Coan, Schwadron, and the matter of management infusion. Bassine, who had built his own $375 million business from the ground up, was helpful, philosophical, and a just plain good ear.

By the time the two couples returned home, Bassine and Ferkauf were solid friends. As he admitted repeatedly afterward, Gene said, "I found a new father image in Charley. He's a great person."

Relaxing once again in his big, brick colonial home in Queens atop the Grand Central Parkway, Ferkauf found himself on the receiving end of a flurry of disquieting phone calls from his adherents in the company. Coan was up to something. No one knew exactly what. There was an aura of extreme security at 1180 Avenue of the Americas. Coan's gang was very tight-lipped. Tension was building but it was impossible to know right away over what. All Ferkauf could do was to urge the "boys" to keep their antennae flapping for the first sonic tremors. He spent lots of time with both Richard Dicke, his close friend and lawyer, and with Charles Bassine, his new friend and father image.

The media, too, began to hear that something was up. The situation was too pregnant to continue unchanged. It was all like a head of pressure pushing a cork up the bottle and ready to pop. But what? The big news, of course, was in Washington where Lyndon Baines Johnson held fast with highly vocal Texan hyperbole against the anti-Vietnam chorus. But in New York's volatile retailing-fashion market, eveyone sensed that something was about to explode in the most visible, most controversial company, Korvettes.

Two days before Christmas 1965, *The New York Times* dipped its journalistic toe into the muddy water. In a lead story, a financial "Sidelights" item, the writer asked whether Korvettes wasn't seeking a new president, again. "Retail and Wall Street sources say it is," the article read. "Management of the nation's largest discount chain vehemently denies the report."

In addition to noting that Hilliard J. Coan had vigorously

denied the report, the article noted that a partner in Carl M. Loeb, Rhoades & Company, which owned 337,089 shares of Korvettes, denied that his company was involved in a search for a new Korvettes' president. The article also noted in passing that Eugene Ferkauf, the company founder, had added the title of president since the June 12 resignation of Jack Schwadron and that Korvettes' earnings for the first quarter ended October 31 had declined sharply from the year before.

The brief story concluded with a statement that trade sources said that the job "had been offered within the last two weeks to an executive of Sears, Roebuck & Company but that it was declined."

Christmas, New Year's Day, Lincoln's and Washington's Birthdays, and Easter passed, and still nothing happened. But the company's stock kept throbbing in anticipation of an imminent move.

In mid-May, Hilliard Coan met constantly with his closest cohorts in the company. He had never quite given up his suspicion that the board room, his office, and all the other principal offices were bugged. So the group met away from the office, or in Coan's office if a thorough search had been made beforehand. In what emerged as a final meeting, Coan spoke with satisfaction. "I think it is time to make our move." His deep, cultured voice was calm but the others could see that he was full of controlled tension.

He stared at them as though the die were cast. "I'll call him to come into the office tomorrow afternoon," he said. "And I want two of you to be here. I want him to see that we are a solid front."

That night, sitting in his "private" den (he didn't even like his family to invade it) Gene Ferkauf had just hung up on the third phone call in fifteen minutes. Each one simply confirmed the other. This was it, this was what all hints threatened. The phone rang again. It was Hilly Coan, inviting him to come in the next afternoon for "a little meeting." Ferkauf's heart began pounding, pounding.

As he sat and listened to Coan, Ferkauf was hardly conscious of the two others who flanked the speaker. His consciousness told him that technically they worked for him but the conviction that hardened their faces was proof sufficient that they were Coan's staunch tribunes. Later, he could not even remember their names. But he could never forget Coan's words, battering at him after an initial exchange of small talk:

"Gene, the time has come for the final step in our reorganization. I can't turn this business around without having the ultimate authority. You're Korvettes' past. I'm Korvettes' future. I want you to turn over the chief executive officer's title to me. In fact, I demand it. If you don't—"

Ferkauf walked out. In an outer office, he phoned Richard Dicke, the partner of Simpson, Thacher and Bartlett, who had been Korvettes' corporate attorney since 1955. They spoke briefly, Ferkauf excitedly, Dicke calmly.

The next morning, Dicke called on Coan. A native of Salt Lake City whose father had sent him to live in New York so that he "could get some of that East Coast patina," Richard Dicke was a tall, disciplined attorney who had developed an excellent reputation as a skilled corporation lawyer but kept a clear strain of the homespun hardiness of the plains. He had a habit of saying not many words, but each one was meaningful. He had told Ferkauf during yesterday's phone conversation, "If you're going to shoot the king, you're going to have to get him with the first bullet."

And now, as Coan stared at him challengingly, he delivered it. "Hilly, you misfired. It's too bad that you asked Gene to step down in front of two witnesses," he said. "That's disloyalty on a public basis. You have completely misjudged Eugene's temperament. He will now never allow you to become the CEO. And there's only one thing left for you to do."

Coan's long, classic face completely drained of color. Perhaps if he and Gene had had a private conversation, perhaps if—but there was apparently nothing more to be said. Dicke rose, nodded solemnly at him, and departed.

A few days later, in his lavish home in Great Neck, Long Island, Charles Bassine answered the telephone himself. It was Ferkauf, anguished, a bit guilty, wanting urgently to see him. After listening for a few minutes, Bassine said, "All right. You might as well come right over. Beulah has some of her friends here tonight, so we'll talk in our kitchen and do our business there."

A day or so later, May 20, 1966, to be specific, *The New York Times* broke the following exclusive story:

KORVETTE HOLDING MERGER TALKS WITH SPARTANS INDUSTRIES, INC.

E. J. Korvette, Inc., and Spartans Industries, Inc., are discussing a merger. If consummated, the joint enterprise would create a retail discount and manufacturing business with sales of more than $1.3 billion a year.

Reports of the merger talks were confirmed last night by Charles C. Bassine, chairman of Spartans, who said that they were still "in the early stages."

Eugene Ferkauf, president of Korvette and chairman of the executive committee, could not be reached for comment.

Although Mr. Bassine declined any further comment beyond a cryptic confirmation of the reports, it is understood that the discussions have been held only between him and Mr. Ferkauf, and their attorneys, with other key executives in both companies remaining almost completely unaware of the proceedings.

A strong possibility was said to exist that Hilliard J. Coan, chairman of the board of Korvette, would either take another post within the organization or resign if the merger was consummated.

Mr. Bassine would become chief executive officer of the Korvette-Spartans combination. Mr. Ferkauf would continue in his present posts, with the possibility that he would relinquish the presidency to another executive. . . .

The next day, Ferkauf also confirmed the merger talks. Coan remained unavailable for comment. The news forced Korvettes' stock to move up 1⅜ that day and financial market speculation centered around the fact that the proposed merger would have widespread ramifications. Among the possibilities: That the consolidation would lead to a spinoff of Korvettes' troubled food operations. That Hilliard Coan would soon go. That George Schwartz, executive vice president, would soon go. That Korvettes' 42 percent holdings in Alexander's Inc. might prove a stumbling block to the deal. And within the Korvettes' organization, concern was expressed about the tenure and security of numerous supervisory personnel. The uncertainty stemmed from the possibility of integrated buying, merchandising, and other functions of the two companies, despite the probability that Korvettes and Spartans would continue as separate chains.

Coan decided to follow Dicke's advice. There was only one thing left for him to do, especially after the kitchen conference between Ferkauf and Bassine and the next day. That very next morning at a special director's meeting, Ferkauf delivered his bombshell. "I have decided to cast my one million shares in the company in favor of a merger with Spartans Industries," he said, with a simple dignity. "That means that Spartans will technically take over Korvettes but we will operate as an independent company. And Charley Bassine will become part of our management." He stared around at the foes and friends, including Coan, seated at the table. They, of course, knew a euphemism when they heard one. Deciding that his words had penetrated, Ferkauf then, as he always did, abruptly walked out.

"We had no warning," Mel Friedman recalled. Bill Willensky and Eve Nelson also were shocked that the announcement came with absolutely no advance hint. The board meeting closed shortly afterwards in turmoil.

Several hitches soon developed, raising hopes in the Coan camp. Ferkauf and Bassine, in their haste to merge, had failed to ask the Federal Trade Commission for an advisory opinion prior to planning the merger. Normally, this is done in order to either obtain tacit government approval for a merger or to determine that such a merger might be considered a violation of antitrust law. And there was the matter of the 42 percent interest in Alexander's held by Korvettes, the retention of which by the merged company might well represent a monopolistic ownership. And finally, there was the matter of some ninety Spartans discount stores as well as another large group of Atlantic discount stores owned by Spartans. Those holdings also raised a question of antitrust holdings.

Both Korvettes and Spartans had scheduled special stockholder meetings to be held in July. But when the F.T.C. intervened and asked for more information on the proposed deal, those meetings were postponed until September of the same year, 1966. And before those meetings were held, the F.T.C. gave its approval but insisted that both companies sign consent orders to take effect within five years. Korvettes agreed to sell its interest in Alexander's. Spartans agreed to divest itself of its Spartans-Atlantic stores. All in all, a small price to pay for a corporate marriage that both companies now sorely wanted.

The two separate stockholder meetings, held to consider one of the largest corporate mergers in the history of American retailing, were scheduled for the same day, September 22. The Spartans' meeting at the Commodore Hotel in New York was calm, quiet, and relaxed. Bassine, always an assured, smooth, commanding presence at annual meetings of his company, was in complete control. When it was just about over, he announced in his florid tones that 3,223,298 shares present had voted for the merger with 314,650 votes against. Motion carried, 10 to 1, with no feelings ruffled.

The Korvettes' special stockholder's meeting was another matter. For more than two hours, stockholders paraded up to microphones at the New York Hilton Hotel to hurl acrid, sometimes confused and venomous charges at the rostrum. There, Richard Dicke, Korvettes' lawyer, tried to deftly field the questions. But the meeting got out of hand several times. Sitting at the head table, but off to one side, Ferkauf stirred restlessly, his face flushing, often seeming poised to make a run for it.

Stockholders, at least the highly vocal ones, were stirred by four things. They appeared confused and annoyed by the fact that a smaller company appeared to be absorbing a much larger one, moreover a much lesser-known, less-respected company swallowing up a better, more respected corporation. Others were concerned that Korvettes had agreed to sell its shares in Alexander's, probably preventing them from buying such shares in a company long rumored to be planning to go public. In addition, there was dismay over the fact that Korvettes' stock had dropped precipitously in the last year. And, finally, there was the gnawing feeling that the dividend policy included in the merger terms would provide only lean fare for the average shareholder.

The owner of fifty shares, Harry Griffiths demanded to know why Korvettes had persisted in an aggressive expansion program in the face of declining profits and a succession of management changes. Isidore Wiener, another shareholder, turned to face those in the audience and told them in impassioned tones, "I urge you to get up and vote against this merger—and show that you are not pawns!" Then he strode to the front and leaned up against the rostrum, asking Richard Dicke, "Why did all the money I paid—the $55 a share I paid for this stock—go down the drain? Last week, the stock sold for $15!"

Calmly, Dicke replied, "We have no way of controlling the changes in the stock market but must concentrate on the affairs of the company."

The divestiture of the Alexander's stock created a flurry of its own. Two professional stockholders took the initiative. Evelyn Y. Davis asserted that the Korvettes' shareholders should be the ones to share in the divestiture if it should be offered in a public sale. John Gilbert asked the meeting's chairman to take a hand vote of the audience to see how many wanted to participate. The lawyer consented and a majority in the room lifted their hands.

Throughout, Ferkauf remained silent, except to wave a greeting when he was introduced at the outset. But he wasn't to be left without a moment of ultimate embarrassment. He had been pale and grim during a barrage of comments from the floor over the proposed engagement between David Bassine and Barbara Ferkauf. But when someone shouted hoarsely over the floor mike, "The whole merger is a dowry!" he stood up and whispered in Dicke's ear. "I've been told to say," the lawyer announced, "that the engagement is off."

The merger was approved by 71.5 percent of the Korvettes' shareholders present, or 3,677,258, against 2.2 percent, or 112,566 against. Motion carried, more than 30 to 1, with feelings ruffled, probably permanently.

Ferkauf had his merger.

PART THREE

The Strategic Years (1967-1971)

8.
Uncle Charley

The atmosphere on the sixth floor of 450 West 33rd Street is bright, vibrant. Secretaries move briskly, their voices on the telephones and intercoms alert and friendly. Executives in the small but modern offices wear responsible, determined expressions. Their rapport, if one can judge from words, glances, body stance, seems good. Everyone appears to be in emotional balance; no hysteria, pressure, no lack of control here. And nowhere, at least in the outer offices, is there the sort of malaise that might underlie a recent merger. Everywhere smiles and warmth bathe the visitor.

It is what is commonly called "a new ballgame." Gone the ratty old offices on the Avenue of the Americas. Here in a sprawling new building across the street from the entrance to the Lincoln Tunnel are the headquarters of some of America's giant merchant businesses, Lerner Stores, Zale Jewelry—and Korvettes. If new trappings denote a change, Korvettes has changed. And if one can capture a mood from a first visit, it is a different, revitalized company.

Now, the visitor is escorted, no, floated on a carpet of good-will, by a secretary and others who lead the way to the human embodiment of all the changes. One enters the new office curiously to see the occupant in his new context. A heavy-set, swarthy man in his late fifties wearing an expensive dark suit comes forward with outstretched hand where two gemmed rings glisten. "Welcome, welcome," he says, his hand crushingly friendly. "It's wonderful to see you here at the new Korvettes."

"Hello, Charley. It's good to see you, too. How's everything?"

"Wonderful, just wonderful."

He motions to a vast, lush sofa and moves to his desk. He stands beside it and there is a sudden sense of astonishment. It is the largest, broadest, most impressive desk one can imagine, certainly five feet wide and perhaps seven feet long, its surface covered with a variety of rich, brown leathers. It is entirely clean of any papers, writing materials, anything. He notices the visitor's surprise and a question forms around his deep-set eyes and prominent nose.

"Charley," the visitor says, "that's got to be the biggest desk in captivity."

He laughs deeply, almost a guffaw, in a baritone on a bass undertone. "Let me ask you a question," he says. "Do you think that the chairman of the board of a $1 billion company should have a small desk?"

The visitor can only shrug.

"I've always wanted to head a $1 billion company," he adds.

"I guess you're not alone," comes the weak response.

He sits behind the huge piece of furniture and a conversation ensues across the room with its large, oriental rug and richly paneled walls. There is to be no interview, he reveals. "A lot is going on, you can believe me," he says, "but we're not yet ready to tell the press. I wanted to see you and show you the new place and maybe meet some people. Later, there will be plenty to write about."

He excuses himself to take some calls. In face-to-face conversations, he is articulate, enthusiastic, even loquacious. His great talent, as the visitor has learned in the past, is his credibility, his ability to convince people. He is a born salesman. Much of his aura, though, seems to depend on personal contact. On the phone, he is laconic. But even on the phone, the short phrases, pauses, sighs, and murmurs have an authority of their own. When he completes his last call, he says, "I want you to meet two people before you leave. They're important in this new organization I am building."

A few moments later, his secretary ushers in Murray Sussman, president of Spartans, and Samuel Weissman, financial vice president. We chat briefly. They are both low-key, obsequious to him. As we all leave, the outside offices seem somehow pale and unimportant. The strength, warmth, and paternalistic power flow from behind that huge desk. The visitor has, simplistically or not, put the man in his new context. If he proved to be Ferkauf's father image, he creates an avuncular relationship with everyone else—tough, demanding, protective, exacting his toll of extreme loyalty.

Uncle Charley.

Charles C. Bassine was born in 1909 in Brooklyn, attended the borough's Boys High School, and took night courses in pre-law at New York University. Later, he finished law school but never took the bar examination. He couldn't afford it. He was doing too well on a job he had taken even as an undergraduate. He had become a salesman for the H. D.

Bobb Company, a producer of men's shirts, and even while studying law had established himself as its star salesman.

Much later when he was a multimillionaire and chairman of his own company, he could observe without any evident trauma, "I am a frustrated lawyer chiefly because I could not afford to give up a well-paying job to complete my law apprenticeship."

In 1936, after becoming one of Bobb's senior executives, Bassine decided, in perhaps his first giant step, to start his own shirt manufacturing company, opening his first plant in Sparta, Tennessee. Taking the company's name from that town, he developed his business as a supplier of basic shirts to the big catalog chains. In about a dozen years, his sales had reached $4 million. He then took the second of his giant steps. He moved his headquarters to New York, increased his sales staff, expanded his line from shirts to a full array of apparel, and became a major supplier to a wider retail spectrum. Always, his own selling ability eased the way to important new accounts. By 1956, or twenty years after he had launched his own firm, his sales totaled $20 million and by 1960 volume topped $40 million.

But he carefully avoided the big arena of major branded garment manufacturing where large advertising budgets are a competitive tool. Unlike Cluett Peabody, Phillips-Van Heusen, or Manhattan Shirts which had a lock on the public with their respective Arrow, Van Heusen, or Manhattan men's shirts, Bassine was the king of the unbranded garment, not only shirts but many other items. No doubt he could have made an important mark in the more prestigious branded field if he'd wanted to, but he liked the low-price, high-volume field with its tremendous leverage.

It was big time, for sure. In 1958, he shipped some thirty-two million garments to Sears, Penney's, Montgomery Ward, and whoever else would buy them and put his own labels on them. That year, he also took another giant step. In an effort to compete with the increasing flow of foreign imports, especially from the Far East, he set up manufacturing operations in Hong Kong. In a few years, it became the dominant portion of his output and he gradually closed many of his domestic plants.

In 1960, he took the penultimate giant step, one which, along with the strong, paternal rapport he had built with Ferkauf, provided the bridge for the later merger. He entered the burgeoning discount-store field. A dynamo in whatever he did, Bassine within four years had twenty-six discount stores in operation under the Spartans' name. If he had drawn attention with his great success in manufacturing, the new venture brought him awe.

By 1966, the year he merged with Korvettes—acquired is probably a more apt word—he was one of the wealthiest men in New York with a fortune estimated at between $30 and $100 million.

Was it skill or luck? The simple answer was that he had both. When he had made the decision to go into business, he knew the possibilities that existed in the South to help him do so. Alabama, Tennessee, Georgia, the Carolinas were all eager to clear any obstacles for ambitious businessmen, no matter where they came from, as long as they had some reasonable capital. Not only was Sparta eager to help, but so was a regional railroad. The town's fathers wanted jobs. The railroad was eager to pull more freight. So Bassine got a building at a very, very favorable rate, and the carrier proved amenable to suggestions on rates and scheduling. It took skill on his part to know and maneuver the authorities but he was lucky that they were, in effect, waiting for him.

He wasn't always skillful or lucky. When he opened the Spartans' discount stores, the expansion was noteworthy, but store-opening expenses and organization-building costs were much higher than expected. They brought first a decline in corporate profits and then a deficit. Bassine was stunned. How could Mister Right be wrong? He gave up eating lunch or dinner in public places because he didn't want to be seen. He wanted to hide.

But he rallied, cut the high expenses, and jarred Spartans Industries back onto the right side of the ledger. In fact, as if to throw sand into the open eyes of the critics, in 1965 he acquired the Atlantic Discount Stores, a forty-store chain, and added it to his own group. And, the next year, he acquired Maro, a hosiery and apparel manufacturing concern.

With that, only months before the merger with Korvettes, he was back on top. And he showed it. There was in his booming voice, erect back, heavy shoulders a sort of coiled strength. His face, dark and lined, sometimes seemed to give off a threat of unleashed, raw power. His prominent black eyebrows gave him a look of imperiousness but he rarely demonstrated it. All in all, what he sold was credibility and trust and his advice was sought by many on both professional and personal matters. Fear is often part of respect, and he sold that, too.

Probably, in that year of 1966, three decades after he had gone into business, everything came into play for him. At the Empire State Club, Club 21, the Harmonie Club, and other luncheon and dining spots, people carefully watched who he spoke to and noted what investments he might be making. The word went out: "If Charley likes it or wants in on it, it's got to be good." Inevitably, he became part of many business deals or at least a soul mate in them.

Bassine, in relation to Ferkauf, was at the same time a supplier to Korvettes and a co-philanthropist and art connoisseur. At one point, knowing that the Korvettes' founder wanted to set up a merger with Alexander's Inc., Bassine

volunteered to make it a three-way merger with Spartans.
Farkas couldn't have cared less. But when Ferkauf found
himself threatened and proposed a two-way merger, Bassine
sighed deeply, hesitated only briefly, and said yes. To many
people, even though Spartans was the smaller company, it
seemed right that Bassine should come out on top. He
deserved it. He had paved the way for that final giant step,
for the good-will and the respect, for thirty years.

All that stood Bassine in good stead when he made the
merger with Ferkauf. The simple fact was that Uncle Charley charmed them all—Ferkauf, Korvettes' stockholders,
Spartans' stockholders and even Hilliard Coan, not to mention Carl M. Loeb, Rhoades—into agreeing to the deal.
Once Bassine saw Ferkauf's eagerness, once he perceived
that the other large stockholders agreed that he would indeed provide the management that Korvettes sorely needed,
the battle was over. Had Bassine made the overtures to an
uncommitted Ferkauf, the bargaining would have been
tougher.

As it was, though, Bassine took all the spoils:

Spartans, the smaller of the two companies, would be
the surviving company, at least in name. A legal tech-
nicality? That's what the lawyers said. But the psychological
and structural implications were clear. It was like the city of
Buffalo taking over New York City.

Korvettes, which was in effect being bought, had to issue
a new set of stock, about 4.2 million shares of junior preferred, in exchange for the common stock of Spartans. The
new shares issued by Korvettes would be convertible into
common stock of the surviving company on a share-for-share
basis. That in itself was unusual, the reverse of the norm
when the buyer dilutes its own stock to lure the seller.

Hilliard Coan, of course, was through, departing the

morning after the September 1966 merger approval by the stockholders. Alan Haberman, George Schwartz, and Norman Rothman also left. Ferkauf may have gotten satisfaction from that. But Bassine was also getting rid of a rival. He would not have stood for that.

As for his own role, Bassine would be chief executive officer, president, and chairman of the board of the resulting, combined company.

Perhaps because I was covering the merger steps more closely than anyone else, Bassine invited me to come, that evening, to the office of his law firm where both Spartans' and Korvettes' top managements were thrashing out the terms of the merger.

I was warmly welcomed by a friendly secretary. As she settled me in a side room, with a sofa, armchair, ash-tray, and a dish of shelled peanuts, she pointed up the hall to a closed door at the end and whispered, "That's where they are meeting. There's about twenty of them in there."

While I sat there reading and wondering just why I was there, a young man in a dark suit emerged from the room of deliberations, saw me sitting there, seemed to become incensed, and angrily spoke to the secretary. I heard his muttered words, "What the hell is he doing here?" Then he spun off down the hall.

The secretary now came to me and told me that the young man, a partner in the law firm, was afraid that "with everything being so confidential" I shouldn't be sitting where I was. The thought occurred to me that to eavesdrop from fifty or sixty feet away through a closed door was quite a feat.

"Well," I said, "that's all right. I was about to leave anyway."

Startled, her eyes filled with tears. "Please," she said. "Mr. Bassine insisted that we have you here. Please don't leave, not until I get word to him in the conference room that you plan to leave. Please?" Sympathetically, I allowed her to escort me to an office somewhat more removed from the combat area. I was dismayed to find that it was the office of the young turk who had uprooted me. He stared at me with an unlikely smile from a large photograph in which he posed with what appeared to be his family. I fidgeted, really wanting to bolt off.

Then the door opened and it was Bassine. I stared. He was in his element, dapper but saturnine, his dark face aglow with sheer, inner light, signifying, I was sure, the triumph he must be achieving in the closed room.

"These lawyers," he said. "They get nervous every time they see a newspaperman. Come, I'll make you more comfortable."

"No, I've got to go. Just give me a number where I can call you—"

But he had already taken my arm and was moving me closer. "I do want you to stay," he said. "It can't be more than another fifteen minutes. Let me take you into a more comfortable office. It will be worthwhile for you, I absolutely guarantee it. You will be the only one with the inside story."

Now I was in still another office and I had lost any sense of direction. Was I closing in on or receding from that all-important conference room? Bassine had disappeared and was no doubt holding forth there. But suddenly the secretary returned, proudly bearing a tray of Cutty Sark, a glass, a fresh dish of shelled peanuts, and two expensive cigars. "Please do make yourself comfortable," she said, her eyes swimming with gratitude. "Mr. Bassine was so distressed."

An hour later, I was still there. From time to time, I stood at the window, looking down at Fifth Avenue, which was awash in moonlight reflected through a slight drizzle and a haze of polluted air. I felt both foolish and as though I were being used. Just about an hour after Bassine had come out, the secretary was back at my side. "Come," she whispered excitedly. "They're ready for you."

I was brought forward to the conference room where a seemingly endless stream of people was slowly exiting. Bassine, his face even more aglow, introduced me to his top team, some of whom I already knew. The same glow of elation made their faces round, joyous, proud. But none more so than Bassine's. "What were you doing while you were waiting?" he wondered, his arm clasping my shoulder. "I'll bet you could hardly wait."

Looking him directly in the eye, I said, "I was wondering what all those people down on Fifth Avenue would think about all this? Do you think they'd like to come up here and wait two hours like I did? Thousands, I'll bet."

Bassine and his men stared at me unbelievingly. Finally, he grinned and slammed me on the back. "What a goddam sense of humor!" he shouted. "That's one thing that I always liked about you." He turned to his people and repeated it as if they hadn't heard. But the way he told it to them, I knew he meant just the opposite.

"Now, now," he intoned, his heavy, black eyebrows dancing, "to fulfill my promise. I want you to talk to someone. Then we'll go out to dinner, the three of us, and you can ask us anything you want. And every damn word will be on the record!"

I replied in low tones that I would have fainted from sheer delight, only my weak physical condition probably would have made me fall in the opposite direction. I was being churlish, but I don't think he heard me because he was already moving back into the conference room.

It was obvious, of course, who he would bring out. Ferkauf. I hadn't seen him in several years. He had avoided the press even more than before, running from its snipping and sniping over the up-and-down earnings, the departure of Schwadron, the power struggle with Coan. Those of us waiting out in the hallway couldn't help overhearing the conversation just inside; it went something like this:

"Come on, Gene, I told you I invited him here. This is a history-making merger. It's only right that he should be here to represent the press. Come out and at least say hello. This is for posterity."

"Screw posterity. You talk to him."

"Gene, what's wrong with you? Are you afraid of a newspaperman?"

"Hell, yes. I just don't want to have anything to do with that pain in the ass. You talk to him—I'll just go out the back."

"That's just like you, Gene. You yourself said that this merger is your lifeline but you've got to come through, too. You have got to face up to a tough situation and bull it through, damn it. That's the way you've got to play this game."

They emerged. Bassine had his arm around Ferkauf, as though supporting him and encouraging him at the same time. The unwilling Ferkauf, at least a dozen years younger than his new partner, looked at least twenty years older. His face was pale, his eyes appeared tortured and red, and he drew his breath with some difficulty. Bassine introduced us as though we hadn't met before. I couldn't help quailing under Ferkauf's hot glare. As we shook hands, he said, "You wrote some rough stuff about me. Is it personal?"

How to answer that? Foolishly, I resorted to desperate humor. "Sure. I'm jealous of that big dowry."

Bassine intervened, fortunately. He guffawed and slapped us both on the back. "Damn it," he said, snapping his fingers at one of his top men, "this calls for a celebration. Who stole the booze?"

Gene revived a bit after some liquids. The three of us

then walked through the ranks of possibly thirty people in the law office on our way out to the elevator, like a triumphant procession after a bloody battle. I never saw so many obedient smiles, heard so much well-wishing. It should have been inspiring and might have been if I hadn't been tired and hadn't felt guilty about Ferkauf.

Down on Fifth Avenue we didn't mind the slight drizzle. The cool air and the spray on our faces were invigorating. I glanced up and could just barely make out the windows of the law offices. Some lights were winking out as I watched; others remained on. How long, I wondered, would they stay on into the night, picking up the pieces?

It was well past ten o'clock when we finally dined at one of the city's best Italian restaurants. Both men talked to me for about two hours. Bassine said that this night had fulfilled his career dream of heading a $1 billion company. Ferkauf said that the night was both the greatest and the worst in his life. I said that the night would force me to file for overtime under the Newspaper Guild contract. This, oddly enough, sent them into raucous laughter.

Bassine, beaming and elated, explained the new chain of command. He said Ferkauf "will continue to hold a position of great executive importance to the corporation with emphasis on merchandising and store operations. I will consider Mr. Ferkauf my adviser and consultant."

Ferkauf, agreeing, said, "It is my preference that for the best interest of the company, the merged company have only one top executive and that will be Mr. Bassine."

He went on, slowly, that the merger was "the right decision after several wrong decisions." There were two reasons for his decision that Bassine become the combined company's chief executive, president, and chairman. One was that Bassine was "a great administrator." Second was that Bassine had become "a father image" for him. "My

attitude today," Ferkauf admitted, "is one of relief. I feel that
I have finally found the man to run the Korvette operation
after many years. I could have made this marriage a few years
ago, but I had reservations. Don't ask me what they were. I
guess I just wasn't mature enough but now it comes at the
right time."

This candidness, this voluntary self-flagellation, didn't
come easily to Ferkauf. The entire interview seemed to pain
him while Bassine, the host, was enjoying himself hugely.

As we left the restaurant and walked down Fifth Avenue,
Ferkauf stopped for a moment or two to stare at the Korvettes' store there at the corner of 47th Street. He said
nothing, just stared. Neither Bassine or I said anything.
Whatever the Korvettes' founder was thinking, it was to
remain private.

When we parted, the two of them left together. Bassine
explained that, even though it was so late, they still had some
things to talk over. Ferkauf didn't say anything, not even
goodnight. It was clearly the end of an era.

Within weeks, less than two months, Bassine, like Coan
before him, moved quickly. He had his own people, Sussman and Weissman, check into everything. Everything that
Korvettes did had to earn its own way. The first thing to go
was the Eve Nelson door-to-door cosmetics business. The
small mountain of inventory was disposed of rapidly by
selling it all at 40 percent off normal prices in the Korvettes
store. Bassine was appalled to find that expense and inventory controls in most divisions of the business were very
loose; he quickly took steps to tighten them all.

But unlike Coan—and certainly unlike Ferkauf—Bassine bubbled with charm and loved an audience. In December 1966, he made his first public appearance as the head of
the combined company when he spoke at a luncheon meeting of the New York Society of Security Analysts. The invita-

tion was flattering, a recognition of the importance of the newly merged company and of investors' interest in it. The morning of the meeting, Spartans Industries Inc., the merged company consisting of the former Spartans and of Korvettes, reported higher sales of $1.976 billion against $923 million of the year before. But net income dropped sharply to $7.98 million from $14.6 million, or to 84 cents a share from $1.58 a share. That, however, didn't faze Bassine.

Often, public companies appearing before the New York analysts are optimistic about their prospects, enthusiastic about ongoing activities. After all, they are reporting to the people who can recommend, reject, or just ignore the stock of their companies. It behooves the speakers to be moderate in their claims and projections in order to achieve credibility. But not Bassine. He flatly predicted gains of 50 percent in earnings in both the then current and the next fiscal years for the newly merged company. There were, in fact, a few gasps from the packed audience, partly because of the humiliating earnings decline reported only hours earlier, and partly in astonishment when Bassine called his estimates "a very conservative forecast."

What was the basis for the glowing predictions? The improvement would come from more efficient operating procedures in all divisions of the company rather than from any proportionate increase in sales, Bassine said. New merchandising controls have been installed in the Korvettes' division, he explained, "which will create an instrument for making money such as this company has not seen before.

"Korvettes has had a sound merchandising policy but it lacked a system of controls on knowing how much goods to buy," he said. "Now," he added, smiling broadly around the audience, "it has that system."

After a "disastrous, hemorrhaging situation" in the prior fiscal year, he went on, the furniture division's losses had been stemmed. Furniture still wasn't making any money but "may be put on a decent, profitable basis in the next six months."

The hour's talk was filled with blunt remarks and many expressions of high optimism. "There were," he summed up in a booming voice, "no disaster areas remaining in the Korvettes' operation."

As one who sat in that audience listening and observing the reactions around me, I couldn't help admiring Bassine for his *chutzpah*. But I also couldn't avoid the feeling that he had hit the wrong tone. Given his "conservative estimate," it seemed to me that he should have controlled his own effusiveness. This was, judging by some of the prim lips and guarded expressions of those around me, a risk he had taken that he might well rue. As the meeting broke up, I spoke to a few analysts I knew and their reaction was surprised and skeptical. Their "advisories," or reports on the talk, I noticed later, were generally of a wait-and-see nature.

But he had accomplished one thing. He had created and embodied a new image—a friendly, bluff, tough "Uncle Charley." He convinced everyone that Korvettes was truly in the hands of a "new broom," an entirely new and different personality who would take it to new heights—or new depths—than it had ever experienced before. Here, indeed, was Management with all that that connotes—decisiveness, conviction, clear goals, and strong beliefs in corporate discipline.

He showed it with a series of decisive actions. The man who had acquired a stellar reputation for handling stockholders' meetings and philanthropic fund-raising sessions with great aplomb and success found little difficulty in persuading his own directors to go along with his plans. He said that quite reluctantly he had come to the decision that Spartans would never make it in the food business with its painfully small profits; that it should move to sell Korvettes' supermarkets. The first steps were taken to do this. Also, since Korvettes already had forty-three stores and was deeply involved in implementing new controls, its expansion should be sharply slowed or even postponed. However, the projected Herald Square store would open in 1967, the year just ahead, as would the large new store planned for Brooklyn's Bath Beach section.

It was a sobering thought. Slow down Korvettes' locomotive, even though profits are down? But no one rose to contest Bassine. Nothing firm was decided at the moment but the signal raised was clear.

Bassine, perhaps capitalizing on his closeness to his son-in-law, Arthur Cohen, chairman of Arlen Realty & Development Corporation, the builder and landlord of a large number of Korvettes' and Spartans' discount stores, reached agreement with Arlen to buy forty-five of those leased properties. Spartans would issue a new convertible security and pay about $50 million of it for the land and buildings. The purchase of about twenty Korvettes' shopping centers and stores and of twenty-five Spartans store premises would make Spartans an owner of stores and shopping centers, not just a tenant. It would make the newly merged company real-estate rich, perhaps compensating to a certain extent for the eventual, enforced sale of its large interest in Alexander's Inc. Arlen would still own a number of the Korvettes' centers and stores. But the move brought Bassine and Cohen, or Spartans-Korvettes and Arlen's, into a much closer relationship.

Now Bassine moved to fill the first vital Korvettes' executive openings. David Brous, formerly merchandise manager for furniture, was promoted to vice president and general manager of home furnishings. Alvin Blank, who had been an officer of the N.A.C. Charge Plan and the Northern Acceptance Corporation before its acquisition by Korvettes, was appointed president of the N.A.C. Credit Division and of Korvettes' financial activities. Abraham Jacobson, who had been Spartans' administrative vice president, was named senior vice president and director of merchandising, working with the general merchandising managers. And Mel Friedman, then a vice president, was appointed senior vice president for store operations.

But, in arranging those appointments, Bassine stressed that he would personally maintain administrative control of Korvettes in addition to running the total company.

Yet, despite those appointments and his evident increasing grasp of the total operations, Bassine smoothly sidestepped two issues. One was the need to name a president of Korvettes. The other was the status of Ferkauf. He was still the ubiquitous visitor to all the stores, the late-afternoon "exploder" of new ideas, and the non-presence in headquarters.

On both matters, Bassine could wait, at least for awhile. An uncle's attributes, in case you haven't noticed, are forebearance, good-will, patience, and a sort of loud joviality in the face of family problems.

So it was, at that point, with Uncle Charley.

9.
Is There a President in the House?

W hy did you appoint *him* president?" one of the stalwarts asks later.

He stares at the questioner, his heavy eyebrows arching in a parabola of incredulity. "Let me get this straight," he says, leaning forward. "You want to know why I appointed *him* president?"

"Right."

Admiration over the other's persistence and disbelief at the question fight for priority on the dark face. But it all disappears in a huge guffaw that rumbles up in the barrel chest. "What the hell's the difference who is president?" he shouts, his voice carrying to the corridors. "It's Bassine's company!"

Bassine, one of the most charismatic personalities on the giant New York merchandising scene, has a unique talent and he knows it. He can make weak men straighten their shoulders and stand tall. He can make uncertain men feel full of resolve. He can walk into a room tight with tension and, by sweeping it with a wide smile, uttering a few slightly self-depreciating, slightly assuring words, transform the atmosphere into one of good will. He is a physical man. Powerful, with strong, heavy bones, he exudes a sense of basic confidence on a one-to-one basis. His warm, hairy hands clasping a shoulder, a friendly smack on the back passes on that confidence to others.

But, he knows too that it's one thing to realize a lifelong ambition of running a $1-billion corporation, and another to actually run it. He has already taken a few steps, the most obvious ones. He has put a cork on further expansion. He has put new, needed controls on expenses and inventory accumulation. He has indicated the need to sell the food business, possibly the furniture business, and has called an end to the door-to-door cosmetics business. But those steps, he tells himself as he flings out of the chair to pace around the handsome, paneled room, are corrective, not creative in nature. New offensives are needed because the situation has changed drastically.

In the first few months after he took over and 1966 crept into 1967, he often closed the door on the rest of the world and leaned back in his chair and shut his eyes. What—he asks himself as he rubs his big, bristly chin—to do? As the new broom ponders his role, the strengths and weaknesses, the triumphs and failures, the company's position in its economic and market matrix is obviously uneasy. Can he stir the pot so that the sediments fall to the bottom and the juices rise to the top? If so, how?

He knows that he has his critics and his sycophants. Some are sincerely envious, and others are sincerely doubtful that he is the right manager for the awesome responsibility. But no one believes that Bassine has inherited an easy or simple job.

While he ruminates over the next, highly strategic steps that the giant company should take, Bassine puts much of his own steam into overseeing the moves he has already generated. He has all his executives backtracking everything they did, he had his own people at Spartans taking a hard look at all that they had inherited. One thing he did not do was name a president.

Of course, he still had Joseph Lamm, the executive vice president for administration, as a sort of right-hand man, just as Ferkauf for a time had had Robert Riesner as general merchandise manager. But Lamm left as Riesner did before him.

"When I arrived at Korvettes in February 1968, there was no president," recalled Lawrence Goodman, who became the company's senior vice president for sales promotion. "Several guys were vying for the job. Leonard Blackman, vice president and general merchandise manager. Mel Friedman, executive vice president. One or two others. The atmosphere was uncertain and unsteady because there was an open fight for the presidency that disturbed people. I guess besides that open battle, the atmosphere reflected the fact that Korvettes internally was never a sophisticated retailer. A lot of the original, 'stickball' crowd was still there but Bassine was bringing in new people from other retail companies. Things were churning and it was hardly a situation that you could come into without trying to know where you stood right off the bat.

"I insisted on being interviewed by Charley Bassine. And I was. I found him smooth, suave—an urbane, sophisticated man. But I could see that he didn't know much about retailing. He was an entrepreneur and he knew the apparel business. Strangely enough, the management group didn't meet very often. In the three years I was there, I was only at two meetings."

Yet, though he found it exceedingly hard—or very intriguing—to hold back on a presidential appointment, Bassine could already point to some successes in his first year at Korvettes.

The 50 percent gains in sales and net profits that he had predicted for the first year didn't materialize. However, Korvettes showed improved profits in the fiscal year ended July 31, 1967, although its sales fell below the prior year's. Volume failed to show a gain because "no new stores were opened during the year," he announced, "and sales reflected the erratic pattern of general retail activity."

The bottom-line performance had responded to "better controls over markdowns, shrinkage, and inventory." The total company, Spartans Industries, Inc., had enjoyed gains in both sales and profits. These came despite a setback in Korvettes' big-ticket durables as well as the "roughest" year in the history of Spartans' apparel manufacturing business. Spartans' earnings in apparel manufacturing were "below what we had expected," he said, because "we had to compete with the dumping of higher-priced makers who were suffering sales reverses."

The company expected to realize about $23 million in cash and "other considerations" from the sale of several of its properties, including the Hills-Korvette supermarkets to Pueblo Supermarkets, the thirteen-store Crank Drug Stores division to the Katz Drug Company of Kansas City, and a small personal-loan company operated by the N.A.C. Credit division.

Spartans-Korvettes decided to divest itself of those properties so as to "streamline ourselves and to concentrate on Korvettes and our apparel manufacturing business," Bassine said. "I want to eliminate the lace and trimmings." The proceeds of these sales will be used to expand the remaining entities, he added. "This has been a year of preparation and now we are ready to move ahead. We believe," Bassine said, "that our potential is enormous."

Four days later, he proudly hosted the opening of the long-awaited Herald Square store in Manhattan. It was a chilly, foggy, early November day in 1967 but thousands of bargain-hunters waited for the flashy, nine-level store to open. It had been built on the shell of the defunct Saks-34th Street store. But the promised neoclassic design, with twenty-six recessed, six-story high pillars and a seven-level corporate tower on top of it all, had given way to economic necessities to produce an odd hybrid. Set on a slightly curved plot to give full advantage to the happy confluence of three streets—34th, Avenue of the Americas, and Broadway—the building from the second floor up was covered with vertical rows of tiles, groups of which were separated by full-length black indentations. The effect was strange, as if a typically pragmatic, utilitarian, suburban discount store had landed in the heart of urban New York with nine levels instead of the usual one or two. The unusual boxlike structure contrasted oddly with the ancient but classic look of Macy's and Gimbels on either side. It was, in a word, a "cheapie" entry. But the appearance of Korvettes' 34th Street store imparted the city's greatest hub of mass transportation with a splash of gaudy novelty—and the lure of bargains.

It was a tremendous coup. Bassine enjoyed every minute of it. He stood shoulder to shoulder, each beaming at the others, with two arch-competitors, David L. Yunich, chairman of Macy's New York, and Bernard B. Zients, president of the Gimbels New York stores. The Korvettes' chief was obviously stirred beyond the mere symbol of operating a $1 billion company. Macy's had taken a full-page ad in the metropolitan papers. "THE WORLD'S LARGEST STORE GREETS A NEW NEIGHBOR," boomed the ad. Other competitive brass was there, too, from the nearby B. Altman, Ohrbach's, and Franklin Simon. Mary Lindsay, the wife of New York Mayor John V. Lindsay, cut the ribbon and then went immediately upstairs for the breakfast in the store's cafeteria.

The day may well have been Korvettes'—and Bassine's—finest. Ferkauf was there, too, but he hung back in the crowd. Korvettes had spent about $1.5 million for new floor and wall fixtures and brought in about $6 million in inventory at retail to open the store. The 260,000-square-foot structure, the largest of the chain's forty-five units and the eighth in New York City, fanned the hopes of Korvettes' top management that the company would now become the biggest retailer in the city. With the Fifth Avenue store, one on the East Side between 44th and 45th Streets, and stores in Brooklyn and the Bronx, as well as the outlying stores in Long Island, New Jersey, and Westchester County, Korvettes was now a formidable retailer. Nothing seemed to stand in its way. Its profit problems were apparently capable of solution. And Korvettes even appeared to have a top manager who was comfortable with pressure, publicity, and people—the three "P's" that had dogged Ferkauf. The merchandise content, too, had a clever premeditation. The store offered an expanded group of some of Korvettes' most successful departments, and added as many smaller departments as they could cram into the narrow building in order to provide a complete department store. They even included that symbol of up-to-date merchandising, an escalator, something that Saks-34th Street had failed to provide in sixty-three years.

It was probably no wonder that in a *Time* Magazine article on the Herald Square opening a handsome, smiling, gratified Bassine appeared in an accompanying photograph. He stood benignly outside the new store, its big logo immediately over his head and on the side a fractured glimpse of Macy's. The focus, literally, was on Korvettes and Bassine. Macy's was an afterthought.

For those who had followed Korvettes' fortunes, the highly successful, crowded opening created a sense of undeniable excitement over the company's success despite all the stumbling and fumbling. In twenty years since three scared, amateur merchants had opened a second-floor store, practically a cubicle, the company had amassed sales of $800 million, had opened forty-five stores in nine states, and was even vying with the elite stores of Fifth Avenue and the giant Macy's and Gimbels on Herald Square. And, as one observed Charley Bassine, glowing and resplendent in his host's mantle, it was impossible not to feel some pride and awe. Out in the Detroit area, the S. S. Kresge Company may have overtaken Korvettes' role as the nation's largest discounter with the K mart division. But Kresge (later to change its corporate name to the K mart Corporation), had been in business for a much longer time than Korvettes. No one could take away the accomplishments of Ferkauf and his "stickballers." And Bassine, urbane, impeccable in a dark suit with white handkerchief, had been handed the company to carry it forward to greater, more ambitious heights.

The opening was a day on which no one remembered Korvettes' problems, and those who did thought rosily that the problems were close to solution. But the problems were very real, and they hadn't gone away.

For almost twenty years, Korvettes had had the discount field all to itself. Now at least three difficult battles have to be fought simultaneously. Korvettes has spawned a host of imitators that have to be fought. Korvettes has to cope with

constantly rising expenses that militate against the low operations cost that discount stores need. And, ironically, the
huge, two-level stores, built during Korvettes' formative
years, have created operational difficulties and now work
against its competitive strategies.

A few years later, Robert M. Warner, a top Macy's executive who joined Korvettes as a senior vice president,
summed up problems, eloquently and with hindsight:

"The reality was that Korvettes found great success for
two reasons. One was that it could sell cheaper and people
go crazy when you can do that. The other was that it had big
assortments. With both of those, people became aware of
Korvettes and flocked to it. But it also attracted rivals who
started copying it.

"We live in a world of knockoffs. It's bad because everything becomes a plastic world, but it's good because the
good, desirable things get spread around. That's what happens when you have a good idea. People respond in an
incredible way, like with Korvettes, McDonald's ham-
burgers, Kentucky Fried Chicken, Bic pens, Hyatt Regency
Hotels. But the great payoff is to be the fast *second* in the
marketplace. So there was Interstate, Arlan's, Two Guys,
Caldor, K mart. . . .

"What happened then was that Korvettes started losing
market share to other discounters and to department stores
that were beginning to catch on to the strategy," Warner
continued. "The result was that their sales per square foot
declined in dollar terms and expenses went up as a percentage of sales. It was inevitable. There were other reasons, too.
When the company started out as a discounter, the essence
was to be able to sell cheaply and to do that the expense
structure had to be low. But, after the first small stores,
Korvettes' management began to build stores which made it
impossible to have a low expense factor.

"Instead of building supermarket-type stores with checkouts, they built department stores of two levels," he said. "But the most important feature of supermarkets and discount stores is the one-level structure where you can take a shopping cart wherever you want to and then to a front-end checkout. So, Korvettes wasn't geared for that sort of operation even though the original concept was discounting. The big, bi-level structures meant that shopping carts could only be used to a minor extent, if at all, and that instead of central checkouts, there were area checkouts with their higher expense burden. In addition to all that, the stores ranged from 180 to 220,000 square feet, about one-third too large to get the necessary sales per square foot out of them.

"Besides all that, the company proliferated too far from home base," Warner said. "This led to problems of distribution, supervision, customer identity, and lack of market dominance. These were some of the problems that Korvettes faced after just about two decades of unparalleled success. What do you do when such success leads to problems of that magnitude? And what does a management do when it is faced with head-to-head competition that has studied all of the original company's triumphs and blunders?"

Warner contends that unless a business learns to take action and shift its approach in its "growth" phase, it will be much more difficult to do so in the "mature" phase. In the growth phase, he adds, it is enough to have the idea but inevitably the experience acquired should point the way to directions to be followed in the mature phase. Market segmentation? Pushing divisions or departments in which "you can become unbelievably powerful"? Raise or lower markups, the former infinitely more difficult than the latter?

"It's not a situation that lends itself to an easy solution," he emphasizes. "There is no easy answer to the dilemma of a company which grew strongly on one concept but finds itself vitally needing an entirely new concept. That's why so many retail businesses that started out on a low-price basis eventually went out of business. The road to failure was taken at that point when the management had to change its concept and either took the wrong road or didn't take any new road at all."

Through the rest of 1967 and into the first few months of 1968, Bassine continued to operate without a president or a number-two man, even though the company's margins had fallen from 5 percent after taxes to under 2 percent of sales. It became obvious that new controls, however effective, would tackle only part of the problem. Something new in merchandising was needed to prop up the profit ratio. Also needed was a new approach to Korvettes' image to bolster and recapture the market share eroded by the new competition.

In January 1968, Bassine took a step designed to prepare for all those perceived needs. Spartans Industries announced the formation of two new divisions, and appointed Eve Nelson to head them as a corporate vice president. On the surface, the decision had an entrepreneurial flavor. Spartans' industrial sales division was established to make bulk sales to corporations' incentive programs and to provide contract sales services for companies and institutions. In addition, Korvettes started a radio sales division that would sell announcement time to its suppliers over the public address systems of its forty-five stores. Besides running those two new enterprises, Eve Nelson would be responsible for the door-to-door cosmetics business, then in the process of being phased out.

However, Eve Nelson, who nonetheless threw herself into her new duties with the same *eclat* with which she did everything, felt distinctly that she was being phased out. It

Opened in 1953 on West 48th Street, this was one of Korvettes' last small stores.

Eugene Ferkauf

Courtesy Discount Store News

and some of "Gene's boys"—left to right, Jack Schwadron, William Willensky, and Joseph Lamm

Courtesy Discount Store News

Willensky and George Yellen at a press conference

Gene Ferkauf with
Israeli Minister to the
U.S., Nachum Shamir,
at Korvettes'
Douglaston Art Gallery

The two-level prototype store that was to prove so troublesome in later years

A grand gesture—Korvettes on Fifth Avenue.

Courtesy Chain Store Age Executive

Eve Nelson,
Korvettes' first
professional sales
promotion expert.

Courtesy Discount Store
News

Korvettes confronts Macy's at
Herald Square...

Courtesy Eve Nelson

At left, David Yunich of Macy's and Charles Bassine of Korvettes (right)

Courtesy Eve Nelson

Leonard Blackman

Courtesy Eve Nelson

Bassine in his element—a stockholders' meeting.

Courtesy Discount Store News

Arthur Cohen, Arlen Realty and Development.

Courtesy Discount Store News

Dave Brous.

Courtesy Discount Store News

Marshall Rose, Arlen Realty
and Development.

Courtesy Discount Store News

One of the new team's management objectives: a clear store.

The Other Korvettes campaign and its hanger symbol.

Joseph Ris
Courtesy Discount Store News

The Willot Brothers, owners of the Agache Willot Group. Left to right: Antoine, Regis, Jean-Pierre, and Bernard.

Courtesy Raphael Fenet France Soir/Scoop

was hard for her to think otherwise when Larry Goodman, who had been vice president for sales promotion at Stern Brothers, the New York division of Allied Stores Corporation, was appointed Korvettes' vice president for advertising, sales promotion, and public relations.

A month later, in February, one of Bassine's problems solved itself. Eugene Ferkauf, who even in his fadeout status had continued to pop up in the stores, ad lib changes in their operations, and still maintained a clear ideological and emotional hold on many of the executives, decided to retire for "personal reasons." At forty-seven, leaner, more intense than ever, but somehow bemused and out of sorts—befitting a company founder who had sold his business—he requested retirement on February 8. Bassine accepted his resignation "with regrets." Ferkauf and Estelle had received about $20 million in stock from the merger and were fixed for life. In making the announcement, Bassine said that he did not contemplate that Ferkauf "would seek employment in another company." The founder's most recent post—chairman of the executive committee—was discontinued. There were no parties for Ferkauf. He shook a few hands that he couldn't avoid and simply left.

Trade sources, the ever-lively grapevine which made gossip about people and companies a never-ending font of conversation, suggested that he might fade away from Korvettes but would soon be involved in one or two things, probably simultaneously. One would be to start a new retail company. The other would be to foster the economic development of the State of Israel by aiding its import activities. The sources were right. He did both.

A month later, on March 11, almost two years after the Spartans-Korvettes' merger, Bassine chose as president Leonard Blackman, the forty-one-year-old vice president and general merchandise manager, who had joined the chain in 1955. Bassine described Blackman's appointment as "a key step" in the further development of Korvettes' management. Mel Friedman, the closest rival as executive vice president, was named vice chairman. The other disappointed rivals, of which there were at least three avowed entrants and several of the closet type, received nothing.

A short, dapper, smiling man with a clipped mustache, Blackman had truly come up through the ranks in little more than a dozen years. He had started as an assistant manager ("I knew Lenny when he was pushing tables around" Eve Nelson said) and had moved up in a variety of merchandise and managerial posts. In 1963, he became a vice president and in 1966 he was appointed a vice president and general merchandise manager. According to some of his closest co-executives—Eve Nelson, Herbert Ricklin, the industrial-relations director, Larry Goodman, and Mel Friedman—Blackman had a high talent for store presentation, the arranging of merchandise in an attractive, effective manner. But they agreed that his abilities as a top corporate manager had, at least up to his appointment as president, not been clearly demonstrated. So his selection surprised almost everyone, shocking some, dismaying others. Leo Cohen, who was Blackman's counterpart as hard goods general merchandise manager, quickly resigned in a tacit protest.

Despite his unexpected choice of Blackman, Bassine continued to play the "Uncle Charley" role, maintaining his paternal-avuncular status, so that some of the executives were not afraid to come to him and ask why he had chosen as he had. Herbert R. Ricklin, who had come to Korvettes in 1959 as industrial relations vice president from three and a half years as an assistant personnel manager at Food Fair Stores, recalls such a conversation he had with Bassine.

"Blackman was glib, street-smart and hard driving but

we all assumed that Bassine would go outside for a president because he didn't seem to be grooming anyone," Ricklin said. "When I asked him about why he had picked Blackman, Bassine said, 'What are my options, Herb? To merge with Sol Cantor of Interstate Stores and let him be president? That's the only way I will get him. Or some other guy from a large discount chain? Who is there? I'm just as well off with Blackman.'

"Bassine," Ricklin continued, "was a brilliant, visionary guy except when it came to some major decisions on his own company and on the merged operation. Spartans manufacturing at the time of the merger was already on the brink of decline with twenty-five Southern factories that were suffering because of the inroads of low-wage competition from the Far East. And when he took over as head man of Spartans-Korvettes, he showed an obvious flaw of failing to surround himself with people of his own stature. His own Spartans discount stores were practically a disaster—converted barns and recycled warehouses . . . some of them were pure junk stores."

Oddly, Bassine's choice of a number-two man went against the current corporate trend. In many cases, top managements and boards of directors seeking to name a new chairman or president in an internal environment of severe competition for such posts will go outside for their choice. The object is to avoid the dissension aroused when an insider is named and rivals are so angered that they fight him. Bad morale hurts progress, the thinking is, but when an outsider comes in everyone rallies to show the new man how good he is. As often as not, the benefits of this technique do not materialize. The insiders tend to react resentfully although sometimes the process does produce salutary results.

In making his internal selection, Bassine's motivation was probably well-intentioned but the choice turned out to be not very effective. Under Bassine's heavy hand and domineering personality, Blackman proved inadequate, uncomfortable in his post, and highly defensive. It was not hard to understand why. When the chairman exploded about the appointment by declaring, "What the hell's the difference who is president? It's Bassine's company!" the word quickly filtered back to Blackman. It hardly bolstered his self-confidence or spurred him on to greater efforts as Korvettes' president.

If there was a general agreement among many of Korvettes' executives, the old as well as the newer ones, that Blackman was far from the best president the company had ever had, some of it can be attributed to sour grapes from unsuccessful rivals and some of it can be pinned to sincere belief.

But what titillated everyone were the wisps that filtered out of Blackman's closed door to the effect that whenever Bassine called his president on the phone, Blackman would jump to his feet and stand at attention as he spoke to Bassine.

In any case, Bassine's decision that, yes, there was finally a president in the house, was not a wise one. As it turned out, it was only a harbinger of worse to come.

10.
How to Throw Away
a Public

They were still looking for a dream, incredible as it may
seem. Analysts had stopped following the company in
1966. Sales were slipping about 15 percent a year. The bottom-line sagged $1 million or burped $1 million. But they
still hoped for a dream in 1968, 1969, and 1970.

Bassine had his $1 billion company, Lennie Blackman
had somehow made it to the presidency, and Arthur Cohen
had that synergistic tieup of a vast real-estate empire looking
to build and the forty-five-store Korvettes chain still wanting
to expand. Trouble lapped all around them but Bassine
kicked at the puddles with his usual aplomb.

The old-timers were distressed. Ferkauf was gone. The
new miracle man wasn't hacking it, not so far at least.
Reports that the founder had been seen peering into a Fifth
Avenue store window heartened Friedman, Willensky, Eve
Nelson, Zwillenberg. "He looks good," as one put it; that

pleased them. "He got old—he looks sixty-five," as another reported; it saddened them. But what distressed them most was that Gene's chosen successor, his father figure, appeared to be pushing them aside rather than taking them in.

The newer people were happier. David Brous, who had only recently come from Macy's, was a brash, pesky achiever on the home furnishings side, eager to be fully recognized. Larry Goodman kept hoping that his professional expertise in sales promotion would give the company the public impact it needed. Herb Ricklin was surprisingly able to attract new professionals who apparently thought Korvettes was still an important company with a good future.

While many hopes were riding on him both inside and outside the company, the heavy burden of responsibility didn't change Bassine's personality. He was enjoying himself, his role as the head of a giant business, especially of Korvettes and he had begun to move into merchandising with an evident zest. And those moves became controversial, although it did not distress him.

He reasoned with them all out loud. Korvettes' sales were waffling but clearly it had its loyal customers. The $600 million plus sales—$200 million had been lopped off due to the sale of the supermarkets and good riddance—meant that the chain still commanded lots of loyalty. But it was not making any money to speak of. It was all a matter of energy not producing any heat. There was only one solution. Raise the markup. Logic: even if some customers turned away from you, many others would stay so that the profit dollars would be much better.

It was at this point in the logic that Bassine added another ingredient that had worried opponents of the Spartans-Korvettes merger from the very introduction of the idea. With a substantial manufacturing-now-turned-import business of low-priced apparel, why not use those products as a prime source of supply for Korvettes? He was surprised to see the evident expressions of disapproval.

"What's wrong with you fellows?" he demanded. "You're owned now by a manufacturer and so you have to buy from the company that owns you. It makes lots of sense to me. It should make lots of sense to you." But the argument was already academic. The buyers had early sensed the new shape of things and had increased their purchasing of all manner of Spartans goods. Before the merger, Korvettes' orders from Spartans had averaged about $3 million a year. By 1968, or two years after the merger, it had jumped to $23 million. Two years after that, under Bassine's push, it ran up to almost $100 million at cost.

At the same time, the initial markup was raised from 40 to 42 percent. To sweeten the bitter pill, Bassine made sure that there were plenty of loss leaders. At one point, he offered shoppers four men's shirts for $5 and sold many thousands of them. Then, over a short period of months, he unloaded warehouses full of women's lingerie and foundations, selling 1.1 million bras at inflated prices. Sales began to rise under the combined thrust of apparent bargains and higher-markup, lower-value offerings. Profits rose too—for a while.

Bassine combined this policy with a tight one on expenses. Blackman carried it out with a vengeance. As Raymond Blank recalls it, "Bassine was on an expense-savings kick and decided that maybe credit was using up too much money. So, in 1970 when we opened our store in Reading, Pa., Blackman decided that there was to be no credit-card budget. The store didn't promote its credit at all like every new store should. The store started off just plain blotto. It took quite a while for that store to get going."

On another occasion, Bassine and Blackman became convinced that they could save money by cutting store hours.

"What happened?" Blank said. "Suddenly, without testing it, we would open some of our stores an hour later. Customers would stand outside in confusion and wonder what was going on." Later, normal hours would be resumed as the management attempted to recover from its misjudgments.

Run impulsively from the top with little input from experienced executives, Korvettes in the late 1960's and into 1970 appeared to be grasping one idea after another. It wasn't that the burly Spartans' founder didn't like new ideas. He welcomed them, in fact, as long as they reflected his own philosophy. But his blend of cutting costs and of infusing stocks with lower-value merchandise at a higher markup defused Korvettes of one of its most important weapons—its competitive clout. For years, he never forgave Dan Dorfman, then a financial columnist for the *Wall Street Journal*, for writing an article based on a shopping tour showing that Korvettes' much-vaunted low prices for books were actually higher than prices of competitors.

Bassine put his figure people on a constant quest to ferret out any waste. Inevitably, they showed him data proving what every qualified retailer already knew—that big-ticket durables, such as refrigerators, washers, dryers, and ranges, were minimally profitable, hardly competitive against non-durables for sales per square foot. True, the big stuff drew traffic, absorbed a disproportionate share of fixed expenses, and so took some of the onus off of soft lines. And, since it had always been Korvettes' mainstay merchandise, durables were in a sense the heart of the company. But Bassine, whether he took the revelation of the numbers to heart or whether he merely wanted to increase the flow of his Far Eastern plants to Korvettes, cut back on the durables operations. The heavy promotional guns were shifted to apparel and other soft lines in a direct offensive against an array of powerful competition from Macy's, A.&S., Gimbels,

Alexander's, Ohrbach's and others in New York; and against Strawbridge & Clothier, Gimbels, and John Wanamaker in Philadelphia; the Hecht Company and Woodward & Lothrop in Washington and the Baltimore areas; and similarly in other cities.

The result was predictible—a tough, uphill fight that Korvettes could not win. It was not battling from strength. Shoppers thought of the chain as the place to buy records and tapes, books, cameras, housewares, and still to a great extent refrigerators, furniture, and carpets. Even after some of these departments had been dropped, customers came in looking for them. It proved a hard-to-swallow truth: The public doesn't easily change its mind or quickly adopt new perceptions. The public is tough.

Yet, the dream persisted. Bassine kept busy, stirring the pot. Blackman nervously tried to live up to his new role, occasionally winning plaudits for his determination, uneasy as it was. At the December 1967 annual meeting, Bassine told a packed audience of restless stockholders that Spartans was "deconglomeratizing," leaving only its Korvettes' stores and the manufacturing business. The sale of everything else—the Spartans-Atlantic Stores, the Korvettes' supermarkets, the already consummated disposition of Crank Drug stores and a small Baltimore finance company "would enable Spartans to concentrate on proceeding along two main highways, Korvettes and the soft-goods manufacturing business. There will be little need," he emphasized, smiling broadly around the big room at the old Commodore Hotel, "for outside financing to achieve growth."

And there was, he added, "no sense of urgency about it," referring to the divestitures, including that of the 42 percent interest in Alexander's Inc.

But the three-hour session erupted into frequent exchanges between Bassine, some discomfitted stockholders, and a pair of frequent meeting-goers, Evelyn Y. Davis and John Gilbert. Urgency, at least on the part of the shareholders, filled the air. A particular target, Professor Theodore D. Ellsworth of the New York University School of Business, showed his embarrassment when Gilbert and Miss Davis insisted that he shouldn't be re-elected a director unless he were also a stockholder. After some 10 minutes of a three-way discussion involving the two and Bassine, the professor shook himself out of what appeared to be utter unhappiness, rose, and conceded, "If there is any question, I'll buy 100 shares." He won smiles and re-election.

Irked by other petty exchanges that extended the meeting into its first hour and a half, many stockholders shouted from their seats and implored Bassine to comment on more pertinent matters. "What's the present and future of this company?" was a common plea. And Bassine, who had learned the technique well in running such meetings at his own company, reassured everyone in unctuous terms which soothed their concern like Pepto-Bismol coats a disturbed stomach.

"Korvettes continues to improve its profitability in the new fiscal year," he said. "The new store at Bay and Shore Parkways has exceeded budgeted sales. And the new store at Herald Square in Manhattan is doing tremendously well. It has already become the best store in the chain."

On that point, "We have weathered some strong efforts from our adversaries on Herald Square," Leonard Blackman said in an interview in *The Times* in 1968. In one year, the striking, elliptical store had smoothly assumed the role as the flagship in Korvettes' fleet. It was also among the chain's most profitable units and had topped expectations by achieving more than $30 million in sales the first year. Capitalizing on its opportunity and its success, Korvettes had reduced all non-selling space in the Herald Square store "to grant maximum opportunity for selling," Blackman said. The effect of this, as well as Korvettes' entry into that mass-transit hub, was to step up competition among Macy's, Gimbels, Korvettes, as well as the nearby Ohrbach's and Franklin Simon. Macy's Dave Yunich and Gimbels' Bernard Zients confirmed that rivalry had increased. And, with evident pride, Blackman pointed out that the one-year-old store was blessed with good inventory turnover and relatively small in-store inventory because of the close proximity of the big Seventh Avenue fashion market. Frequent, almost daily, hand deliveries come in from apparel suppliers. As a result, he reported, dress departments "turn their inventories in the store every three to four weeks compared to Korvettes' Fifth Avenue store where the turnover rate is four to five weeks."

Now Bassine picked up the ball. Two years after the merger when he had decided that there were to be no new stores until the company had consolidated its position and improved earnings, he announced that Korvettes would resume its expansion program. The two-year lag was over. With forty-five stores accounting for sales of almost $700 million, Korvettes now would open twenty-eight more stores within the next three years, adding between $300 to $350 million in volume. Three new units were already earmarked, including another in the metropolitan New York area in Suffolk County, an entry which was calculated to heighten the Macy's-Korvettes' rivalry. Did it mean that Korvettes' profits had improved? Bassine implied that that was so, but insisted in an interview that current disclosure laws prevented him from furnishing such information to "any single newspaper."

Nonetheless, Bassine's announcement satisfied the considerable curiosity that had been aroused by the expansion hiatus. Obviously, if Spartans-Korvettes had such ambitious growth plans, things must be improving, right? Conversely, even if profits were better, was such a heavy resumption of new-store building more bravado than sincere intention? Discussion about the matter went on for some time in both the retail and financial communities. Bassine, however, did not care to amplify. But it was soon accepted that Bassine had a fortuitous, not-so-secret weapon. His son-in-law, Arthur Cohen, chairman of Arlen Realty & Development, which had built many of the Korvettes' stores, was as eager a builder as Bassine was an entrepreneur. Together, they were a powerhouse. So it came as no surprise—although it intrigued many that this case of nepotism was curiously expansionist rather than conservative or cautionary—that Arlen would construct almost all of the new stores. Actually, as events later showed, only seven of the proposed twenty-eight new units were ever built.

Inside Korvettes, work was proceeding on both a new image and a strategic change in name.

Aimed to complement the renewal of expansion, the company was changing its corporate logotype, designing new packaging and shopping bags, and, perhaps most importantly, reducing the corporate name by removing the longtime "E. J." from it. "It's all in the interest of providing a shorter, more recognizable company signature," Blackman explained. He said it followed a trend in retailing, citing the fact that Sears, Roebuck & Company had switched to using only "Sears" as its designation. If the move served to underline Eugene Ferkauf's fadeout (he was after all not just the founder but the "E" in "E. J.") no one said it openly. But there was, to be sure, an admission among many that it was probably a worthwhile idea to simplify the name after twenty years of existence.

With Larry Goodman, the new sales promotion vice

president, standing by, Blackman proudly displayed the new packages and bags in blue and yellow. The old script signature was now a modern, block logotype. Five "K's" for Korvettes were featured on the bags and packages, superimposed on a five-K background. Smiling confidently, Blackman further explained that the name and graphic changes were "a major effort to create a new outside image following a series of internal changes that have built a new inside image." The most important of these internal changes, he said, was the appointment of twelve vice presidents "who will help me run the business and assume responsibility for direct-line functions."

In fact, he declared, executive recruitment now also was geared to "attract a more sophisticated professional retail executive." A number of them had already been hired under the new management from other leading retailers, he said. "Our aim both internally and externally is to develop the image that Korvettes is now a young, swinging, professional organization," he added.

One couldn't help feeling that perhaps much proselytizing was going on. But there were some solid accomplishments, too. At the December 1968 annual meeting, Bassine said that the company expected to get about $20 million from its 42 percent interest in Alexander's, which after many years had finally decided to go public. And with the sale of the divisions that it didn't want, he said, Spartans-Korvettes "was finally on our way. We'll earn more money from operations than we need to retain."

The combined company, he went on, "now has a good capital flow from both internal efforts and the sale of our subsidiaries. We have dropped certain furniture units in Chicago and St. Louis and we are negotiating the sale of our beauty salons to a leased operator."

He noted by way of passing that Eugene Ferkauf, who

by then had started a new chain, Bazar, on Long Island, had recently sold "several hundred thousand shares" of his stock in the company.

And after disclosing that the Hartford, Conn., store was the only one in the chain that was losing money, Bassine asked the audience "if forty-four profitable stores wasn't a pretty good record at that?"

A year later at the next annual meeting, Bassine had definite good news, leavened a bit by some unpleasant disclosures. For the first time in more than three years since the merger, the company would pay a dividend of fifteen cents a share on its 5.5 million common shares. The quarterly payout, equivalent to sixty cents a year, equaled the one that had been regularly paid on the Class A stocks. After the expected solid applause from the hungry stockholders, Bassine narrated for a few minutes the progress of the company's revitalized expansion program. Then he told the meeting that "Our fortunes have improved and we have a better working capital, which has permitted us to share our good fortune with you."

Then came the small shockers. For unexplained reasons, shoplifting had boomed in the Korvettes' stores. Twenty thousand suspects were apprehended in the fiscal year just ended. Were the security procedures too loose, not enough staff available to detect shoplifters? Or was there some internal thievery which had caused the rise in inventory "shrinkage"? Bassine shrugged at the questions from the floor. In a reassuring voice, he said that the company was now pursuing "a strict policy" of prosecuting dishonest employees and shoplifters, after having been less strict before.

But a seed had been planted in the minds of those who heard. Was the expense-cutting program hurting, allowing merchandise to walk away? Too much self-service, too few salesclerks? As if to stoke the stockholders' concern, Bassine in the next few moments announced that a stack of blank checks had been stolen from the company's vault. Spartans had immediately notified the banks involved because it had the check numbers recorded and had successfully stopped payment. And the District Attorney's office had apprehended a man who had been caught with the checks after forging the name of Spartans' treasurer on them.

That unsettling news aside, the company's chairman declared that "we believe that we will continue to report higher earnings than last year." (It didn't happen, as events later showed.) And, with his famous smile, he closed the meeting by raising the possibility of yet another Manhattan store, which would be Korvettes' fourth, sometime in 1971. Macy's only had one. Gimbels, two, A.&S., none. Korvettes' new likely site would be the upper West Side. (It never happened.)

That wasn't all, by any means. Some months later in 1970, Bassine announced that Korvettes would soon enter the Florida market, particularly the Miami-Fort Lauderdale-Coral Gables area. There would be as many as six stores. "We will start with two or three," he said, "and then add others. Florida is just the right market for us." (No one ever learned if the statement were true. Korvettes never entered the Florida market.)

In retrospect, it's apparent that Bassine was simply playing to his strength—selling. Willy Loman in Arthur Miller's *Death of a Salesman* may have learned that successful selling takes more than a smile and a good shoe-shine. It takes, in addition, well-grounded credibility, exuberance, an undeniable self-confidence. In addition, while proposing that Korvettes was planning additional out-of-town stores, Bassine may also have been simply fooling everyone.

The simple fact was that Korvettes' out-of-town stores, in Philadelphia, Washington, D.C., Maryland, Chicago, Detroit, and St. Louis, were not doing well. After a strong start in most of those cities, the stores became sluggish and their progress—starting about two years before Bassine's Florida announcement—should have been worrisome. Enough so to make the Florida plan hardly a serious one.

"The out-of-town stores began losing money beginning in the late 1960's," said a former top Korvettes' executive. "They had made a profit in the early years. But the St. Louis stores were losers from the outset. The Chicago stores were losing money, too, while the return in the Philadelphia stores got razor-thin. But it wasn't only in the out-of-town units. The Fifth Avenue store did well for the first few years. It really didn't belong there in the middle of the big, fancy service stores.

"It didn't have the right kind of merchandise, the decor, or the service. But it did have the price—and people flocked to it just for that and the fact that they could get it on Fifth Avenue," he said. "But then Charley came along and raised the markup and brought in the cheaper stuff. That effectively removed the one *raison d'être* the store had. It didn't lose money, of course. It continued to make about $1 million before taxes on $20 million—but it was a store that wasn't going anywhere. It was sort of like a bird with its wings clipped."

All along, Bassine had been getting more involved in merchandising, buying, and pricing. He was convinced that Korvettes needed to operate with lower costs and at the same time push up its margins. An executive who was there in that period related what happened: "Bassine's approach was entirely different from Ferkauf's. Gene always tried to get good quality, operating on a gross margin in the low 30's so that customers would get good value and good merchandise.

"Bassine was accustomed to a low-end, low-price business, not only in his manufacturing operations but in his decrepit Spartans-Atlantic stores. He saw Korvettes in trouble and decided that he had to raise the initial markup and the gross margin. He boosted the gross margin to the mid-30's, at least two more points. And he did it not on the good stuff that we had always had, the merchandise that cost us more, but on an increasing amount of stuff he made in his own Far East plants. And he took the higher margins on branded goods, too."

On Kodak film, Korvettes had always underpriced Macy's on a particular line, $1.60 to $2.00. Bassine boosted it to $1.90, hardly enough of a price differential to keep the Korvettes' customer loyal. Macy's had its own brand of men's shirts at $6. Korvettes had its store-brand shirt of a similar type at $4. Bassine raised the price of the shirt to $5, and then to $5.50, mingling in the stock a rising number of cheap shirts made abroad.

And despite all of Bassine's efforts to cut overhead, costs remained high for a discounter. The combination of those high operating expenses and the higher prices dulled much of Korvettes' competitive edge. "By the end of the 1960's, the other discounters were beating down Korvettes," said the former top executive. "K mart was coming up fast everywhere and things were changing in all markets."

The low-margin operators hit Korvettes hard on pricing," he recalled, "the department store got the name brands, the mall locations and the upper-middle income customers. The only way that Korvettes could do any big business was on its advertising, cutting gross margin on as many items as it could to get the traffic. Combine that with half of the stores, the out-of-town units, doing less and less well, and what did we have? The twenty-five profitable stores in metropolitan New York supporting twenty-five unprofitable stores out of town."

Some of that, if you will, was sour grapes. Like most big companies at the time, Spartans wasn't breaking out its divisional sales and profits but including them in its corporate totals so that Korvettes' real performance was entirely masked. Yet it became clear by 1970 that Bassine was having a difficult time jarring Korvettes back to a profitable track. But he was not letting the world in on it. Bravado, the big smile, and the heavy pat on the back were his best means of covering it up.

In the meantime, the old-timers were beginning to leave, not because they were actually pushed but more because they were either shunted off to unrewarding jobs and tasks or plainly ignored.

"I began feeling not very happy when Bassine took over," said Bill Willensky. "He ran his own show. He had his own people. I had less and less authority, even though I had been president of the company. I didn't leave for a few more years—but it was clear what was happening."

Eve Nelson: "I left in 1971. I was sick at heart. I couldn't take Lennie Blackman but when I told Bassine it was time for me to change, he said, 'Listen, Eve, you've got a job here for life. I'll make you a corporate officer.' I gave in for a while—but it was hard to stay. You just see something grow and grow and then fall apart, brick by brick."

Others left, too. Murray Beilenson. Joseph Zwillenberg. Leo Cohen. Bassine saw them all depart with regret, a reassuring arm around their shoulders. Some left because they had to in order to have a job they believed in. Others out of conscience. Bassine did some unusual things but who could fault him when he was the boss?

One of those odd pursuits was connected with his dichotomous activity on raising markups while at the same time continuing to convince the customers that Korvettes was still a bargain house by offering them the familiar loss leaders. But he did it his way. He created a mythical "Department X." It existed only on paper and was not considered a profit center as every other merchandise department was. As promotional goods arrived, a substantial portion of them were assigned to "Department X." The objective was not to burden many of the true profit-centers with promotional costs. The corporation paid those costs but it came out of a non-profit center. It was not only legal. It was convenient, too.

Despite its proliferating problems, Korvettes sold considerable tonnage of goods, using its immense size as the clout to obtain favorable terms. It obtained distributor terms because of its ability to deliver sales. As David Lapine, who with his son, Mark, operates one of the Eastern states' largest manufacturer's sales agencies, recalls, "Trade discounts to distributors in the 1950's and 1960's were 50 percent off the list price and a discount of 10 percent off the list for co-op ad allowance. On a $10 list, that meant that the distributor paid $4.50. But they charged the department stores $5.40, or 16 percent more.

"But in the mid-1960's, when Korvettes put in its own warehouses, the vendors shipped them direct rather than through distributors," Lapine said. "That allowed Korvettes to get the same deal as the distributor—$4.50 wholesale. But the department stores were paying $5.40. That gave Korvettes the edge in electric housewares, at least, and they sold tons and tons and tons of them. We know. We did a lot of business with them."

Dealing with Korvettes' merchandisers and buyers, all of them under intense pressure, was a hectic, emotional affair, the Lapines recall. The Korvettes' people would make difficult, impossible demands and usually get them. A particular favorite and nemesis of the vendors and sales "reps" was Leo Markman, first housewares buyer and then merchandise manager of small electrics. Burly, hoarse, lovable and hateable, Markman was "a screamer and yeller of the first rank," according to Mark Lapine. There were six men in the housewares office and when Leo would express himself in high decibels the tiny office would resound with the others replying in kind.

Markman, now in the closeout business, was an incorrigible, gutsy executive who built a legend for himself. When Bassine moved the company's headquarters to the big, bluff building opposite the Lincoln Tunnel where only the very top executives had offices with windows, Markman was nonplussed. But he remained as creative as ever. He took a Polaroid shot of one of the walls of his cell-like office, blew it up and posted it with a sign, "My Window."

The Lapines represented Dominion Electric Company, a small Mansfield, Ohio, producer of electric housewares, which was the first such manufacturer to sell in quantity to Korvettes. While the company also sold to the major New York stores, as well as to Masters, the only other discounter to rival Korvettes early and then fade into a smaller competitor, Korvettes' growing size and push proved synergistic to Dominion. The relationship gave the discount chain a ready source of toasters, waffle irons, hair dryers, skillets, and other household items it could discount while Dominion became a sizeable supplier from the volume it racked up with Korvettes.

Korvettes, in its early days and even through the Bassine years, was remarkable for the tremendous amount of mundane household items it dispensed to the public at almost ridiculous prices. "I was often amazed at the volume of goods they moved in such items as ironing tables, shopping carts, folding chairs, and card tables and chairs," Mark Lapine said. "They moved millions of them. They knew how to 'beat the hell' out of such items, outpacing everyone around with such merchandise at the lowest price categories. The public loved them for it, too. It helped to ingrain Korvettes as a true discounter in the public's mind."

Yet Korvettes by 1970 and early 1971 was moving away from pure discounting. The push for better margins was jutting the chain up against the department stores while the other successful discounters were pulling away an increasing share of Korvettes' customers.

Bassine seemed tired at times, as well as he might be. He had an immense vehicle to pull along but the horsepower lagged. And while he was indomitable in the office, he was apparently meeting competition at home. After thirty-seven years of marriage to the former Beulah Kinsman, Bassine's troubles with his wife climaxed in 1970 when she filed suit in the New York State Supreme Court, accusing him of fraud and misrepresentation in handling her finances and sued him for $6.2 million. Beulah, an artist who was achieving some small recognition among gallery owners, claimed that she had begun a financial arrangement with her husband three years after their marriage in 1933 in which she would receive a 20 percent share in his business enterprises. This was her due, she said, because of funds she gave him at various times to invest.

Her suit was based on Bassine's "misleading" her into authorizing the surrender of her stock in the Kardell Corporation, a holding company controlled by her husband. When he urged her to give up the stocks in May 1966, she charged, he promised to pay all taxes resulting from the transaction. But the next year, Bassine told her she would have to pay $1.2 million in taxes accrued from the stock transfer. Before that, she claimed, her holdings amounted to about $8 million. But after paying the taxes, she said that her assets from the transaction amounted to $2.8 million.

She also said that her husband contributed Kardell stock

to charities at her expense, "thus enabling my husband substantially to enhance his reputation as a great philanthropist."

The suit was later settled out of court, prior to the Bassines' divorce. But the publicity created by the suit, and, perhaps more to the point, the years of dissension and evident competition at home, hurt Bassine at a time when he was struggling to put Korvettes on a better footing. His son-in-law, Arthur Cohen, was a valued confidant, apparently not only on the business but on the personal problems, too. But Arthur, whose Arlen Realty at the start of the new decade appeared to have only a golden future, had, it developed, another, totally different influence on Bassine.

"Charley was having a very rough time," said a close friend, who prefers to remain anonymous. "He was being castrated by the troubles with Beulah and by the great success Arthur was having in his business. It's kind of hard to think that a tough guy like Charley could be hurt by what was going on in his own family. But even the toughest guy can take only so much. Maybe if things had been going well at Korvettes—"

Maybe.

On July 21, 1970, somewhat less than four years after he had "bailed out" Ferkauf, Bassine made the most significant, most controversial move of his charmed business career. He proposed a merger with Arlen Realty, involving a $180 million exchange in stock, thus allowing Arthur Cohen to "bail him out."

PART FOUR

The Hopeful Years
(1971-1979)

11.
"I Cordially Wish You
Such a Son-in-Law"

At the opposite ends of the long ballroom table, they sit a bit self-consciously. The bulky, dark-haired, older man and the slim, blond, younger one occasionally direct smiling glances at each other. If it is an important, even unique occasion, they aren't showing it.

In the minutes before the special stockholder's meeting opens that morning of February 26, 1971, the 250 people milling about the floor study them and those who flank them. The curiosity that drifts toward them is a palpable mixture—awe, concern, unhappiness, disbelief, skepticism—and hope. Two or three times, a stockholder, friend or whatever, approaches Bassine but he quickly raises a gently restraining hand. It is all going to be strictly according to legal procedures, no informal chats or personal kibitzing which might later appear as an official conversation on someone's brief. Observing it, Emanuel Klimpl, Spartans' outside corporate counsel, nods firmly in his prim way. But no one approaches Arthur Cohen at his end of the table. He seems remote, though he smiles vaguely, a handsome, almost too young, too pristine a figure to be involved.

Quite a pair. Walter Matthau and Robert Redford.

To an observer, it was curious that even now, just before retailing's most unusual merger in many years—and an unusual one for any industry—both principals were behaving so much in character. Even in these final moments of running his $1 billion company, Bassine was still acting out the Uncle Charley role, holding up a paternal but warning hand to improper questions, exuding his warm personality, indicating that he was not only above all of it but assuring everyone that regardless everything would work out fine. And Cohen, the epitome of the great American business "whiz kid," cool, withdrawn, but giving the definite impression that he was surely the answer to all the problems, whatever they might be.

The restless crowd is something else again. Although they are in age, sex, income, and general lack of knowledge of corporate activities a microcosm of the thirty million American investors in business, they are not quite a cross-section of Americana. Their company is largely represented in the big cities so that most are urban and suburban residents. Sears, Penney's, K mart, and others draw many more small-town investors because a large number of their stores are in smaller cities as well as in the big ones. Korvettes, and to a smaller extent Spartans and Arlen's, had become lures to many investment-oriented, middle-income families in the East. It had, like A.T.&T., Consolidated Edison, Macy's, and other highly visible, highly regarded corporate monoliths, achieved much credibility, not only as a dramatic success but as a vital retail entity in their lives. They are, although many had sold or reduced their number of shares, reluctant to give up on Korvettes. Many believe that the company will yet turn around, and its fading stock rise again. Yet more than a sprinkling in the generally middle-aged audience are visibly emotional, some even angry. Even as the meeting begins with the sound of Bassine's gavel on the rostrum, excited pockets of conversation and hot, local debates continue. They slowly melt with the warmth and assurance of Bassine's greetings.

This quiet attention, however, doesn't last more than fifteen minutes. One by one, stockholders rise, often defying the agenda to criticize management and the proposed merger. "Why do we have to pay so much for this merger? Who is Arlen, anyway, just a private company!" "What happened to our dividends?" "What does Arthur Cohen know about retailing?" "What's happening to Korvettes— first it was swallowed up by a garment company, now it will be swallowed up by a real-estate company—what's happening?" "Is it because Arthur Cohen is your son-in-law that you're making this merger? Shame on you!" These are only a few of the questions and comments that cause the meeting to last three and a half hours. More than once, fists are raised in the audience and a curse or two is heard.

Stoically, with a wide, seemingly frozen smile, Bassine listens and answers when he gets a chance. He has been warned by his cohorts. There would be noise, *strum und drang*. Profits at Korvettes have been dragged down by the new-store opening cost. Worse, the older stores, the more than forty built through 1966, were being hurt by strong competition and have been virtually flat in sales or up only about 6 percent, not much more than the inflation in merchandise, each year for the last five. Certainly, new stores, the eight new ones, do produce sales, but only about enough to keep the total chain volume a bit ahead. Patently, Arlen would be getting a company that wasn't progressing at the bottom-line where it counted. And what assurances did the unwashed public have that a non-retailer could do better with an important retail chain?

After letting some of the ire and invective run their course, Bassine stresses that the merger of retailing and real estate has to have "synergistic results. I must tell you that real estate is the best area of economic activity for many years ahead—if management has the expertise and Arlen has it.

"Besides, the tax shelters provided for real-estate activities," he added, "will enhance the combined company's profits and we will be able to expand Korvettes as never before."

Arlen, after all, he continues, glancing at the still-smiling Arthur Cohen, is an immense company with commensurate assets. It has pro-forma revenue of $910 million this year, is the largest real-estate developer in the country and the nation's largest owner and developer of regional shopping centers. Korvettes, despite some of its problems, still has immense potential which can only be intensified by its affiliation with Arlen. But there is more than just Korvettes involved—there is also Spartans' apparel importing business (the manufacturing division in the U.S. had been closed to concentrate on the Far East ventures), the Spartans and Atlantic Discount Stores which will eventually be sold, and a 38 percent interest in Tech-Aerofoam Products, a foam-rubber producer which Spartans bought into not long ago. In a word, upon merger, Korvettes would become a muscular, diversified, almost $2 billion business.

But the questions wouldn't let up, especially those on the suspected nepotism. Finally, charged with resentment and self-righteousness, Bassine tells the audience, "Do you think this is like that television caricature of the dim-witted son-in-law who races around in an auto that his father-in-law bought? Absolutely not!"

Gesturing toward the immobile, blond figure sitting on his left, Bassine declared, "I'm proud of my relationship with him. He has over many years developed an organization of about a thousand people and it is now the largest single developer of real estate in the United States. They are all well known in all levels of government where his advice is eagerly sought.

"I cordially wish you all such a son-in-law. He's a better man than I am."

The merger was approved by 77 percent of all the shares voted.

And so, there it was, Korvettes' third merger in little more than twenty years—first with Hills Supermarkets, then with Spartans, and now with Arlen Realty. With each, owners and managements moved in and out. Gone were Ferkauf, Hilly Coan, Jack Schwadron, Bassine, and in no time at all Leonard Blackman. Each had had his day; some had longer days than the others. The two mountains among those peaks were, of course, Ferkauf, who as founder and evanescent genius, reigned for eighteen years, and Bassine, as his successor owner-operator, had had only a brief five years. The charismatic, respected older man had, however, proved incapable of carrying Korvettes further, despite all the good-will and force of his personality and lofty promises. One reason for his failure, some analyzed later, was that he brought a lot of burdensome baggage along with him to the merger—a low-price apparel manufacturing business that he later scrapped to become an importer, a pair of down-at-the-heels discount-store chains, Spartans and Atlantic, and a drug store chain. Another reason, others said, was that he really lacked the ability to manage a large retailing enterprise because he was intrinsically a manufacturer. What's the difference? Don't they both at the core have to satisfy the public? They do, of course. A producer, though, excites retailers to take on his products; the retailer excites the public. The end may ultimately be the same—but it is the retailer who must be able to slug it out in the arena of the marketplace, manipulating the artillery in a way to keep his offensive lean, hard, and constant. Many a producer who has ventured into retailing has had to give it up—it has a different set of economics, merchandising thrust, and competitive challenge. An actual, different dimension.

As an observer of Bassine and his way of doing business for almost a decade, this writer has yet another reason why the man whom everyone respected and whom Ferkauf regarded as "my father image" couldn't make the Spartans-Korvettes merger succeed. He lost interest. It's a fallacy that successful businessmen always want to succeed. After a long string of successes, some businessmen, especially if they get into their sixties, decide reluctantly that it doesn't really matter, they have hung up quite a record already. Will another bauble on the escutcheon really mean anything? Especially if getting it is tough, grindingly so? Bassine tried, all right, but it's likely that a combination of his age, his personal problems, and the difficulties of the task defeated him. He wanted out.

Early in 1981, I asked one of his oldest friends why Bassine didn't deliver at Korvettes.

"I've had trouble perceiving why Charley didn't do all the good things expected of him," the friend said. "Maybe it was too much put together too soon. In 1965, the year before the merger, Bassine acquired Maro Hosiery, then the Atlantic Stores and he had already bought Crank Drug Stores. On top of that he had his Spartans manufacturing and the Spartans discount stores. And suddenly, he's got Korvettes, too. It was an awful lot to digest . . . Of course, Bassine was that way. He liked to make decisions himself but sometimes he would ask for advice." Not enough, perhaps? The friend shrugged.

Not that Charley didn't like to know where he was putting his foot before he stepped into a mushy surface. "As a condition of taking over Korvettes," he continued, "Charley insisted on getting a substantial bank line of revolving credit of about $80 million to pay for the substantial needs of Korvettes. He was careful that way—but in other ways, I guess he bit off too much . . ."

As for Leonard Blackman, he left soon after the new merger was consummated. He successively became president of Federal Stores, Detroit, and of M. H. Fishman Company, two discount chains which found themselves eventually compelled to file Chapter XI bankruptcy proceedings. Their problems reflected those of the discount industry in general—overhead that inevitably crept up and eroded their competitive ability—resulting in a ten-year shakeout bridging the 1960's and 1970's.

"But Blackman was a smart fellow," said Bassine's friend. "Whether or not he was responsible for each company's problems, every time he got into a troubled situation and had to give up the job, he collected a great severance. How many guys can do that?"

Despite everything, the golden glow that hovered around Korvettes somehow remained. The chain had $600 million in sales transacted in fifty stores, although racking up only small profits, but it had prime locations in New York, New Jersey, Philadelphia, and Maryland. Its stores in Detroit, Chicago, and St. Louis were struggling. But in the

East, at least, the aura of leadership still lingered. The generation that had matured after World War II and filled their first homes with appliances, furniture, carpets, and TV sets from the exciting Korvettes' stores still remembered. If they, their children, and parents became confused by the retailer's abrupt switches in merchandising and promotion, they still regarded Korvettes as a price leader in housewares, audio, appliances, records, tapes, books, women's accessories, sporting goods, auto accessories, and other goods. The loyalty, of course, had been reduced. Korvettes had lost its role to K mart several years earlier as the nation's largest discounter. Even in the New York metropolitan area, although it had the largest number of big stores, with twenty-five units, it had slipped to the number three position behind Macy's and Abraham & Straus after pushing the former hard only a few years before.

But the new merger—once the charges of nepotism and a "family deal" had died down—began to be viewed in a different light.

For the first time, it appeared, Korvettes would be affiliated with a larger, dramatically successful company with unquestioned management expertise. Arlen's growth had been the greatest in the American real-estate industry in the prior decade. Its chief executive, Arthur G. Cohen, was widely considered the most skillful entrepreneur in real-estate development. He had undoubtedly inherited that trait from his father, who had established his own successful record in the field, but had added his own flair for creative empire-building. If Cohen regarded Korvettes as a great potential growth vehicle, it was an important vote of confidence in its viability. Besides, if one studied his executive team, one could only increase one's sense of confidence. Working with him were Arthur Levien, Jay Solomon, Peter Lebowits, and Marshall Rose, all experts in sensing and developing entrepreneurial opportunities. Jay Solomon later became director of the General Services Administration, the Federal government's procurement agency, and Lebowits emerged as president of Cadillac-Fairview Shopping Centers, U.S.A., the American arm of the big Canadian-based developer of that name.

Perhaps Americans make too much of corporate or institutional connections. All the same, the combination of a struggling company, however large, with that of an unqualified success with considerable physical assets, is hardly to be ignored. And it was the demeanor of Arthur Cohen himself, smiling, cool, judicious, capable of putting together a top team, which probably gave the new affiliation the glow of promise.

Shortly after the merger, the reasons behind that glowing expectation were outlined in the combined views of Bassine, still lingering on as Korvettes' executive committee chairman, Arthur Cohen, chairman of Arlen's, and Marshall Rose, now doubling as president of both Korvettes and of Arlen's. In a calm discussion, they said:

"The tax shelters provided for real-estate activities will enchance the profit of the combined company, enabling Korvettes' for one to benefit from an expanded cash flow. All of Korvettes' earnings might be tax-sheltered as a result of traditional differences in tax and financial reporting of the real-estate operations."

As a major shopping-center developer, "we can obtain the best site selection which will allow Korvettes to open new stores in choice locations around the country."

In fact the Arlen Group's shopping-center operations were booming. In 1970, the company built 1.7 million square feet of new centers while in 1971 it appeared that about 4 million square feet of facilities would be built. And in 1972, about 4.8 million square feet of construction is on backlog.

"These and other building projects probably will provide financial and operating benefits to Korvettes and to Spartans . . ."

But, they were asked, wouldn't Korvettes be downgraded as a priority business in such a merger, assuming that many of these high expectations will depend upon the shifts in the national economy and availability of money? Bassine himself answered:

"For several years, Korvettes has been consolidating itself and has not opened nearly as many stores as it did in the early half of the sixties. Now, with the benefits of our tax-shelter and our expertise in the site-selection field, we are planning to open seven new stores this fiscal year, which will produce between $60 million and $70 million in sales annually. We plan about the same rate of expansion the year after than and subsequently we will step up the pace."

Won't the merger place more of the combined holdings in the hands of the Cohen and Bassine families, creating a restricted ownership structure which might make decisions too unilateral and inbred? Won't the appointment of Marshall Rose as Korvettes' president put a non-retailer at the head of a retail company?

Bassine smiled as he glanced at the other two smiling faces. A few weeks earlier, he had stated, "The root management problem at Korvettes has been a superstructure that we developed, consisting of control and management systems, that was too large for the company." Now, he said, in direct reply to the question about Rose's appointment, "Korvettes has become staffed with professional, specialized retailers while what was really needed was a hard-nosed administrator, a money manager, who has leadership abilities. Marshall Rose has those abilities."

And, as to the question about restricted decision-making because of the consolidation of control in two families, he added, "You remember what I said at the special stock-holder's meeting. I have the greatest faith in Arthur Cohen. I am very proud of him for the administrative talents he has." Then Bassine's smile widened as if asking for some indulgence because of repetition. "I cordially wish all such a son-in-law. He's a better man than I am."

Not unexpectedly, perhaps, one of Arthur Cohen's first moves had been to tap his friend and closest associate, Marshall Rose, to take on the direct supervision of the new entity. A young man—he was still only in his thirties—Rose had an investment-banking background gained from his association with Lazard Frères in New York. He had not only displayed a keen, analytical flair but he had also quickly proved in the Arlen organization to be a skilled trouble-shooter. Arthur took to him and gave him increasing responsibility. There was a chemistry between them that seemed to surprise and intrigue people. Both were low-key, outwardly unexcitable, but whereas Arthur combined opportunism with a hit-and-run instinct, Marshall was an opportunist who preferred to see things take root before he was gratified enough to move on. It was simplistic to decide that Cohen was the leader, Rose the follower. They were just a great team, together providing much of the impetus and the direction for the infrastructure.

A slim, handsome man with dreamy eyes, Rose played it very straight, putting aside any preconceptions as he studied the new company. He knew something of Korvettes from having dealt with its top management as a developer. Now, he studied the management, the space, and the business. Within a few months, he came to two basic decisions and Cohen backed him.

The first decision was to close thirty of Korvettes' furniture stores with a total space of 1 million square feet. The

furniture operations were to be transferred to adjacent or
nearby regular Korvettes stores while the vacated furniture
stores, which were mostly next door to the regular stores,
were to be rented to other retailers or service organizations.

Many of the older Korvettes' stores had stockrooms that
were larger than needed as a result of both mechanized
moving systems and a greater use of the chain's Bayonne,
New Jersey, distribution center. After a detailed study of the
existing Korvettes' store space aimed at obtaining better
supervision, traffic flow, and cost benefits, Rose decided
there were both economies and potential revenues to be
derived from closing the existing, free-standing furniture
stores.

In addition, the study found that space was wasted in the
"dead-storage" floors in four of the major New York area
units. This could be corrected by shifting basements and
some upper floors from "dead-storage" to selling floors. The
result: the four stores, including those on Fifth Avenue and
on East 44th Street in Manhattan, would have their space
expanded between 25 and 30 percent.

Both parts of the space-saving project made sense. The
important furniture warehouse-showroom trend was beginning to rev into high gear and there were only two ways to
compete with the Levitzes and the Homestocks. Either
compete with them on a head-to-head basis, offering vast
showrooms full of furniture with adjacent warehouses from
which the customer could literally carry the sofa home on his
back, or compete with a selective assortment, also providing
immediate or nearby delivery, and by operating on a more
economical scale one could maintain a good sales per square
foot. Rose's plan, of course, was the latter.

Providing more selling space in the four stores also
worked to the advantage of a more productive establishment.
Weren't suburban branch stores already being opened with

much more selling space? Why not follow suit with older stores by reducing storage area? Korvettes, after all, could readily use all the favorable economics it could get.

Rose's second decision was highly strategic and, as it turned out, fateful. But Arthur Cohen had agreed, too. After some months of study of Korvettes' assets and liabilities, Rose decided that the retail chain needed a merchant to head it, someone with merchandising expertise who could implement a tighter, more disciplined policy. Someone who could pull the still somewhat bemused executive team together. Who? The hovering spotlight then fell almost inevitably on a short, chunky, charismatic man who had been at Korvettes for seven years after having been a furniture buyer at Macy's New York.

David Brous, a Harvard Business School graduate, was one of three brothers gifted in the art-science of merchandising. David had reached the level of home furnishings vice president of Korvettes. Philip had a similar post at Miller-Wohl Stores and was clearly slated for the presidency. Frederic operated his own appliance chain in New Jersey. David, hired by Norman Rothman in 1965 just a year before the Coan-Ferkauf split, had risen to head all of the company's home furnishings operations before being promoted to executive vice president by Bassine in 1967. Although he was only in his late thirties, he had already bridged the Ferkauf-Bassine and now the Cohen-Rose regimes. And he had writhed through much of it as he had watched with frustration the gropings from trading-up to trading-down, from keeping margins down to raising them and from playing up to denying the role of his own hard goods. He was ready for a personal and professional breakout; as sometimes happens (but not often enough) the opportunity opened to admit him.

He was terribly eager. Sometimes, his colleagues said

later, his desire to run things seemed to have a life of its own. He spoke at break-neck pace, his words occasionally stumbling over one another, as he would gesticulate aggressively. But he had that innate confidence that came from working at Macy's, he had the Harvard degree, and he was clearly a merchant. But during the days when Blackman was Korvettes' president it seemed to Brous that he had made the mistake of his life to come to Korvettes.

Inconceivably or not, he got the job, as though it were, to quote the oldest of cliches, "a dream come true."

His hopes had been raised when, only three months after Rose assumed the presidency, Leonard Blackman was fired. Cohen and Rose then called in Brous, who had been the top merchandiser of home furnishings, and asked him to become executive vice president and top operating officer. After they became a close, working team, Rose recommended that the scrappy little Brous be named president of Korvettes. Rose would continue to keep a sharp eye on Korvettes from his own office in Arlen's big suite at 888 Seventh Avenue and Brous moved into Bassine's massive office.

After seven years at Korvettes, Brous had an intimate knowledge of what the problems were and this knowledge guided the priorities that Rose and he quickly formulated.

"We had to stem the incredible decline in sales, about 6 percent a year, and the slipping sales out of town," Brous recalled. "That was the main priority. The next one was that we had to stop the proposed expansion in Florida. And we had to regain credibility with our customers and our suppliers. And we had to do all of that as fast as we could."

The move by the predecessor management to "bring in cheap shirts," lower-grade goods at a higher markup, had proved to be disastrous, said Brous. "The department stores were trading up but making sure that they kept enough of a promotional posture that they wouldn't lose old customers as they gained new ones," he added. "But for several years, Korvettes had given up its credibility on price and value. In the metropolitan New York area, we were losing ground every year and out of town K mart was killing us."

It was decided that the effort to turn the business around required help. Doyle Dane Bernbach, the consumer-goods-oriented advertising agency, was appointed to define what Korvettes' image was and the Daniel Yankelovitch market-ing-research agency was tapped to develop the demograph-ics that would be needed for the turnaround program.

The internal and the external search soon combined in pin-pointing a basic problem—Korvettes' image was seri-ously blurred. Even that was only a symptom, not an effect of an even more underlying problem. What was it? "We were not running credible merchandise," Brous said. "Opera-tionally, we couldn't make any money. We were practically losing our shirts."

When all the data came in, and when Cohen, Rose, and Brous decided that a new approach should then be taken, the decision was simple and yet startling. Korvettes could no longer be a discounter. If the big department store operators such as Macy's, A.&S., and Gimbels, were trading up to bolster their profits and the discounters were trading down to stay alive, there was a niche in the middle—a sort of promotional department-store—that Korvettes could fill. It would take some hard study, lots of work, and certainly new people, even new types of people.

First, it was clear that the Florida expansion, involving at least three stores, which Bassine and Arthur Cohen had enthusiastically wanted, must be halted until the company could recover its viability. Cohen had considerable real-estate interests in Florida, including the famous Avventura multi-purpose complex, while Bassine loved Florida and saw great commercial potential there. But, Korvettes needed another respite from expansion, they finally agreed. The metalwork that had already gone up on Fifth Avenue in Miami Beach was abandoned.

It was obvious, too, that Korvettes would have to improve sharply its fashion business by enriching inventories and creating an exciting image to customers. If that presupposed higher prices and an even higher expense rate—and it did—there seemed, in the eyes of the whole new top team, to be no alternative. Korvettes' stores were simply too big (at least twice the size of the typical K mart stores) and so burdened with high labor costs since the chain was fully unionized that they had to be shifted to a department-store approach. They were all in agreement on that point. They were going to have to take the opposite direction from the earlier owner-management. *Finis* the discounter. Henceforth, Korvettes would be "the promotional department store chain."

There was, Brous insists, no alternative. "We were losing lots of money on top of a sharply eroding sales base. Our priorities became clearer every day."

Very much part of regaining credibility, Brous, Cohen, and Rose decided, too, was to attract new senior executives who knew the department-store business and could guide them into the new niche they wanted to occupy. With the help of Herb Ricklin, Korvettes' industrial-relations director, outside executive recruiters, and anyone else he could get hold of, Brous went about the business of attracting top new people. That, too, became a priority item.

In the midst of that, the matter of expansion, which always seemed to raise its head when Korvettes least needed it, arose again. This time, it was the moribund S. Klein stores, once a vital bargain chain which had been taken over

by Meshulam Riklis' company, the McCrory Corporation.
The then nineteen-store chain had been losing money for
years and Riklis, a wily, controversial financier who seemed
almost always to come out ahead on a trade, suggested one to
Arthur Cohen. If Korvettes would take over six of the Klein
sites in the metropolitan New York area, he, Riklis, would
gladly assume the sites of Korvettes' two unproductive stores
in St. Louis.

"Deal?" asked Riklis.

"Deal," the three said.

The details, worked out in June 1974, represented a
stunning development for both Korvettes and McCrory Corporation. It was the biggest single expansion move by any
New York-based retailer in many decades and, in addition, a
strange decision for Korvettes considering its losses and
current efforts to stage a turnaround. But when one consid-
ers that Arthur Cohen had built a real-estate empire by both
construction and acquisition, it's not hard to see an aggressive strain emanating from Arlen at the time. As for McCrory
and its parent company, Rapid-American Corporation, the
agreement was tantamount to breaking a log jam, the need
to begin divesting some, if not all, of the failing S. Klein
stores.

And so Korvettes, with twenty-five stores already in the
metropolitan area, took over the huge Klein stores on Long
Island in Hempstead, Valley Stream, Commack and Hicksville, as well as in Yonkers, N.Y., and Wayne, N.J.

In an interview in July 1974, Marshall Rose and David
Brous emphasized that Korvettes was buying "selected real-
estate, not Klein's as a company." "Korvettes is committed to
a policy of increasing saturation in existing market areas
where the market knows us and we know the market," Rose
said. The Klein's acquisition is "consistent with that policy,"

he added, and "provides us with rents that are below what it would cost to build new stores and also allows us to increase our penetration in this area."

He said that Korvettes expected to achieve a profit in the unprofitable Klein sites as a result of "our efficiencies of scale and the fact that our average sales-per-square-foot of gross space is in excess of theirs." And Brous said, "There is a dearth of sites for large retail stores in the area. We feel that we sidestepped this problem."

Seven years later, asked if the six-store site acquisition had been a sound one, Brous was still defending it.

"We saw a chance to add stores in the New York area," he said. "It also put us into three area malls, Valley Stream, Hicksville, and Wayne, something that had been difficult for us because as discounters we were largely kept out of the malls. Besides, we sold the 'key' to the Yonkers store to Alexander's and made a $4 million profit on it."

But, wasn't that biting off a lot at a delicate stage?

David Brous smiled, a precocious, small-boy's smile, and shrugged. "It was an opportunity we had to grab hold of," he said. "It might never have come around to us again."

12.
The Hot New Team

S ometimes, in those pressure-filled but hopeful days of
the mid-1970's, Herb Ricklin would glance around the
conference room table at the other members of the executive
committee and he would feel a great pride. "I used to think,
'What a crew,'" he said. "They could run not only Korvettes.
They could probably have run General Motors. Their average IQ was probably 170."

The long-time Korvettes' industrial relations director,
Ricklin paused in his recollection and his eyes glistened.

"It could have been the hottest executive team in New
York . . . but maybe there were too many egos in it," he said.
"At that point, it was certainly one of the talented teams in
retailing and one of the most expensive. We were groping for
a handle between department and discount stores but so far
it was neither fish nor fowl. So there was a lot of argument, a
lot of intellectualizing going across that table."

The talent to mold that new type of store was clearly there. From 1972 through 1975, David Brous, never one to shrink from a confrontation, raided Macy's and Abraham & Straus for some of their best top executives. The new affiliation with the highly regarded, asset-rich Arlen Realty helped to attract. And wasn't Arthur Cohen on Citicorp's board? It was hard to climb higher in the rarified strata of corporate America. Korvettes also offered much more responsibility than they already had, also a lure. And top money, too. A general merchandise manager who received $75,000 to $80,000 at Macy's got $125,000 from Korvettes. A senior vice president who commanded $75,000 from A.&S. easily got $90,000 to $100,000 at Korvettes. And it wasn't just the top people who could get a good pay boost. A buyer who wasn't much more than thirty years old and earned $25,000 was induced to come to Korvettes for $40,000, and he wasn't alone.

So they came to work.

Kenneth Kolker, A.&S.'s senior vice president—just about the fourth- or fifth-highest executive in the entire group of stores—became chairman of Korvettes' executive committee. His appointment was a great coup, so respected was Kolker's ability to analyze, plan strategy, and motivate. He had a rare combination of intellectual honesty and scientific acumen. Later, he became chairman of the May Merchandising Company, one of the largest department-store buying offices.

Then there was Thomas Larkin, another A.&S. senior vice president and a general manager, who became Korvettes' senior vice president for stores. After leaving Korvettes, Larkin was named president of the Gertz Stores division of Allied Stores Corporation.

Julian Taub, A.&S.'s vice president for research, became Korvettes' sales promotion vice president. Later, the intense, meticulous Taub joined Gertz in a similar capacity and after that became vice president for planning at Bloomingdale's.

Robert Warner, already mentioned, had been Macy's senior vice president for home furnishings and, in an earlier post, general manager of Macy's Herald Square store. He became Korvettes' senior vice president and general merchandise manager of home furnishings. Later he became general merchandise manager of soft lines, fussy on detail and avid on strategic planning.

Gary Ozaroff, merchandising vice president of Macy's, came to a similar job at Korvettes. Very tall, knowledgeable, and with a good market sense, Ozaroff seemed to do well everywhere. After Korvettes, he became senior vice president of J. L. Hudson Company, Detroit.

Robert Kahn, Macy's merchandising vice president, was placed in a similar job at Korvettes. There, he became known as an aggressive merchant, like Ozaroff a man well over six feet with a meaningful stride.

Israel Hurwitz, Macy's vice president and administrator, who was put in charge of systems for Korvettes. Analytical and scholarly, Hurwitz was a carpet and wine expert, an odd combination perhaps but the result of career developments at Macy's.

The debate concerning Korvettes' future continued apace, the three strongest personalities—Brous, Kolker, Warner—always bubbling to the top and shaping the decisions. One of the big issues was the nature of daily business versus the number of promotions. Kolker insisted that Korvettes develop the kind of strong daily volume effort that built A.&S. into one of the strongest department stores in the U.S. Brous advocated a barrage of "key events," the kind of heavily advertised promotions that had always made Korvettes so exciting. Warner insisted that what was needed was

to take the departments that were really the best and develop them into "fantastic" businesses through deep and
wide assortments, "great, simple presentation and excellent
cashiering techniques." It was not an argument that could
be readily resolved. Some on the committee were clearly
skeptical that Korvettes could be maneuvered into that narrow niche between department and discount stores. At
times, the discussion turned acrid, even nasty. A few times,
Dave Brous cut through the committee hullabaloo and
slammed a decision down on the table.

"We can't afford to be a discounter when expenses are so
damned high," he stated repeatedly. "What we need to do is
to move up to the kind of store where our wives will be happy
to buy their clothes."

That remark, some said later, really raised eyebrows. It
was one thing for the husbands to work at Korvettes—but it
was another for their wives to want to shop there, too. How
much can a company, Arthur Cohen, Marshall Rose, Dave
Brous, ask, anyway? The resulting laughter was friendly, if a
bit hollow.

Word filtered out, of course, about the heated debates.
The crew of highly paid discount-store merchants, it seemed,
were really department-store guys. All that experience
being channelled to a retailing vehicle most of them never
really knew much about. All that expensive talent trying
hard to turn the fish into a fowl or was it fowl into a fish? If
they couldn't do it—

Perhaps it's unfair to make comparisons. Twenty years
earlier, a bunch of Ferkauf friends and relatives also coped
with an uncertain business. Only then, it was on the up-
swing, fighting its way through entrenched competition and
fair trade. Now, it was Dave, Ken, Bob, Tom, Julie, Herb,
and Gary. Then it was . . .

Gene, Joe, Murray, George, Mel, Dave, Bill, Leo, and all the rest. Running, jumping, darting, yelling, exhorting, schlepping but somehow sustaining two of the busiest, most profitable stores in the metropolitan area . . .

Whatever they do wrong comes out right. Whatever they forget turns out better forgotten. Whatever they neglect someone does for them. Every misjudgment becomes self-correcting. Every unfortunate development manages to right itself. And just when they get to feeling they don't know anything, they turn around and find the pros studying them like they know plenty . . .

The pros were in now. And they were a bit discomfitted. Which the old-timers didn't mind at all.

"When I was negotiating to join Korvettes with Brous, Rose, and Cohen," said Bob Warner, "I kept wanting to see the figures at the company but they were reluctant. I signed a good contract and then they showed me the numbers. I was shocked. They showed a 5 percent compounded sales decline in comparable stores. In fact, if I had seen the numbers first, I wouldn't have signed the contract.

"I thought later that they were just trying to conceal those numbers but I decided afterward that they were really just a bunch of optimistic guys. But I regarded those figures as a sign of terminal cancer. They were aghast when I said it looked like they were headed for bankruptcy.

" 'Do you think it can be turned around?' Cohen asked.

" 'I'm not sure but we'll certainly give it a shot.'

" 'How long will it take?'

" 'Three years.'

" 'Well, we'll do everything we can to make that happen.'

"From the beginning, I told the management of both Arlen and Korvettes of the problems but they were only somewhat receptive. Fundamentally, the main thing I urged them not to do was to raise the markup, to keep it where it was and to keep lowering their expenses. But the markup was moved up and the expenses kept moving up, too."

Warner, who spent eight years at Korvettes from 1971 through most of 1979, described the experience as an "enjoyable" one and the company as a "very pleasant place to work." David Brous created a "pleasant ambience," resulting in a "very informal organization." Everyone was on a first name basis, the pressure coming "from the business, not from the people."

Not everyone on the new team agreed that the atmosphere was pleasant. One member, who prefers anonymity because of his critical observations, insists that "it was a hectic, disorganized management. There were long, even confused meetings. Brous talked a lot but didn't listen enough. Some poeple were confused by him. Fundamentally, he is a very intelligent man with a very good mind, very charismatic, and a good speech-maker. But he didn't tie things together and he didn't follow up."

One of the continuing performers through that period, David Rothfeld, who was in charge of records, tapes, books, and audio, says, "Nobody bothered me, they left me alone to do my work. Brous was very enthusiastic about my operation and would constantly go out of his way to brag about how good a formula we had—volume at a discount that produced excellent profit dollars. We were lucky, too; we got an enormous amount of co-op ad money from the suppliers, mainly because of our leadership in the field. They got an awful lot of exposure from us.

"But in soft goods," Rothfeld noted, "we just couldn't get the name brands. I used to tell Dave, 'Why not get all the closeout buys you can? And then from that, you can build a traditional business just like Barney's, the big men's store, did. They started out as a discounter, built a big clientele, and then went full-price, full-service.' But I guess that was easier said than done. The problem was that discounters like Korvettes could get identifiable values from good makers but getting the names to put on them was still tough, even after fair trade began fading out."

Mel Friedman, who was one of the last "originals" to leave, observed, "Dave Brous wanted the company to operate department stores, not discount stores. One day he took a closeout shirt that I had gotten and threw it at me. 'I don't want that kind of business, Mel!' he shouted. 'I want us to be a real department store.' There was no mistake about that and that made things a lot tougher."

When Bassine left in 1972, Friedman recalled, the company had a general expense rate of 2 percent on sales of $600 million. But David Brous brought it up to 4 percent, adding almost $12 million a year to the cost of operation, he said. "Whatever you want to say about Bassine, he understood expense control," added Mel Friedman. "Brous didn't. I think our expense structure became the highest of any discounter and was even higher than most department stores."

An important member of the new team, Norman Matthews, offered some sweet-sour recollections. First Korvettes' general merchandise manager of soft goods and then of hard goods and afterwards the chairman of the Gold Circle discount stores division of Federated Department Stores, Matthews said:

"We felt that we were beginning to make progress. But there were lots of headaches. We had very little leverage. Our information wasn't good enough. Until Arlen approved hiring the pros, the management wasn't highly skilled. But even the pros had to prove themselves. We spent much of our time trying to develop a marketing strategy.

"Yet Korvettes had a place and we knew that plenty of

customers and suppliers were supporting us. It was a great group sitting around that table and considering all the effort and thinking we put into it, things could easily have gone the other way."

Competition, of course, developed within the new team. It involved both Matthews and Bob Warner. When the two switched their G.M.M. jobs, Norman wound up with hard goods and Warner with soft goods. For his part, Warner recalls an almost constant need to improve his morale. "When you're in a business that you really feel won't make it, you can't go to work every day feeling that way unless you want to be damned unhappy. While I felt in my heart that we would not make it, I tried every day in my own way to see that we would make it. When you're in your fifties, if you're lucky, you get alternative job offers but not significantly better. But I felt loyal to Dave, Arthur, and Marshall," said Bob Warner.

"Korvettes wasn't exactly alone in its problems. There was Macy's, too, big, powerful, but only making out, just barely, until Ed Finkelstein came along. It was a mature business with a high expense structure and it had lost a lot of its glamour. It was, well, you could almost say that Macy's was going down the tube. What Korvettes needed was what Macy's needed—an Ed Finkelstein, no reflection on anyone else. He's a man with great ideas, he's very charismatic, innovative, gutsy. There's a key thing to remember: it takes a different kind of manager to keep a successful company going than it takes to turn a company around. Finkelstein had the experience of being a turnaround guy at Bamberger's; Mark Handler, his number-two guy, kept it going successfully," he said.

After thirty years as a corporate executive, Warner believes that businesses, like people, die at different ages— thirty, sixty, one hundred. If Korvettes was to die young—at thirty or thereabouts—it would mean that its management performance was less than average. Its mixture of talents wasn't rich enough. And yet, the talent of the collected Harvard MBA's was there, ready to be turned on. "Most managements are in the middle level of performance," he observes. "Some are terrible, some are fantastic but most are in the middle."

At the same time, not everyone has the same degree of talent or the same type. One of Korvettes' problems, as always, was to mold, to intertwine, to activate the talents it had "sitting around that big table." Adds Warner: "A turn-around guy might not be successful in an already successful company because he might want to do too many new things. Sears, Roebuck, big as it is, needed a turnaround guy in the late 1970's just as Korvettes did in the early 1970's. Was Brous right, would Kolker have been right as top man, any more than Ferkauf was right?"

In the retail business, though, there is a difference. The merchant has to remain paramount. "And that's where the rub comes in," Warner insists. "A retail company becomes successful because first there's the merchant. Then he turns into or is succeeded by the corporate executive. And next there is the Wall Street manipulator. Why did Macy's run into troubles? They had too many administrators. Why did Korvettes run into all its troubles? The administrators took over . . .

"The new team knew it. So here was a bunch of highly paid, pretty well-motivated professionals, arguing with each other, throwing sparks, anxious to come up with the answers. Somewhere, maybe, there was a strategy looking for a problem to latch on to . . ."

All they had to do was to find it. The strategy was, perhaps, already mistily clear—to upgrade, to create merchandising excitement, to shore up credibility, and hopefully to increase it. And, quite clearly, to expand the confidence that the company already had in its profitable housewares, records-tapes, books, audio, camera, and photography departments into other departments. There were some clear areas of dissension. One was the matter of acquiring the six S. Klein units. Brous, Cohen, and Rose wanted them for the greater exposure. Others on the executive committee felt it was a risky diversion, that the company should first solidify itself. Despite some qualms on the part of the Federal Trade Commission that the six-store buyout would hurt competition in the metropolitan area, the agency approved the takeover in March 1975. And so that became a *fait accompli*.

Another area of disagreement was the big-ticket merchandise. In 1972, Korvettes had already decided to close thirty furniture stores and rent the space to other retailers. Furniture operations were shifted to nearby or adjacent regular Korvettes' stores. But between 1972 and 1976, both the furniture and the carpet businesses continued to lose about $4 million a year even though they produced average sales of about $40 million annually. The primary problem was competition, as it had been in the earlier years. The success of the Levitz Furniture warehouse showrooms, the entry of W.&J. Sloane into a proliferating chain of local Clearance Centers, and the spread of franchised stores by furniture producers hurt Korvettes' big-ticket activity. Department stores, too, were visibly affected in their furniture departments and began to scale them down.

The debate about the matter got heavy at times. Between Brous and Bob Warner, not to mention the merchandise men and buyers, there was plenty of know-how about furniture and carpets and that should have been reassuring. But did Korvettes—now expanding again despite razor-thin profits—need the space-consuming, labor-intensive, mini-mally producing furniture and carpet business? But then, didn't those departments produce the kind of store traffic that accrued well to the more profitable soft lines divisions? After all, if you are going to aspire to the department-store concept, how can you not have the big tickets, too?

Right? Wrong.

In October 1976, Korvettes announced that after more than twenty years it was discontinuing its furniture and carpet operations in twenty-eight stores in the metropolitan area. About five hundred employees would be displaced. The announcement was partly cushioned by the fact that a year earlier the company had dropped its major appliance department and since then had phased out furniture and carpets in most of its stores outside the New York area.

Both Marshall Rose and Dave Brous stated at the time that Arlen would reimburse Korvettes for the closing costs and relieve it of its real-estate obligations for the separate, adjacent stores that housed the furniture-carpet depart-ment. But while Korvettes would use the vacated space in some of the stores for apparel and other soft lines, most of the vacated buildings would be leased to others. Korvettes wouldn't tarry about its divestiture. In a week, a general public clearance would be held for inventory with a cost value of at least $5 million.

Why the decision to drop the final big-tickets, certainly a vivid symbol that the pioneering discounter was kicking over all its traces?

In his normal, rapid-fire conversational tone, Brous spelled it out in clear terms, with an undertone of relief, as one might describe the reasons for therapeutic surgery. "The decision to drop furniture and carpets is more impor-tant than our discontinuance of major appliances," he said. "We lost money on that business for a variety of reasons.

First, there's the high cost of delivery. It costs as much to ship a $200 sofa as a $1,000 sofa. But as a moderate-priced retailer, we could sell only the lower-priced item. Then, there's the quality problem—lower-priced furniture has less of it than higher-priced goods, and that can be a sales problem. Then there's the rapidly rising labor costs of warehousing. The increased commissions for salesmen. And the credit problems—bad debts in furniture really hurt because the price tag of the merchandise is high. And, not the least of all, the high advertising expense of promoting furniture and carpets."

Pausing for breath only briefly, he went on, "We have followed a planned strategy of getting out of big-ticket merchandise which requires home delivery and commissioned salespeople. The reasons are that these departments require large warehouses, customer service departments, and substantial promotion costs.

"But," he added, with a broad smile, "we expect the change to increase our profits substantially. We will be removing the $4 million annual loss and using the capital for furniture and carpets to expand our inventories in more profitable goods."

In the meantime, he and Marshall Rose said that Korvettes expected to report the second consecutive quarterly loss in that current quarter, totaling about $5 million pre-tax. Korvettes' business had turned erratic for the first seven months of the fiscal year through August but had picked up since. But both executives predicted that the expansion of profitable departments into a good portion of the vacated space would put the company into the black in that fiscal year.

Obviously, debate or not, the new team was backing into a strategy of concentrating on those departments with best profit potential for Korvettes with inventories and prices deemed proper for the "new niche." It was enough to work on even if the grand plan wasn't in place yet.

Even so there were some disquieting wisps of rumor that crept into the sixth floor of 450 West 33rd Street where the new team had taken over their predecessors' offices. Sitting behind the same huge, ornate desk that had represented Bassine's dream of managing a $1 billion company, Dave Brous managed to maintain his perky bravado in the face of those wisps.

Arthur Cohen, as cooly remote as ever, showed no outward sign of concern, nor did Marshall Rose, with his clear, careful articulation. But indications were that Arlen Realty and Development Corporation, that most respected and enterprising of all real-estate developers, was beginning to have problems. Its earnings were under pressure and there were hints that its appetite for acquisitions had outpaced its ability to digest and to capitalize upon them.

The fears of 1972 became the bitter realities of 1973. That year, Arlen lost $22 million after a prior year's net profit of $21 million. Several unhappy forces had combined to clobber Arlen. Two of Bassine's pet enterprises, his Atlantic discount stores and the Far East importing business, were proving very unprofitable and costly to dispose of. On the corporate side, Arlen was fighting the combined effects of rising interest costs and a declining cash flow.

Despite that, Cohen, Rose, and their astute associates were convinced that the year's losses were what financial analysts liked to euphemistically label "an aberration," one of those odd, unaccountable things that happen, go away, and never come back. As for Korvettes, more than a few on the new team had concluded that Cohen, Rose, *et al* liked their new relationship with what was still one of the biggest, most important discounters—or promotional department stores. There was an obvious cross-fertilization of ideas between corporate and subsidiary and there was something else, too. The Arlen brass had considerable confidence in Korvettes, otherwise why did it back Brous's attracting some of the brightest retailers in New York at top dollar?

Slowly, deliberately, the new team moved into an overall game plan. The effort showed the care that comes only with experience.

First, it defined its financial objectives. Korvettes was to seek a profit of $8 million of a sales base of $606 million. It would generate capital by reducing inventory at least $6 million at cost. It would maintain a capital budget equal to depreciation expense for the year. And it would seek to provide funds of $10 million required for the acquisition of the six S. Klein stores.

Second, it was vital to establish management objectives. It was the only way to formalize the goals by which the financial objectives could be reached. There were five parts to establish the "management-by-objectives" program. A formal system of M.B.O. was to be introduced at the senior management level. A group of operating committees was to be established to formulate company policy and oversee its implementation. Formal quarterly-performance reports were to be prepared for submission to the parent company. A three-year company capital program would be set up. And guidelines for decision-making authority would be established, as well as a system of company bylaws.

But how was all this to bring about a real turnaround in Korvettes' fortunes? Management and financial objectives were necessary, of course, but they were only ideals without an action scenario which would realize them.

According to information obtained from members of Korvettes' executive committee, the merchandising plan in the mid-1970's called for the following:

1. Expand the merchandise emphasis

Emphasis on all soft goods areas would be expanded to reach the objective of 44.4 percent of the total business, an increase of 2.3 percent, targeting the following specific areas: Sportswear, Parent Department, growth rate objective, 15 percent; Junior Sportswear, 33 percent; Lingerie, 7 percent, Mens Habo, 6 percent; Men's Clothing, 5 percent; and Boys and Girls Clothing 8 percent.

Emphasis would also be expanded in certain hard goods areas—those lines that were accepted by consumers, were promotable, and generated high traffic and profits—namely: a growth rate objective of 20 percent in automotive, 10 percent in records, 6 percent in linens, 8 percent in cosmetics, and 10 percent in housewares.

Emphasis would be expanded throughout all merchandising areas, "table goods," and other special promotional buys, with a standard objective of 7 percent of total sales.

2. Contract the merchandise areas

The objective was to identify those merchandise areas which were unprofitable, required excessive handling or expert selling, and to prepare a plan to contract and reduce the emphasis on these areas. Specifically targeted areas were Fabrics, White Appliances, Skis, Men's Suits, and Pharmacies.

3. Shore up troubled departments

Objective of this effort was twofold. First was to redefine the direction of and initiate immediate remedial action in those departments Korvettes considered "troubled." The departments considered "troubled" were Dresses, Women's Shoes, Sporting Goods, Giftware, Juvenile Furniture, and Fine Jewelry. Other departments, considered "recession prone" (TV, Bicycles, Radios, and Audio) were to prepare defensive merchandise postures.

4. Tighten financial controls

5. *Upgrade quality of merchandise*

The objective here was to set specific standards on quality control and formulate a list of acceptable vendors.

6. *Develop the ability to respond to specific stores*

This objective aimed to tailor merchandising programs to specific store's needs according to the individual market, store size, demographics, and competition.

Besides the merchandising plan, the team developed additional objectives to implement the plan largely through sales support or operational activities.

Personnel was to be tightened up and consolidated where possible. Store tables of organization were to be developed so that management would perform only executive functions with a timetable of when and how to do this; use of part-time employees was to be maximized; and as many warehouse functions as possible should be passed on to central operations.

Attacking the problem of heavy merchandise theft and losses, the program called for ensuring that store directions were to be "articulated and monitored in accord with written standards." Apprehension reports and employees' dismissals should be monitored at the regional level. And all stores were to set up shrinkage control task forces where there was an inventory loss of over 3.5 percent of sales and where it had grown .75 percent over the prior year.

On the financial-administrative side, a study was to be developed involving the complete utilization of IBM equipment with the goal of achieving a "paperless" company. Criteria were to be established to allow the company to expand the acceptance of its own credit card. And bad-debt guidelines would be set up and implemented to meet the national department store average of 1.75 percent of sales.

In personnel, a goal of 75 percent internal promotions

was to be reached. An "ombudsman" was to be appointed. His function "shall be the maintenance and preservation of the dignity of the individual employee within the structure and who shall be protective of the customer's rights."

But, despite all the debate, all the planning, and all the backing and filling to make it effective, the results in the 1975 fiscal year were heavily disappointing. The fifty-eight-store chain had 60 percent lower net income in the year ended February 28, to a total of only $3 million against $7.6 million the year before. And sales inched up only 1.6 percent to $694.3 million from $683.3 million. Actually, Korvettes' income from operations had gone up slightly but the high cost of borrowing had almost wiped it out.

To be sure, Korvettes was only one of hundreds of retail chains severely hampered in the final quarter. Starting in late September 1974, the nation's economy had been stunted by a dramatic reversal in consumer buying. Retailers had permitted their inventories to drift up for many months, anticipating a continued honeymoon of enthusiastic purchasing by millions of consumers. But, suddenly, only a week or two after Labor Day, Americans found themselves worried by inflation, unemployment, and a general malaise. The effect on retailers and manufacturers in what was called "the almost biggest recession" lasted almost a year. And at Korvettes, where hopes had risen, the dismay was evident on lots of well-groomed faces.

At Arlen, the fears had materialized into realities. Seventy-five was the worst year that company had ever had. It more than doubled its 1974 loss of $22 million with a whopping deficit of $59.8 million. Ironically, about $48 million of that loss was attributable to the operating deficits and provision for closing the Atlantic stores and the import operations. Arlen had its own problems to which had been added the encumbrances acquired in the 1971 merger with Spartans-Korvettes. Was Korvettes, too, then, an encumbrance? Or was it the other way around?

It was, of course, too early to be sure. But one thing could already be told. Despite everything the new team at Korvettes had come up with, something else was needed, something harder, more specific, more stimulating, more urgent.

13.
The Rakish Hanger

If you walked through any one of Korvettes' fifty-eight stores those days, whether in New York, Washington, Chicago, or St. Louis, and observed with clear eyes, it was obvious that customers were simply cherry-picking Korvettes into an early death.

Even when they realized it and marveled at the pure casebook example, the new pros couldn't quite get used to it. Every store, they well knew, represented something different to the public. They used to say that Macy's was the housewares mecca. Gimbels was the store to shop others against. Marshall Field was where you went to find Grandma's doilies, or the best pewter. Neiman-Marcus, of course, was the store to get the best custom-tailored men's shirts if you could afford it. And B. Altman or W.&J. Sloane was the best source of the fullest selection of Baker furniture. And Ohrbach's was where you found the absolute but absolute best buys in women's coats.

Korvettes was ironically an attraction for two things and each had its own peculiar customer. First, there were two, distinct types, grades, and incomes of customers. The up-scale consumer, with family incomes from $15,000 to $50,000, thronged into the stores for housewares, books, records, tapes, audio, and radios. *They* recognized value, brand, and quality. But the downscale consumer, with family incomes of under $15,000 but probably averaging $7,500, came in for low-priced apparel, domestics and linens, children's wear, and daily specials. *They* appreciated value, brand or non-brand, and quality for a price.

That divergence, it became quite clear if you were a pro, accounted for the big gap of dollars in Korvettes' soft lines, especially the erosion under the growing onslaught of competition of sales throughout most of the store. Is it possible to survive with two distinct kinds of customers? What about the middle-income shopper? How could you promote effectively to both and still maintain the public recognition of overall credibility? Was there ever a store that succeeded with its head in the clouds, its feet on terra firma, but its broad middle portions amorphous and floating? Even Filene's in Boston, with its fashion customers for upstairs and its bargain-hunters for the famous, low-price basement seemed to have a bridge appeal that brought the upstairs customers down and the downstairs customers up.

But once the new team agreed on the problem, it was clear what had to be done. A major demographics and preference study had to be undertaken among Korvettes' and non-Korvettes' customers to find out what the perceptions about the company were. From that, it would then be necessary to decide how to change the perceptions for the better. It could be an entirely new approach.

When Shirley Young, executive vice president of Grey Advertising, New York, heard from Edward H. Meyer, the agency's chairman, that it had been contacted by David Brous, she was surprised and uncertain about taking on Korvettes. The chain already had had Doyle Dane Bernbach. But it appeared that Brous and his colleagues were not happy with "the loud sale advertising we're doing" and wanted to talk to one or more other ad agencies. The time: June 1977.

As creative head of Grey, Mrs. Young knew that any arrangement made with the retail chain would fall directly upon her. She was surprised that Korvettes had come to Grey, which was widely known as a retailer's specialist agency, because the discounter had always pushed a price rather than a merchandising image. Her reluctance stemmed from the rumors that trouble was brewing for Korvettes. Would it have been a comedown or a conflict for Grey to work with Korvettes? She denied both possibilities. Mrs. Young was already a director of the Dayton Hudson Corporation, which had its own discount subsidiary, Target Stores, while Edward Meyer was on the board of the May Department Stores Company, which operated the Venture discount stores.

"There was no thought of a comedown if we took on Korvettes," she said. "It was primarily that time was our most precious commodity and we were already quite busy. And we weren't sure we were interested. Korvettes may already have been in too deeply to help."

She found that Grey had been recommended by John S. Reed, senior executive vice president of Citicorp and its subsidiary, Citibank. Reed was on Arlen's board and had a close, advisory rapport with Arthur Cohen. When Mrs. Young and Meyer met with Brous, he was very candid. "We've got an overall strategy," he said, "but we need more professionalism in our marketing."

Giving the Grey executives a briefing, he went on, "We'll let you have all the background material you need.

But we'd like you to come back with a point-of-view, an approach, in other words. We have got to reverse the decline in sales. We have got to increase our margins. We have got to increase our store traffic. We have got to upgrade our merchandise." He paused, then added, "Maybe the toughest question of all is just how much we should raise our prices?"

He then related the findings of an outside research firm that Korvettes had hired, to the effect "we've got lots of problems." They were: "The customers don't think our merchandise is good enough . . . Our cashiers' lines are too long . . . Service is no good . . . The stores don't look very attractive . . . The bargain tables should be taken out."

The list of criticisms was very long, Mrs. Young recalls, running to at least twenty-five items. "We've got all these things to do," Dave Brous told Grey Advertising, "and we need a set of priorities." The agency decided to accept the assignment even though "the fee offered was modest," she said. As usual for the start of a new client program, a team of five was set up, including Mrs. Young and Edward Meyer, John G. Marder, account executive, Manny Rubin, creative director, and Joel Wayne, executive vice president, creative. "We went back through all the research that had been done," she said, "and we talked to the Korvettes' people about it. There was even more to it than Dave Brous had told us. The company had credit card problems, problems of cleanliness. The management felt that Korvettes needed to increase its proportion of soft goods merchandise. To go to more middle price-points. Instead of 60 percent low, 30 percent middle, reverse it with 10 percent at the high point."

The agency's "task force" did "a lot of work" and engaged in some research of its own, Mrs. Young said.

"We found that people do not go into department stores for records or hard goods," she reported. "But Korvettes' main problem was not traffic. Well over half of the shoppers in its trading area were shopping at least every few months. But while there was good penetration, the Korvettes' shoppers weren't buying enough other types of goods because of the chain's great reputation for hard goods. In fact, the customers were not even looking at the company's soft goods. We found, too, that no one thought that Korvettes' cashiering was very good. And that if the fashions were to be more successful, they should have more appeal."

The typical Korvettes' customer was found to have an annual income of between $10,000 to $25,000 a year. While this finding may have been low because of the peculiarities of spot-sampling, the agency nonetheless felt that the income bracket was close to reality. And so Grey told Brous and his staff, "Let's concentrate on those customers who like you—not on the wives of your own type who probably prefer Bloomie's."

In carrying out its own original research, Grey's staff would go to a Korvettes' store in all the New York area's shopping centers or neighborhoods where the stores were located and interviewed about 125 customers. Typical questions were: "What's most important to you in shopping Korvettes? . . . Have you bought any clothes at Korvettes? . . . What's your image of Korvettes? . . . What do you think of . . . its fashion . . . prices . . . service?" And one clear overall response was that Korvettes was "not good" on quality and fashion against the competition but was "good" on price.

The Grey staffers now attempted an interesting experiment. Fashion ads were clipped and four, distinctly different layouts were prepared, pasted on white sheets. Look #1 had mostly polyester suits, pant suits and dresses, conservative, practical, simple, basic, normally low-priced suits. Look #2 featured trendy, up-to-date clothes. Look #3 consisted of classic apparel. And Look #4 had junior sportswear.

The researchers fanned out again to the Korvettes' stores and flashed the sheets at women shoppers.

Question: "Which of these fashions do you like most?"

Most responses: "I like Look #3 and #4. I'm not really looking for #2 (Bloomie's type)."

Question: "Which Look do you think you can get at Korvettes?"

Most responses: "Look #1, the polyester pant suits."

Based on these answers, the question arose at Grey, "Was that perception image or reality?" The next stage of the experiment involved a personal fashion demonstration aimed to answer that very question. Several of the women working on the Grey unit bought clothes at Korvettes representing Looks #3 and #4, the classics and the junior sportswear, respectively. They were shown to about one hundred Korvettes' women shoppers by the team members actually wearing the clothes. The shoppers were asked, "Does this outfit come from A.&S., Macy's or Gimbels?" Each store was suggested by the respondents but no one volunteered that the source might have been Korvettes. In addition, the erstwhile models also wore clothes representing all four Looks and asked the shoppers which of the four might have come from Korvettes. Most responses were that #1 emanated from Korvettes.

"This convinced us that the shoppers' perception of the fashions sold at Korvettes was much worse than what was actually in the store," Mrs. Young said. "It was like looking at someting with a jaundiced eye. And we began to see what had to be done."

Obviously, Korvettes had to change people's minds about what it had to offer. If it was true that women shoppers choose to come to a department store because of fashion merchandise, then it would be necessary to improve the general perception to the extent that Korvettes did have the kind of fashion goods that women liked. At the same time, and just as vital to the project, was the need for the company to largely shift its inventories to offer Looks #3 and #4, the classics and the junior sportswear.

"Up to that point, we had devoted four or five weeks at a modest cost of our own to our research with no fee from them," said Mrs. Young. "Then, we put together some story-boards to illustrate the message that Korvettes had to deliver. 'You have all those customers who come in for the hard goods, use that to advantage and tell them that you have the soft goods, the attractive fashions. Make sure you have the merchandise. Advertise it properly. Display the merchandise and highlight it. All three of those pieces have to work together or none of them will mean anything.' And having told them that, we said, 'Now, we have given you a strategy.' "

Brous, Norman Matthews, Bob Warner, and Gary Oza-roff listened to the presentation and were impressed. But they were nervous about it. Arthur Cohen was there also, along with his daughter, who registered much interest. "They all liked it," said Shirley Young, "even if they were a bit shaky about its prospects. But we apparently did the best job of any of the agencies that they had asked to make a presentation," she added, "because they asked us to give the presentation to their bankers. It was the first time that we had ever made a pitch to bankers. Maybe Arthur Cohen was being very smart. *If* the bankers bought it. Apparently they did, because Arthur asked us to come back."

But he and the Korvettes' brass kept asking, in effect, "Can we really promise it to the customers and will they really believe it?"

"We assured them that it would, based on our research," Mrs. Young said, "and they gave us the go-ahead."

"But what are we going to call it?" they wanted to know.

"We were prepared for that. We said, 'Well, it's really about the side of Korvettes that the shoppers don't know about—'"

"Right—"

"Let's call it, 'The Other Korvettes.'"

For almost all of its first twenty-five years, Korvettes had been gradually increasing the amount of advertising and promotion that it used and its dollar outlays grew accordingly. By 1970, its annual expenditures for advertising-promotion reached about $16 million, or a bit less than the normal 3 percent of sales that department stores allotted to that activity. Added to that figure was about $8 million in co-op advertising allowances contributed by suppliers. That created a kitty of about $24 million, about 95 percent of which was given over to pure sales advertising. Approximately 4 to 5 percent of the total outlay was channeled into television advertising and its thrust was almost entirely institutional.

In the early 1970's, few of the department stores in New York, Washington, Philadelphia, Chicago, Detroit, or St. Louis were using television for anything more than institutional imagery. Special sale days, of course, received an intense, limited push, as did holidays, such as Christmas, Easter, Mother's Day or Father's Day, when specific item promotions were presented on the tube. The heyday of big-store TV advertising was still a few years ahead. And so Korvettes through 1974 advertised generally as most discounters and middle-price department stores did. Price, hot value, and loss leaders were the mainstay in print media with heavy play on comparative prices.

Korvettes in its quest for a more meaningful advertising approach was attracted about that time to Doyle Dane

Bernbach, which was generally considered the most creative advertising agency of that period. But, as Dave Brous recalls, "They were too sophisticated for us. What they suggested, we felt, was too far ahead of the public perception of Korvettes. It wouldn't have worked for us."

Turning to George Lois, whom "we felt was a brilliantly creative guy," Brous asked the advertising man to come up with a "handle, something that would give us a certain difference or distinctiveness." Brous himself liked the concept of a "spokesman." A well-known personality or, if not well-known, a personality whose warmth and charisma would create a bridge between the newspaper reader or television viewer and Korvettes. In 1970 and 1971, Korvettes had used Bill Cullen, the TV-radio master-of-ceremonies and talk-show host, in its furniture and carpet TV advertising. George Lois, charged to produce a "spokesman," proved a fertile source of ideas and soon emerged with one that Brous and the new team approved.

In 1975, the "Mayor of Korvettes" appeared on television spot commercials. They featured a short, chunky man wearing a fire-chief's hat who rushed on the scene, shouting in a shrieky voice that he was dashing to Korvettes where there was "a hot sale" or "a fire of a sale." He was, of course, an intended allusion to the much-admired Mayor Fiorello LaGuardia, whose trademark was rushing to fires in the city or reading newspaper comics to children over the city's radio station.

In some commercials, the "Mayor of Korvettes" would trade quips with shoppers or appear in a Korvettes' store in the role of a zealous salesman.

The "Mayor" was also used in newspaper ads and on radio commercials. The application on those two media appeared effective. But the TV presentation appeared shrill, amateurish, and somehow off-center for Korvettes, a sort of "cheapie" that wouldn't create any real benefit for the chain. It was obvious then what Korvettes was doing—attempting to build a personality which would humanize the company. And perhaps build on the LaGuardia-like credibility.

But it didn't work. The commercials were withdrawn after about five months. Years later, Brous was to say, simply, " 'The Mayor' didn't present the image that we wanted."

Yet, it was one of the few relatively sustained advertising approaches which the retail chain, then still the nation's second-largest discounter, had employed. Two years were to pass before the next one was paraded before the public.

Because Arthur Cohen and the Korvettes' management were still uncertain about how much impact the new marketing strategy would have, it was agreed that some more testing should be done first. In summer of 1977, the Grey staff prepared a number of "The Other Korvettes" ads, showed them to Korvettes' shoppers and took them afterwards into the stores to see the actual merchandise. The favorable reaction encouraged the doubters who then fully approved the start of the program.

"We began to run the advertising and lo and behold it ran for ten full weeks in spot commercials on New York television in fall of 1977," reported Shirley Young. "During that period, sales of soft lines at Korvettes' New York stores went ahead 6 percent while in the out-of-town stores business went down 4 percent. In hard goods in New York, sales rose 15 percent and only 6 percent ahead in the other stores. This proved that the thirty-second and sixty-second ads were making a difference."

Was the emphasis on soft goods bringing in women and their husbands to also buy the automotive accessories, radios, audio, and housewares? It appeared likely—and quite startling—to judge by the results.

The effort to convince Korvettes' shoppers, and any others who were listening, needed some sort of a symbol. Ed Meyers of Grey suggested that since the program basically involved apparel a likely symbol might be a coat or dress hanger. This idea was accepted as a visual prop. In one of the main Fifth Avenue windows, a tremendous yellow hanger, at least ten feet high, created attention. One day, the probably apochryphal story goes, the hanger slipped on its overhead strands and hung there tilted about thirty degrees. The diagonal position continued undetected from inside the store for hours. But outside, it attracted considerable attention, intriguing hundreds of pedestrians whether for its rakish angle or simply because it might have been a mistake on the part of a display man with a hangover.

From then on, the hanger symbol assumed a tilted position in advertising and in store presentation and signs. Somehow, it fit the "corrective" nature of the program, the pitch of the hanger perhaps underscoring the error of the wrong perception about Korvettes. But, more likely the ironic or playful tilt added just the right touch to the rather stolid style of "The Other Korvettes." And it's not hard to envision more than one Korvettes' employee jaded by the fits and starts of the swinging executive turnstyle wondering out loud if "it takes a cockeyed hanger to set us straight."

The commercials involved a series of scenes in which both women and men wearing routine clothes were tapped by smiling salespeople and instantly transformed into paragons of the latest fashions from the racks and stocks of Korvettes. If the delirious rapture displayed by the transfigured shoppers was just a bit hard to take, the point nonetheless came across, clearly, if a bit heavily.

Within the stores, the dress-up, paint-up, clean-up campaign to support "The Other Korvettes" also led inevitably to wider renovations of most of the other stores. Despite

Arlen's mushrooming problems, Korvettes was generally protected against providing money to the parent company under the retail chain's loan agreement with the banks. Not only did that arrangement bar Korvettes from providing money to Arlen, according to Dave Brous, but the Korvettes' board had also adopted a resolution against transferring funds to Arlen.

The marketing program was renewed in spring of 1978 for another ten weeks. It was also extended to additional markets where it similarly improved the sales trend. Grey and Korvettes decided that the program would benefit from a wider employee participation. "The Other Korvettes" badges were provided for employees and signs were posted throughout the stores. Morale picked up with word that business was responding. Employees who sat at home at night and watched the TV commercials were buoyed up. Korvettes finally seemed aggressive once again, nipping at the heels of its competitors. That fall, a presentation for all the company's top brass, the merchandisers, and buyers was given of the merchandise and strategy of "The Other Korvettes" for the 1978 Christmas season. The response of the staff at the preview held at a Bushkill Falls, New York, resort was spontaneous and enthusiastic.

On September 11, 1978, a long, unsigned article in the *Wall Street Journal* reported that "The Other Korvettes" advertising campaign plus refurbishings of many of the stores had helped increase sales and slash traditional first-half losses. Quoting David Brous, the article continued, "Overall sales for the first half were about 11 percent over a year earlier, with one department, junior sportswear, ahead by 40 percent. The junior sportswear departments have been refurbished" in most of the stores . . . The advertising campaign on television and newspapers has played up the department store chain's switch in emphasis from just low price to fashion quality at reasonable prices. The emphasis thus far has been on apparel but soon will include such hard goods as housewares and small appliances . . .

"In the past year, the chain gave up some of its lowest-price business in apparel and built up its medium-price categories, stressing the fashion angle . . . In doing this, the company lost millions of dollars in sales but currently the soft goods sales also are showing double-digit gains. This is true despite the newspaper strike . . . The ambience, the new type of fashion apparel being offered, and the advertising campaign have been the main factors in boosting business.

"Overall, the chain will spend about $12 million during fiscal 1979 refurbishing a number of stores and will continue this pace in fiscal 1980. It costs between $750,000 and $1 million for each store. Just to refurbish the junior sportswear departments chainwide cost about $1 million . . ."

But, because of a pruning process of divesting of several unprofitable stores, a total of eight, leaving Korvettes with fifty stores, the chain had a net loss of $5.4 million in fiscal 1978. Other than non-recurring costs, mostly the expense of disposing of those stores, Korvettes had in that year an operating profit of $1 million, Brous told the *W.S.J.* reporter.

However, things were definitely improving, he stressed. In that particular fiscal quarter ending August 31, the company's president said that he expected to report a lower loss of $700,000 against the year-earlier deficit of $3.7 million and a 1976 loss of $5.2 million in the same period. The trend was also better in the first fiscal quarter ended May 31, 1978; a loss of $1.3 million against losses of $2.3 million in 1977 and $3.4 million in 1976 in the appropriate periods.

But why does Korvettes continue to lose money after making substantial gains? Brous was asked.

The company traditionally lost money in the first and second quarters, he replied, but the most recent losses came after expenses for its advertising and promotion campaign, increasing the credit business and charges for depreciation. "Our goal for the first half of next year is to be even or make a profit," he said, "maybe about $1 million."

How well was "The Other Korvettes" *really* working? Was it possible that a new golden era was unfolding for the company thirty years after its founding and after so many ups and downs?

Usually, retailing pundits insist, it takes from three to five years for a department or specialty store to realize fully the successes—or failures—of a massive shift in merchandising. But in December 1978, or about fifteen months after Korvettes' new concept was unveiled before the public, Research in Perspective Inc., a New York-based research consultant, conducted the latest consumer survey of shoppers in reaction to "The Other Korvettes" program. Earlier, the research company had reported to Korvettes on similar surveys in October and May 1978, in December and October 1977, and had conducted an initial 1976 basic market study.

Submitting its December 1978 findings in March 1979, the researchers reported to Korvettes the following:

"While penetration . . . of the new Korvettes' fashion-oriented advertising has increased . . . further changes in perception or modification of behavior with respect to Korvettes clothing departments have not accompanied the increased advertising awareness. Among both frequent and infrequent Korvettes shoppers in the New York market, unaided and aided awareness of Korvettes' advertising, as well as relevant fashion oriented recall, increased in the current wave of research versus the preceding wave of research (December vs. October 1978).

"However," the report continued, "while measurements

relating to clothing perception and behavior had increased among frequent shoppers on a year-to-year basis, there were no significant increases on these measurements between October and December 1978. These measurements included: The overall rating of Korvettes as a place to shop. Selection of Korvettes as the favorite department store. Perception that Korvettes is better than it was a year ago. Attribute ratings related to Korvettes' clothing departments. Likelihood of buying clothing at Korvettes. Past year and most often shopping patterns in Korvettes' clothing departments and specific departments within men's and women's clothing departments. Ratings for departments other than clothing. Interest in shopping in departments other than clothing."

In fact, said the report, there were declines from October to December 1978 in the ratings given to Korvettes by frequent shoppers for having excellent or very good men's clothing and children's clothing. "Additionally, there were period-to-period declines in frequent customer shopping behavior with respect to Korvettes' children's clothing. Further, some declines in interest in shopping for 'hard goods' at Korvettes were registered."

In other selected findings, the researchers said that while the concern made great progress in improving the "perception and the shopping patterns relative to its clothing departments, Korvettes' clothing continues to have a less favorable perception than does Korvettes' non-clothing merchandise. But "significant progress has been made among Korvettes' frequent shoppers in high ratings" on such questions as "Carry the styles and kinds of clothes I like; clothes are in good taste; in-store displays give you fashion ideas . . ."

Frequent Korvettes' shoppers have shopped the men's and women's clothing departments in "significantly greater numbers" than the year before.

But frequent and infrequent shoppers in New York,

Washington, Detroit, Baltimore, and Philadelphia rated Korvettes' non-clothing merchandise "significantly higher" than its clothing in terms of such things as "being well made, the advertising is believable, a good value, being good quality, a wide selection and variety . . ."

Wrapping it up, the report stated that "the lack of increase in consumer attitudes or behavior relative to Korvettes between October and December 1978 suggests" three conclusions. "The need to strengthen the position of Korvettes relative to children's clothing and men's clothing. The need to develop and execute a strong 'hard-goods' oriented marketing, advertising, and merchandise program. The need to begin to look for the 'second generation' to the basic 'Other Korvettes' positioning if the current advertising/in-store programs do not begin to cycle upward in future waves of research."

In other words, "The Other Korvettes" had had some success, was promising, but needed significant further push. The bulk of the $3 million advertising of the total $30 million advertising-promotion budget was being expended on the fashion program. More would evidently have to be spent, displays and presentation would have to be improved, additional merchandising efforts and promotional clout would have to be given men's clothing, children's wear, and hard goods. And just to play safe, unless the basic concept format didn't give any additional benefits, a new wrinkle or "second generation" effort would be necessary.

But events were overtaking the ambitious merchandising and promotion effort. A harsh spotlight was swinging to Arlen and the implications for Korvettes were fateful.

14.
A Case of Mutual Indigestion

On the 45th floor of 888 Seventh Avenue in Manhattan, the smell of wealth, power, and success filled one's nostrils.

But in the penthouse on the 46th floor, where only the top-top executives stayed and only the most distinguished visitors were hosted, the feelings of well-being and achievement were the greatest. There was ease, too. The informality, the kidding, the occasional horseplay were evidence that the most successful do not take themselves seriously, at least not so that you could notice it.

The penthouse was the headquarters of Arlen Realty and Development Corporation, America's largest real-estate owner and developer, headed by Arthur G. Cohen. Through the 1960's and much of the 1970's, Arlen was an exciting testimonial to the verve of both youth and experience, brilliance, creative venturism, and rampant empire-building.

The management appeared to be the epitome of American industry, their cool, hard showmanship flashing through the nation's real-estate industry, staging an act that was hard to follow. There was a graciousness in the manner in which they handled the accumulation of properties and the building of new ones, a sign of their self-confidence and sleek business acumen.

Bankers courted them. Developers studied them. Retailers waylaid them. Insurance companies sought to entice them with all sorts of emoluments. For a long period, Wall Streeters stared at them open-mouthed. And when any of them was invited to the 46th floor for breakfast or lunch from the on-site kitchen, there always seemed to be moments when they were left alone to glance out the window and see where Arlen stood. On the top of the world. For beyond, above and below the concrete promontory over the Hudson, was the vast view that beckoned. It was a panorama of upper and lower New York and the bread-basket of New Jersey that on good days was awash in half-sunny mist and on bad ones suffered not much worse than a deep purple hue.

Arthur Cohen's breezy greeting was both youthful and unaffected. A sign of vast success? Of course. Marshall Rose's matter-of-fact yet warm greeting, a bit more formal, was, well, both youthful and unaffected. The perfect administrator to Cohen's empire-building instinct? Maybe. Arthur Levien's more hesitant but friendly, "Hello, there. Nice to see you again,"—wasn't it perhaps a signal of a different kind? Did he wear Arlen's brewing problems more openly on his sleeve? Could be.

The visitor could only sit and wonder about them in 1972, 1973, and 1974. The ease with which Cohen and Rose could discuss Korvettes was disconcerting. If a bunch of highly paid professionals could agonize around a table some twenty-five city blocks away, how was it, the same visitor wonders, that the parent company's senior management could discuss it all so blithely? "Things are definitely improving . . . they've got a handle on things . . . we're proud of that new bunch . . . they're finding their niche . . ." Arlen's words about Korvettes weren't even delivered with either the hoarse or the hyped tones of a sales pitch. It was all low-key, confident, just halting enough to be sincere.

More important, if underneath the surface, there was panic about Arlen itself—didn't it creep out of the cracks, the silences between the easy words?—there was no evidence of it in the jaunty way they moved, poured coffee, trivialized momentarily over the aches and pains of the local ball teams, and switched to a sober, almost scholarly comment about the national economy. A cool response to hot problems is certainly graciousness under fire. But it also serves to deter, to blunt hard questions. Asking them in such a milieu would have been an affront.

Yet disaster lapped at the doors of Arlen's lavish offices.

Its losses, beginning with the $22 million deficit in 1973, simply exploded in the ensuing years. More expansion than almost any other American developer and a related lack of digestive ability were responsible.

In 1974, the loss was $9.9 million. In 1975, it mushroomed to $59.9 million. In 1976, it was $23.8 million. In 1977, it more than doubled to $48.7 million. And, in 1978, it catapulted to $110.9 million. About $275 million in losses in six years.

The havoc that hovered came not so much from the immense losses. These were bad enough. After all, much of it was on paper, a minus against corporate funds and stockholders. The bad news lay in the reaction of the banks, including, ironically, Citibank, on whose board Arthur Cohen sat. The bankers were getting impatient and very worried. True, the country's real-estate industry was in a shambles and Arlen, as the largest company, could hardly have escaped the general upset. But what especially concerned the lenders was the immensity of Arlen's size and of its obligations. One commercial banker and two investment bankers sat on Arlen's board. Since the banks and Wall Street had financed much of the growth that had turned sour, they felt put upon and under intense pressure, too. Year after year, as the decade of the 1970's waned and the losses grew, they sat and fumed. Finally, in mid-1978, they acted.

They insisted that Arlen strengthen its management by hiring Robert F. Stewart as president and a director. A senior vice president for strategic planning of United Technologies Corporation from 1975 through mid-1978, Stewart had previously been vice president of Rockwell International Corporation from 1971 to 1975, president of its consumer operations group from 1974 to 1975, and president of its industrial products group from 1971 to 1974. The stolid Stewart, who never seemed quite comfortable in what was obviously an inspector general's role at Arlen, was given a four-year contract with a base salary of $225,000, a bonus of $112,500 for the fiscal year ending February 28, 1979, a minimum bonus of 50 percent of his annual base salary after that, as well as perks including an apartment, an automobile, and so on.

Although later Arthur Cohen admitted that Citibank had recommended Stewart for the post, he said it was Stewart's experience and record in control and operations that got him the job, not the nudge from Arlen's biggest banker. Soon after, Marshall Rose resigned from his twin posts at Arlen's and Korvettes and became a consultant, declining to involve himself in either company's affairs after that.

The bankers also insisted that the divestiture of the Atlantic discount stores be speeded up. The 100-plus Atlantic stores, which had been sold in 1971 under the divestiture order with the F.T.C. to Heck's, Inc., discount chain, had been repurchased by Arlen in 1974, whittled down to only fifty-six stores, and was proving to be more and more of a drain to Arlen. Business was quite bad, not only for the down-at-the-heels Atlantic stores but for much of the discount industry. Almost two dozen blue-collar type discounters had either availed themselves of the Chapter XI provisions of the Federal Bankruptcy Act, obtaining court protection while they worked out a repayment of debts, or had gone out of business. Finally in 1975, Arlen closed the Atlantic chain, absorbing a loss of $34.5 million that year because of it. But the costs of liquidation, continuing obligations, and severance lingered, like an albatross unwilling to be cast off, accounting for an outflow from Arlen's funds of more than $100 million by the late 1970's.

And the bankers also pressed for some more substantial protection for their institutions if the financial lifeline to Arlen were to be further played out. The financial matters involving both Arlen Realty & Development Corporation and Arlen Realty, Inc., its majority-owned real-estate subsidiary, were complex. In the fiscal year ended February 28, 1978, the parent company and its subsidiaries had outstanding debt of $916.2 million. But in March, April, and June of that year, parent Arlen and several subsidiaries borrowed another $47 million, $23 million of which was to be used to repay existing current bank debt.

Certain properties owned by the real-estate subsidiary were used as collateral for its new bank-loan deal. In its newest borrowing, the parent company pledged all of its shares in Korvettes.

Arlen and its sundry subsidiaries were obviously up against the wall and the bankers, their patience already strained, would not take much more. How much would

Arthur Cohen, his associates, and his backers give in? Some of them were wealthy friends and neighbors in Cohen's home village of Great Neck, Long Island, who had joined him in creating some lush tax shelters by investing in his shopping centers. One can imagine their dismay at the pit their paragon had fallen into.

The implications were pointed enough in Arlen Realty & Development's 10-K statement to the Securities and Exchange Commission for that year ended February 1978.

"The Company is engaged in discussions with its lenders with respect to the restructuring of the provisions of certain loan agreements. If the Company is not able to continue to obtain deferrals of such payments and to obtain waivers and/ or to restructure such agreements, a significant portion of its indebtedness would be subject to acceleration. If repayment of such loans were required in the near future, the Company would probably not be in a position to repay such loans without selling a significant portion of its assets. The sale of assets under such circumstances would probably not realize the values which the Company believes could be obtained if sold in the normal course of business."

"The Company," Arlen said further in the 10-K, has "a negative net worth." It added that "as a result thereof, of the uncertainties described above and those set forth in their report accompanying the financial statements, Coopers & Lybrand, the Independent Certified Public Accountants of the Company, have given a 'qualified' opinion with respect to such statements . . ."

The ironies in Arlen's distress were painfully clear. Given the tough realities of the difficult real-estate industry's straits, which would eventually cost the company some $75 million in losses, it was the expansion by merger into retailing and apparel seven years earlier, the marriage with Spartans-Korvettes, which had sent Arlen reeling. However, it wasn't so much Spartans and Korvettes which had proved to be the albatross, as the Atlantic chain added by Charles Bassine to his Spartans discount stores. Hindsight asks: if it hadn't been for the Atlantic stores, how different would both Arlen's and Korvettes' future have been?

But the seventeen banks that provided Arlen's financial lifeline, and especially the three on its board, weren't interested in probing the ifs or the ironies. About $350 million in debt had to be restructured in the next few months. And it was. But the banks exacted their own safeguards. To obtain its survival, Arlen's management and directors agreed to exchange with the banks a number of properties, mortgages, and other assets. As it moved to surrender some of its lushest holdings, the biggest question about Arlen's properties was raised but remained unanswered through the late summer of the pivotal year of 1978. It was simple enough.

What would happen to Korvettes?

At Korvettes, three separate dimensions were evident, three separate attitudes, three patterns of behavior. As Korvettes began to round out its thirty years of existence in the unfolding year of 1978, a sense of hope filled the hearts of senior management, filtering down the ranks. But it increasingly lost its depth as it descended. The executives who manned the stores in other cities were hardly as motivated as those in New York. Communications were lacking, as they are in most retail companies; those in the field are convinced that they are mostly either forgotten or ignored. In Korvettes' case, the field staff was increasingly confused by what was happening in New York—each day brought new rumors both up and down on the scale of dire or happy prediction. When the top brass, imbued with hope over "The Other Korvettes" but knowing that they were still under scrutiny, would descend on the stores, the effect was often very disturbing. "Brous or Warner or Ozaroff would come into the store and start throwing orders around and you could only conclude that things were desperate," recalled a department manager in one of the Maryland stores. "They would tell me that things were picking up, that we all had to put our shoulders to the wheel—but hell, we had been doing that for years. Still, it was good to see them once in a while. It made us feel part of something. It made us feel that there was some hope."

Besides hope, there was also deep concern over the worsening situation at Arlen. True, the parent company had moved back in 1975 to tacitly remove Korvettes from any direct connection with its problems. As with Arlen Realty, Inc., the real-estate unit, Arlen's set up Korvettes, Inc., as a separate wholly-owned subsidiary. Both Korvettes and Arlen Realty thus had their own financing arrangements and issued separate financial statements. In Korvettes' case, the action was taken to convince suppliers and creditors that the retail chain had its own resources, wasn't beholden to Arlen, and could pay its own bills. But, the top team on West 33rd Street knew that only the simple-minded would be fooled by that. As a token gesture, it yielded only a token result. Arlen was deep in hock to the seventeen banks and it was suspected—and later confirmed—that the parent company had pledged its ownership in Korvettes to the banks in order to maintain its credit and borrowing lines. If the banks were to suddenly call in their loans, or if they were to compel Arlen to "liquify" itself (sell off its assets to bring in needed cash) and include Korvettes in that process, where would they be? There was only one solution to the problem, of course. Pray that Arlen would make it, and work like hell at Korvettes to get back on a solid profit track.

That led to the third attitude: Concern that the suppliers might hold back substantial orders in the fear that Korvettes would be hard put to pay its bills. The chain's top team knew that some vendors were already very nervous and uptight. Often, Philip Kaplan, the executive vice president for finance, spent time reassuring manufacturers and wholesalers that the company was making progress, that its cash flow was strong, and that prompt payment would be made. But suppliers already burned by the 1975 bankruptcy and liquidation of W. T. Grant, as well as the Chapter XI filings by a host of discounters and specialty store chains, couldn't help but be concerned. Even the possibility of Korvettes' petitioning for a Chapter XI dogged them, since in most cases a reorganization under that part of the Bankruptcy Act took several years to accomplish and settlements were rarely more than thirty cents on the dollar.

Despite all that, it was evident that there was motivation and hope. Some of it was based on sheer pride and competitive spirit. After all, they had Ken Kolker, one of the top merchants in the Federated Department Stores system, who probably should have become chairman or president of A. &S. They had Brous out of Macy's, a natural cheerleader. And Bob Warner, a top, creative man by way of Macy's. And Matthews, Ozaroff, and the whole new bright team. The hope was based, too, on the general perception that men, even *a* man, do make a difference. Look at what Carl Bennett had done at Caldor, Harry Cunningham at K mart, Ed Finkelstein at Macy's in California and now in New York, Edwin Roberts at J. L. Hudson, Joe Brooks at Lord & Taylor . . .

But who was to be *the* man at Korvettes? If there were at least six top men on the executive committee, there were probably as many insufferable egos. The tough truth is that too many ideas are sometimes worse than too few. Who could tell if an idea was a good one until it was tried? With dozens of ideas passing back and forth across the table, there had to be instant editing, decisions based on merit or on one-upmanship, or on pure principle or prejudice. "Kolker was like a machine-gunner when it came to ideas," said an executive committee member. "He just shot them out. About 30 percent of them were just too exotic for Korvettes and had to be automatically rejected. But he had more good ideas than anyone else. And he had convictions, too, that were based on his experience at A.&S., just as we all had operating principles that we believed in that we had been trained in where we came from."

It was on one of those principles that caused Kolker and Korvettes to come to a parting of the ways. Kolker insisted that Korvettes could succeed only if it built a strong, daily business, just as A.&S. had done so successfully in the years he had been there. But others objected. They cited the fact that the chain did about 23 percent of its total year's business from Thanksgiving Day through Christmas, well above the average. That meant that its daily volume the rest of the year was small or erratic, given to lows and highs. In addition, daily business at Korvettes responded directly to a constant diet of key events or "item" promotions. The prolonged debate was, in a great sense, a question of how to time the shift into a niche between department and discount stores. A steady trend in day-to-day volume was the department-store *metier*. Item events were the discounter's mainstay. Successful, entrenched stores of each type could effectively blend the two approaches. But Korvettes was struggling under the pressure of new or reawakened competition. And what was its vigorous Christmas business but the public's traditional response to the chain's barrage of seasonal hot items?

Brous held out on this point, backing the supports of the key events philosophy. Kolker couldn't accept it. He resigned. "That decision," said an executive committee member, "was a big loss to Korvettes."

Brous promptly closed the ranks, graciously lauding all that Kolker had contributed. But even with his departure, stressed Korvettes' president, there was much to be thankful for. "The Other Korvettes" was pulling. Arlen was supporting the turnaround effort despite its accumulating problems. To offset the eight stores that it had closed because of their unprofitable performance, Korvettes had added the Klein stores at favorable lease arrangements. Morale at the rank-and-file level still seemed high. Everyone was still putting out a good day's work.

On the question of morale, Brous may have been overselling. Interviews with two branch-store executives, both of whom requested anonymity on the basis that their remarks might be held against them, had this to say:

"They would come into our store and constantly annoy us with their inspections. They would concentrate on how well we were supporting 'The Other Korvettes' program. Hell, half the time we didn't have the merchandise that they were advertising on TV partly because the vendors were shipping us irregularly. It was like it got cut off someplace. I remember one woman shopper came in, looked around, and said, 'Where's the Other Korvettes?' She was serious, too, but I don't know if she meant the merchandise they were advertising or if there was supposed to be another store called 'The Other Korvettes.' I guess I played the wise guy. I said to her, 'Lady, this is the only Korvettes I know of. If it isn't, I've been working in the wrong store for the last ten years.' "

Said the other branch executive:

"They would knock us out, they were so jittery and changeable. Maybe I might seem like I'm exaggerating but every week or two one of the brass would come into our store by himself or with some other guys and instruct us to change everything. A department that was fixed up one way under instruction from New York would be completely changed by the new guy. Our regional vice president would run in one day and ask us if we waxed the storeroom floor. Waxed? What for? From then on, every time we knew he would be coming in, I would have two people wax the storeroom. Another vice president was a bug on neat arrangements in merchandise. Every shelf had to be so many inches from the next one. One stack had to be a 90-degree angle from the next one. The guy would show up with a ruler and a slide rule or calculator. So when we knew that he was coming, we would house-clean for him. In between, we'd forget about it except for normal house-cleaning. That was the kind of nonsense we had to take when all the customer really wanted was good prices and good values."

Brous held several merchandising orientation sessions. It was not an unusual activity for a retail chain eager to impress its buying and operational staff on what it had to offer for a forthcoming season. But in Korvettes' case when the company was under severe pressure and needed to conserve expenses, many executives were taken aback when as much as $300,000 was expended for a weekend meeting at the Nevele or Kutsher's resorts in the Catskills or Tamiment in the Poconos. As many as 400 executives from headquarters and the branches were invited at company expense to these presentations which included fashion shows, merchandising and promotion presentations, and introductory and concluding talks by Dave Brous. The company's president, bouncy, super-optimistic, alternately chiding and complimentary, put much effort into his remarks. But comments from some who were there. showed, at least a year or two later, that the end result was confusion and dismay. There seemed to them to be an immense gap between the official euphoria in New York and the realities of uncertain business and severe competition in the stores themselves.

During this period, the marketing strategy was refined by the top team based on the ongoing surveys by the outside research company and the reaction to "The Other Korvettes" program. An internal memorandum of April 1978 spelled it out:

KORVETTES MARKETING OBJECTIVES ARE TO BE:

A reliable store which serves the general merchandise needs of the family in the $10,000 to $30,000 income range, with special emphasis on the $15,000 to $25,000 family.

A store which fills a clear segment in the middle between discount stores and full service department stores.

A store which garners an increasing share of its existing, frequent-customer's disposable dollars.

A store which garners an increasing penetration of its existing markets through development of loyal customers who shop more frequently on a day-in, day-out basis.

<u>Merchandise</u>

A store with quality and fashionable ready-to-wear at price points just below the national brand leaders.

A store whose ready-to-wear appeals to the merchandising needs of the present, frequent Korvettes' durable goods shopper.

A value-oriented store with wide assortments of durable and fashion hard goods.

A store which at all times and with special emphasis on promotion, offers solid values vis-a-vis general competition.

A store whose key merchandise is solidly in an in-stock position.

Store Ambience

A *clear store, where merchandise and service areas are fully defined and simple.*

An *attractive and tasteful store, which puts great emphasis on contemporary visual techniques to enhance the merchandise.*

A *smoothly functioning store, geared to self-service where appropriate, and adequately staffed by knowledgeable people.*

A *friendly store where all personnel are trained and motivated to be courteous and helpful.*

Communication

A *store whose advertising and graphics are harmonious with the merchandise and store ambience to produce a consistent image.*

A *store whose advertising clearly portrays the three fundamentals of Korvettes merchandising: quality, fashion, and value.*

It was an ambitious plan for a company which in 1977, the year before, had lost about $4 million on sales of $590 million, a dip of 3 percent under the 1976 level. But Dave Brous and his team were not cowed by the erosion of business or profits. In March 1977, they had drafted a series of steps to achieve the marketing objectives. The company's business goal was to achieve a return of 4 percent pre-tax on net sales by 1982 which would be 10 percent on post-tax on invested capital. It was a lower profit projection than what had been sought earlier only a few years after the new team had been formed. As mentioned in Chapter 12, the financial objective had been to get a pre-tax profit of $8 million on a sales base of $606 million. Now, based on an internal memo distributed to many executives, the management hoped for well less than that, 4.1 percent, on 1982 projected sales of

$730 million. It was predicated on anticipated 5 percent year-to-year sales gains for 1980 through 1982.

How was it all to be accomplished?

Single-store markets were to be deserted, such as Harrisburg, Pa., Hampton, Va., and Albany, N.Y., as well as the six-store Chicago market. Trumbull, Conn., was to be investigated as a possible new market.

All non-retail assets were to be divested through sale, merger, or liquidation. These included three small companies that Korvettes had accumulated—the Warren Refrigerator Company, a Texas distributor; the Rockaway Metal Products Corporation, a steel partition manufacturer on Long Island; and the Curtis Partition Company, a dry-wall supplier in New Jersey. No mention was made of the company's Horn Brothers, the Long Island housewares distributor.

An important ingredient in the plan for soft goods was to move from current price "points" to more middle-level price "points." The objective was to keep the chain's lower-income customers but to add department-store customers "by having national brand quality, taste, and fashion at 20 to 30 percent less in price points than department stores. This is a void in the market. The lower price points are covered by discounters; the higher price points by the department stores. Sears covers the middle but with less fashion than we want. Alexander's does not have complete assortment in middle price points."

On that score, management sought to shift the ratio of 60 percent low prices, 35 percent middle, and 5 percent high to 30 percent low prices, 60 percent middle, and 10 percent high. The game plan was to "keep the better quality merchandise in our present low end. Drop the poor quality low-end merchandise. Add significantly to the middle." Monitoring would be established in low, medium, and high price points by department. Goals for each bracket would be set up for all departments consistent with company objectives. To ensure that goals were being met, there would be quarterly monitoring of sales and inventory by units from IBM runs.

As to soft goods vendors, changes were necessary. The bulk of suppliers were mass merchandise or discount type vendors while only a small percentage were department store vendors "who have better quality, taste, and fashion levels." The plan: Over half of the goods should come from department store vendors. The balance was to come primarily from chain vendors and better discount vendors with somewhat less direct imports.

How fashion-aware was Korvettes? "Too slow in moving into fashion trends," management decided based on the research. "Too slow in moving out of declining trends." What should be done? "Identify fashion trends early. Test new fashions early. Explode winning fashion trends. Keep stocks liquid so that the company can react quickly to trends up and down. Bigger percentage of markdown dollars allocated to liquidation rather than promotion. Earlier action on clearance merchandise."

Since 30 percent of Korvettes' shoppers were convinced that the company offered poor quality, it was necessary to develop quality control standards and to use them to upgrade the goods purchased. Existing inspection procedures should be increased to 10 percent of all merchandise inspected at random at the warehouse. Every major vendor's factory should be inspected annually. There should also be a formal development of size standards by the quality control department. Any vendor not achieving 80 percent of the standards was to be reviewed by Korvettes' general merchandise manager and would be dropped unless he could supply an acceptable written plan for correction.

Attacking the problem that 16 percent of the customers believed that Korvettes had too much soiled, shopworn goods, management decided on a drastic step. It would allocate $2 million on top of the spring markdown budget to clear out shopworn merchandise. It was also decided to bring in smaller quantities of goods at the start of each season so as to leave ample room for reorders. A bigger share of markdowns was to be allocated to clear out problem merchandise. A reporting system should be established to age inventory. Efforts were to be made to increase turnover by 10 percent.

On hard goods, management wanted to "retain and increase dominance in records and small appliances and build dominance in photography and automotive departments." No significant change was deemed necessary to achieve this goal, other than broadening the assortments in the automotive and photography departments. But, refining what it already had, the chain was to identify classifications for expansion and broadening of assortments in both departments.

Value perception in hard goods was another matter. The most recent survey found that 25 percent of respondents had a favorable reaction to the value offered compared to other retailers. That left, of course, the major percentage-plus which thought otherwise. The top team ordered that daily prices should reflect a highly competitive stance through the maintenance of a monthly departmental competitive shopping report on twenty of the most identifiable items (SKU's). This would yield competitive prices in each geographic area. On advertised prices, a minimum of 10 percent of advertised items were to be highly identifiable and at prices below the normally advertised prices of competitors. At least 50 percent of total advertising was to be committed to constant repetition of name brands at "value prices." And a program was to be started to compare the value of Korvettes' private brands against national brands.

Responding to the need for better quality cited by shoppers, the company recognized that it was occasionally lowering its quality standards on individual items and decided on a two-pronged corrective approach. It was to "continue major emphasis on brand names and to develop value-oriented private-brand programs with 10 to 25 percent savings against the national brand." The latter would be achieved by developing specific standards of performance for non-name-brand merchandise. All private-label and import goods were to be submitted to a quality control department for approval prior to selling. A timetable was to be set up to eliminate existing products that didn't come up to standards.

Fashion, of course, was almost as important in hard goods as in soft. The Brous team admitted that the stores were "moving with the fashion trends in an uneven way on a department basis, some very good, others not good." To recoup, the plan called for "exploiting fashion trends in a timely manner." This was to involve identifying trends early and testing items early. An approach would be developed to capitalize quickly on "thrust" classifications by increasing space allocation, increasing advertising allocation, and increasing inventory allocation." The chain would move quickly out of declining classifications and would have an "aging" report on prior stock.

Overall, the business strategy called for a boost from an 0.6 percent sales decline in 1975 from the year before to a 5 percent gain in 1982 over the prior year or sales to rise from $557.2 million to $730 million. Profitwise, the projection was for a $5.4 million deficit in 1975 to a $29.8 million profit on an adjusted, pre-tax basis in 1982 or to $17.9 million on an adjusted, post-tax basis. And the pre-tax profit percentage on sales was slated to rise from zero to 4.1 percent.

It was an ambitious, yet realistic plan. One senses a dimension of urgency about it, which it certainly had, given the circumstances of the time. Considerable effort was put behind it and among many of Korvettes' 11,000 employees hope lingered, flickered, then sparked anew. Many of them had been with the company for ten, twenty, or even thirty years. Their livelihoods and lifetimes had been invested in it. Despite the grousing and fading motivations that always accompany abrupt changes in the fortunes and policies of an employer grappling with major problems, the bulk of Korvettes' employees were still proud of the famous, pioneering company and thus hopeful that the latest plan would take hold.

But an unexpected announcement in Paris, of all places, changed everything in mid-August of 1978.

All during 1977 and 1978, the tug-of-war had continued between the banks and Arlen. The $110.9 million loss in the latter year which ended February 28 was bad enough. But indications were that the red ink would flow even more heavily in 1979. The real-estate industry was beginning to pick up in 1978 yet it was obvious that it might take Arlen and its subsidiaries several years to catch up. Cohen huddled with Emanuel Klimpl, the chief Arlen attorney, with Robert Stewart, the company's president, and the others, only to conclude that there was just one thing left to do. The already dismembered company would have to be carved up some more so that more cash could be offered the banks to either delay commitments or to further restructure the entire loan agreement.

The inevitability of selling Korvettes is probably the only certain concession which emerges from interviews with a number of the principals involved. Discrepancies in their statements abound. According to Dave Brous, "The banks insisted that Arlen divest itself of Korvettes and get some money into the till. Shearson Loeb Rhoades was empowered to find a buyer." But Arthur Cohen states, "The reason we had to sell Korvettes is that the capital requirements to bring it successfully to the middle-market were more than we were prepared to put into it." A third, top source, who requested anonymity, reports, "Everyone decided that Korvettes had to be sold because it wasn't producing enough return for Arlen and interest rates to keep up financing were just too damn high."

Other sources gave yet different reasons. Korvettes itself was too undercapitalized to remain a thriving company. It had a $75 million net worth, $25 million of which was in real estate, so that effectively it was operating on a $50 million capital on sales of $600 million annually through the last two years. This was a net worth-to-sales percentage of only about 8 percent, compared with about 15 to 18 percent for most discounters and about 25 percent for department stores. It had only half the backing it needed, according to this theory. It was like a Broadway show that had to go on every night, matinees on Wednesdays and Sundays, with only a little cash in the box office and no indication of how large or small its audience would be. Another problem was that the original Spartans-Korvettes and Arlen merger was ill-conceived since it was dependent upon at least one, preferably both partners being profitable. If, in other words, Arlen hoped to avail itself of Korvettes' cash flow and/or profits, that could work only if the retailer produced enough cash flow or profits to make the arrangement sound. And if Korvettes' profits could be protected by the tax shelter advantages of being owned by a real-estate company, that could work only if Arlen's lenders would not insist that Arlen's live up to its loan agreements rather than be in default, which it was.

In any case, the inevitability of Arlen's selling Korvettes

appears to have existed almost from the very moment that the 1971 merger was formalized. But selling Korvettes wasn't an easy task. Its turnaround progress was slow. It would need a major infusion of funds. And its trade creditors remained concerned about its viability. But perhaps the greatest difficulty in selling Korvettes were the many interlocking obligations with Arlen's, the many intricate lease arrangements, so that a buyer would discover only a maze of complexity.

Despite the complexities, W. R. Grace & Company, the chemicals, natural resources, and consumer services company, almost bought Korvettes from Arlen. David L. Yunich, the former vice chairman of R. H. Macy & Company and later the executive director of the New York Metropolitan Transportation Authority, had been functioning as a merger-acquisition consultant for W. R. Grace and brought the two companies together. But Grace, which had an abortive merger deal with King's Department Stores, another large discounter, bowed out before a final deal with Arlen was put on paper.

In the meantime, Becker, Perry and Warburg, the investment-banking house which had formerly been called A. G. Becker & Company, had been seeking an American retailer for a French company. Societé Foncière et Financière Agache-Willot, commonly known as "The Agache-Willot Group" had already made feints at Gamble-Skogmo, Inc., the diversified retailer and finance company in Minneapolis, and at Goldblatt Brothers, the promotional department-store chain based in Chicago. It failed to find a friendly reaction in Minneapolis and withdrew its interest in the Chicago company after studying that company's timeworn stores and unfavorable profit record.

In the spring and summer of 1978, representatives of Agache-Willot met in New York and Paris with the managements of Arlen and Korvettes. The French company had enjoyed some success in buying and turning around lagging companies on the Continent. But a purchase offer was delayed. The canny French realized that Arlen was under severe pressure and thus hardly in a position to bargain from strength. While the transatlantic deal lagged, other buyers for Korvettes continued to be sought back in the United States.

And then in mid-August, a terse announcement came from Agache-Willot's Paris headquarters that it had made a $31 million offer to Arlen for 51 percent of Korvettes. The two companies had signed an agreement in principle.

The transaction, completed eight months later in April 1979, represented Korvettes' fourth and last merger.

PART FIVE

The French Years
(1979-1981)

15.
The New Marketing
Strategy: Surgery

A lain Mathieu sits at the airport of a desk, his thin face and frame dwarfed by the grandiosity of the furniture and the paneled office. But a smile of satisfaction softens his ascetic features. A French *directeur générale* of an American company? The smile settles to an expression of assurance, of belongingness. Why not? Why not indeed, when the company now has a French parent? More and more foreign nationals are heading prominent American corporations— Britons, Dutchmen, Germans, Australians. Is the world coming to the rescue of American commerce and industry? He shrugs, acknowledging that perhaps the statement is too strong but its tenor may be apt. American productivity surely needs a prod.

It is June 1979, only two months since the Agache-Willot Group has become the owner of Korvettes. Up till now incommunicado, the forty-one-year-old Mathieu, holder of a master's degree from l'Ecole Polytechnique in Paris and a doctorate in economics from the University of Paris, is granting his first press interview as the new chairman of Korvettes. He nods confidently to Nicholas Pahlinich, Korvettes' new president, who has been promoted to succeed David Brous. Brous left shortly after Agache appointed one of its own, Dr. Mathieu, to the chief executive's post at its new American subsidiary.

"Questions, please," Mathieu prompts the gaping reporter. The Frenchman, who seems an unlikely type to head Korvettes, appears more now to reflect his reputation as an expert in turning around newly acquired companies for Agache.

The questions come. The replies, in halting, muttered English, are smoothed over by Pahlinich. It is ironic perhaps that the thirty-nine-year-old Pahlinich has replaced Brous. A Notre Dame graduate and a former Macy's executive who joined Korvettes in 1965 to rise to senior vice president for the metropolitan New York division, he was brought into the company by Brous and was a sort of protégé.

The dialogue proceeds, Mathieu increasingly assisted by Pahlinich . . . *What do the new owners intend to do with Korvettes?* "Our main objective is to improve the profits . . . By being better retailers, cleaning up our inventories, becoming more competitive, motivating our people better, and increasing store productivity." *How were your results in the first quarter ended May 26?* "Last year in that quarter, we had a net loss of $1.2 million. This year, the quarter's loss was $6 million. The big problem was that the $129 million loss by Arlen Realty in its recent fiscal year hurt our standing in the credit community and with suppliers so that from January through April we didn't get enough fresh merchandise, especially in soft lines. But after we bought Korvettes, our business improved because we got new shipments. May sales were 3.2 percent higher than in 1978, while April had been 6 percent below last year. Sales in the quarter were 2.8 percent under last year." *You mentioned being more competitive. Does that mean that Korvettes will have the lowest prices in town?* "Over the last year or two, we have experienced a slackening in our traditional value image. Now, we want to make sure that on basic, highly identifiable merchandise we are realistically priced with our competition. You can't be lower priced than your competition on everything. But our objective will be that on a typical market basket of one hundred items that you buy at Korvettes, you will pay less than for the same merchandise elsewhere . . ."

Mathieu's voice trails off. Is he giving away too much? He raises an eyebrow at Pahlinich, who shrugs. The Frenchman continues somewhat more hesitantly. One of the surprising things he says in the interview is that he plans to motivate 100 executives on profit performance as part of a plan which, if successful, will be extended to more executives. And Agache-Willot has guaranteed $8 million in revolving credit that will enable Korvettes to remain current on payments to vendors. But it probably won't be needed, he adds. Korvettes has obtained a delay in its amortization payments for more than eighteen months from the banks. In addition, the owners hope to increase the chain's 3.1 annual inventory rate to 4 in the next fiscal year by reducing inventories and accompanying promotion, by cutting imports, and by taking more timely markdowns.

The interview ends with a question on whether the problems of turning around a retail business are more difficult than in any other type of business. What does Mathieu reply? "Not at all. The store business is a business like any business. We don't need geniuses in our business. We need people who can execute things well."

Gratitude is expressed for the interview. Mathieu nods in his taciturn way. As the reporter leaves, he pauses for a moment to stare around the large, handsomely appointed office. There are ghosts here. Mathieu stares at him quizzically. Then the moment is over and so is the meeting.

In some respects, the growth, success, and controversy surrounding the Agache-Willot Group reflect much that characterizes a number of American conglomerates. Humble beginnings, the advent of a second generation to management, the hiring of tough financially oriented professionals to assist in the identification and aggrandizing of acquisitions are marks of both the French concern and the American companies. Loews Corporation, Norton Simon Inc., Gulf & Western Industries, Rapid American Corporation, International Telephone and Telegraph Corporation, and at least half a dozen American corporate giants owe their stunning accumulation of assets to some or all of those factors. One of the differences between Agache-Willot and some of the U.S. companies is that the French firm appears to have operated under the family management of the four Willot *frères* while those here largely were prodded by hyperactive individuals whose empire-building and financial drives led to immense corporate growth.

Another difference was the relative lack of governmental scrutiny of financial dealings in Europe contrasted with the opposite in the U.S. where increasingly stringent regulations by the Securities and Exchange Commission kept the American conglomerate makers constantly glancing over their shoulders—while they continued to snap up other companies. Not that that difference really affected the U.S. corporations more than the French one. The French equivalent of the S.E.C. eventually caught up with what it regarded as violations of securities laws and charged Agache-Willot with them. Here, the S.E.C. charged a number of large American firms with disclosure violations and imposed fines and, in the case of monopolistic acquisitions, enforced divestiture actions. But most of it amounted to little more than a slap on the wrist (although it's probably safe to say that the eagle eye in Washington kept the Americans from making even more daring forays than they would have otherwise).

Agache-Willot began its existence in 1907 as "M. et J. Willot & Cie," a family-owned business producing sanitary and hygiene products. But it was only since 1954, when the four Willot brothers—Bernard, Jean-Pierre, Antoine, and Régis—were managing the company, that its rapid expansion began through internal growth and acquisitions. Between 1959 and 1967, several small acquisitions were made in the French textile industry. The big move came in 1967 when the company merged with Etablissements Agache, a major public textile company, to become Agache-Willot. And in 1968, aiming to diversify, the textile assets were collected in a new subsidiary, Consortium Général Textile. A parent holding company was formed, to be known as "Société Foncière et Financière Agache-Willot," and a string of new, more important acquisitions followed.

In 1969, Agache-Willot acquired the Belle Jardinière chain of apparel department stores in Paris, Marseilles, and other French cities, a company that was also a garment manufacturer. The same year, the Saint Frères textile products company was bought. In 1970, Agache acquired the Au Bon Marché department stores in Paris and Caen; in 1976, the Conforama home furnishings chain of company-owned and franchised stores; and in 1978 the Galeries Anspach, a large Belgian department store group. Also in 1978, Agache

bought the Boussac complex of textile and apparel manufacturing businesses, which owned the still important cou-
turier name of "Dior."

When the Willot *frères* successfully bid for the Boussac
empire in France and began seriously eying Korvettes in the
U.S., they already had one of the largest family fortunes in
France, were a formidable industrial and commercial force,
and had had several brushes with the country's securities
authorities. The initial family business was founded by their
grandfather. Their father died relatively young so that the
brothers went quickly into the firm and put their own acquisitive stamp on it. Even in the 1960's when they had
purchased only a few companies, the Willots adopted a
policy of returning them to profitability or wringing more
return from them by paring expenses and discharging those
they felt were extraneous executives and workers. The
rather rough handling of people, unusual in European corporate management where a paternalistic style is the norm,
as well as their empire building, free-wheeling ways made
them controversial among their peers.

But the Willots behaved as though they couldn't have
cared less. At the time they bought Korvettes, a year when
their corporate sales were nearing the $3 billion mark, they
were stolid, tough-looking men with hard, granite-like
faces. As Paul Lewis, a correspondent of *The New York Times*
in France, put it, "They look alike, reportedly think alike,
attend Sunday mass together, and share a single office in the
northern French industrial town of Lille, where they were
born and raised." Their patience until Arlen Realty, increasingly battered by losses and an inability to share in the
real-estate industry turnaround, would meet their low bid
for Korvettes was typical of how they had acquired companies. It should have come as no surprise when the Willots
appointed Alain Mathieu as head of the new American sub-

sidiary, although few Americans knew of him. Mathieu joined Agache-Willot in 1972 as financial officer of Au Bon Marché and a year later was named its president. Before his American appointment, Mathieu had already served as Conforama's president. In both cases, as Agache-Willot noted in its announcement of his U.S. appointment, he was credited with turning around the European chains.

The April 1979 announcement of his and Pahlinich's appointments also included that of Philip Kaplan as executive vice president for finance and administration of Korvettes. Kaplan had been a senior vice president since 1971.

The Agache-Willot purchase of Korvettes and the quick appointment of Mathieu hit the Korvettes' top staff with a combined sense of shock and foreboding. There was a scramble to find out as much about the French as could be obtained. The Retail Clerks International Union, whose locals represented the Korvettes' workers, assembled a collection of press clippings on Agache-Willot. The reports of their stern handling of people and the sharp cutting of expenses were hardly promising. It would probably be simplistic to say that everyone waited for the axe to fall; some senior executives were still hopeful that the new owners might take steps to straighten out Korvettes and retain those people who had been productive and creative.

But the axe did fall, and it fell swiftly.

Two months after his appointment, Mathieu terminated four senior executives. Brous had already ended his fourteen-year association with the company when Mathieu was placed over him. Now, Philip Kaplan, who had been promoted to the number-three spot only two months earlier, was let go, along with Bob Warner, senior vice president and general merchandise manager for soft lines; Arthur Shapiro, vice president for warehouse and transportation; and Bill Willensky, real-estate vice president. Willensky had been the last of Eugene Ferkauf's "boys" to remain with the company. With his departure, all ties with the original Korvettes finally had been cut.

Korvettes, of course, did not announce the discharges. But a company spokesman, John Cook, an account executive of Harshe, Rotman and Druck, which represented the company as public-relations consultant, confirmed the reports of the terminations and said that a staff reduction of middle managers also had been under way for several weeks. He said that Korvettes would replace all four and that Mathieu would assume Kaplan's duties as chief financial officer. New systems and procedures were being implemented and "it will be easier" in Mathieu's view if he "brought in his own people." But it was common knowledge inside and outside the company that the top and middle rank cutbacks were part of an expense-reduction program that would begin slowly and grow in intensity.

Four months after his appointment, Mathieu, who was getting used to or perhaps liking press meetings, called a press conference and announced that 1,200 employees had been cut from Korvettes' staff of 9,300. Four hundred had been reduced from the headquarters' organization—including the receptionist—and about 800 from the stores. All these changes had been under way since March, a month before he arrived, so that presumably he wasn't responsible for all them. "We have tried," he stressed, "to make sure that we cut the fat, not the muscle."

He and Pahlinich said that the dismissals had cut general and administrative overhead by $5 million and correspondingly had boosted store payroll productivity by $5 million. Methodically, as if the result followed naturally from all that had happened, Mathieu ticked off other expense reductions. Annual advertising outlays had been reduced to $23 million from $28 million; other expense-cutting measures and increased real-estate subrentals totaled $4 million.

The stores? Although only about half of the Korvettes' units were profitable, Mathieu said that no consideration was being given to closing any at the time. However, all fifty stores would be reviewed after the 1979 Christmas season. But he said that twenty of the thirty Korvettes stores in the New York metropolitan area were profitable.

Yet the chain's overall performance was worrisome, he said. In the first half ended August 25, the loss had risen to $12.9 million from $2.2 million in the same 1978 period. The second quarter also suffered a higher loss of $5.8 million against a loss of only $840,000. Sales in the first half had dropped 6.7 percent to $233.4 million while volume in the second quarter was down 10 percent.

But while sales were worse and the losses deepening, he said that the parent company would make an additional financial commitment to Korvettes, including a guarantee of $25 million to 360 suppliers and a $10 million advance to the chain "to increase the vendors' confidence level." The new funds would bring the French commitment to the chain to $61.5 million, Mathieu said.

That was September 25, 1979. On January 8, 1980, Agache-Willot said that another 300 Korvettes' employees had been dismissed, bringing the total terminations since the April takeover to 1,500. On January 30, Korvettes announced that it planned to sublease more than 13 percent of its store space to other retailers in an effort to improve profits. John W. Magee, real-estate vice president, said that some 2 million of the company's 9 million square feet were extraneous. Isn't the paring of that much space tantamount to closing five or six major stores? He didn't think so. "The size of many of our stores has not been in proportion to our volume," he said.

And on February 4, it came, the long-awaited bombshell. Mathieu announced the immediate closing of the fourteen most unprofitable of Korvettes' stores. It was the most drastic step Agache-Willot had yet taken, eliminating another 1,300 employees and shuttering two stores on Long Island, one just outside Albany, N.Y., and eleven in four Eastern states besides New York. The action summarily lopped off $100 million in sales but also eliminated about $8 million in losses. That would leave Korvettes with 36 stores, 10 in New York City or 26 in the metropolitan area, and 10 stores in other cities and suburbs. In making the announcement, Mathieu said that the closings and a pending arrangement for additional financing were "integral parts of our new marketing strategy and will enable Korvettes to generate more profit from fewer stores." To which Pahlinich added, "The new marketing plan would emphasize Korvettes as a promotional department store reflecting good value, broad assortment, fashion, and consistent quality." The company, which has determined that its customers have incomes between $15,000 and $30,000 a year, will continue to position itself between department and discount stores, he said.

The closing of 28 percent of all of Korvettes' stores shocked many who worked in the company, suppliers and others, who by now considered the chain a landmark in retailing. Some, however, waxed philosophical about it. If Korvettes was ever again to return to a profitable footing after its $25 million loss in fiscal 1979, its unprofitable stores would have to go. Agache-Willot had turned around losing businesses before. Perhaps the French could do it again, this school of thought reasoned.

But two days after the announcements of the closings, an unpleasant release from Paris raised new doubts about Agache-Willot.

The Paris stock exchange's operations control commission accused the management of Boussac Saint Frères textile

group, the Agache-Willot subsidiary, of misleading shareholders by turning a loss into a profit in the latest financial
report. The commission, which for years had been criticiz-
ing the Willot brothers' accounting practices, charged that
the Boussac Saint Frères group told shareholders in December that it had turned a profit equal to $2.8 million in the
eighteen months ended June 30, 1979 when it had actually
had a loss of $4.3 million. By using accounting methods
"open to criticism," the commission said that the management integrated into earnings special tax-free provisions of
$4.2 million rather than the $930,000 that the shareholders
had been told they were. The textiles group also marked up
as earnings special funds transfers from other subsidiaries of
the Agache-Willot empire. Such transfers should have been
accounted for as special profit in the 1978-1979 balance
sheet, according to the commission.

The commission's authorities said that they would continue their probe into the Willot *frères'* practice of conclud-
ing unwritten subcontracting agreements between the
parent firm and its subsidiaries that allowed it to submit
earnings reports in an "arbitrary fashion." And the commission demanded that the Willots immediately discontinue
those methods.

Those who were dismayed by these charges on top of the
store closings soon had more reason to be nervous. Within
the next few weeks, rumors swept the New York market that
further corrective or austerity moves were under way at
Korvettes. It is interesting, if not of educational value, that
every one of those rumors denied by Mathieu-Pahlinich
through spokesperson John Cook eventually turned out to
be true. They were: (1) a new shuffle was impending in top
management; (2) Alain Mathieu might soon go; (3) A man
named Joseph Ris might be his replacement; (4) additional
out-of-town stores would be closed; (5) Korvettes' Fifth Ave-

nue store would be sold and turned into a building for diamond merchants.

Those "rumors" were denied on March 11, 1980. Underlying all of them were persistent indications that in the year since the French had taken over Korvettes and applied the cut-expenses, cut-the-staff, cut-the-number-of-stores strategy that had been successful in Europe, the American company's business remained in the doldrums. The niche between department stores and discount stores that Korvettes hoped to fill continued to elude it. The suspicion was beginning to grow that Agache-Willot, for all its interest in the American market, didn't really understand it.

In April, *Chain Store Age Executive* Magazine reported in an article written by Lynne Bershad, "One of Agache's first moves has been to drop the expensive promotional effort. Now 'The Other Korvettes' is another Korvettes, namely, a low-price, high-volume retailer, selling goods for 20 percent less than department stores. Korvettes' newest incarnation is positioned between discount and department stores, with its target audience earning between $15,000-$30,000. About 25 percent of its most expensive price points have been shaved off and added to the bottom.

"'We felt that our customer did not fully accept the movement of our assortment of price points into traditional department store price lines,' explains Pahlinich. Furthermore, he added, while 'The Other Korvettes' strategy was showing some positive signs, the increases simply weren't enough to justify its high costs.'"

That promotional program, according to the trade magazine, was to cost some $50 million spread over the five years from 1977 through 1982. Clipped off two years early, it more likely cost Korvettes more than $30 million. But added to that was another $20 million for a massive, refurbishing program intended to support "The Other Korvettes" promotion and to make the stores look much more fashion-oriented than they had been. Agache-Willot cut that program off, too, but much of its expenditures had already been made. Together, this meant writing off and largely pouring down the drain about $50 million that had been put into the grading up effort over three years when the new owners cut spending to a bare minimum.

What was happening inside Korvettes?

To the executives, both the newer and the older ones, Alain Mathieu was an enigma. Other than Pahlinich and Phil Kaplan in the beginning, he ignored practically all the others. It was obvious to them all that he was taking orders from Paris but they had difficulty understanding why he didn't confer with the men who had had the experience of running major elements of the business. He was smart, all right, they decided, but it was figures and book smart. He'd study the daily sales figures, extrapolate them and hypothetical goals on a calculator, and arrive at conclusions without testing them on many of the executives involved.

While he rarely asked anyone for an opinion, he would call in an individual or a group and issue edicts, such as "We must discharge another 1,000 tomorrow." There was a language problem, too. His English was correct but obtuse and it was delivered in a sort of throaty murmur that made understanding him even more difficult.

His demands were often peremptory and hard to meet to the letter. Several top executives recall that he summoned them to his office on a Thursday in February, 1980, and told them that he wanted the Philadelphia, Baltimore, and other outlying stores closed the next day. The resulting scramble made for some painful recollections.

There was a basic problem of misunderstanding, some of the department heads concluded. It was the matter of a different entrepreneurial environment in the U.S. compared to France. Here, entry into retailing is usually based on cooperation between the owner of the business, the banks, and the suppliers. Each is an important cog in the wheel, each providing some grease to keep the wheel rolling. The wheel moves, of course, only if there is economic and market viability in the new business. In France, they learned, a retailer needs a license to open a new business. If there are too many retailers in a locality, the license is not forthcoming. But once he obtains the license, the retailer has obtained a fiat which he exercises with a relative sense of noblesse oblige. His manner toward bankers and suppliers is condescending and even dictatorial. Such behavior in the freer American society would prove counterproductive and self-defeating. Cajoling, a quid pro quo understanding, and a dimension of equality usually underlie most American business relationships.

"Mathieu mostly alienated the creditors and banks by insisting 'We are Agache-Willot and this is what we want,'" said a senior Korvettes executive. "He told them repeatedly that he had two or three times successfully carried out the turnaround formula that Jean-Pierre Willot, Sr., had developed. He said that he was J-P's chief administrator in the U.S. and that he was to be accommodated. Who could like that or go for it?"

But Mathieu seemed to recede, to fade into the furniture when his superiors from France descended on Korvettes' home office. The major figure was Jean-Pierre Willot, Sr., at fifty-four years old the second-oldest of the four brothers and reportedly the most dynamic. His son, Jean-Pierre Willot, Jr., had been dispatched months earlier, shortly after the purchase of Korvettes took place, to occupy an office in the American subsidiary. The wispy, twenty-six-year-old J-P Jr. spoke decent English and busied himself in studying and talking to the Korvettes' executive staff. When his father was in New York, the son acted as his interpreter. But, otherwise, according to some of the Korvettes' executives, his principal role appeared to be that of an amiable pipeline to France.

On May 4, Willot *père* made a regular visit to the New York office and granted an interview to this writer. The short, pink-faced Frenchman spoke not a word of English but sitting alongside him on a sofa J-P Jr. assisted as translator. Also present at the meeting, held in Mathieu's office, were Mathieu; a tall, strapping, genial man, Joseph Ris, who was identified as an aide to J-P Sr. in Paris; and John Cook, the public-relations man.

There had been reports from Paris that J-P Sr., general manager of Agache-Willot and a member of the management board, had come under pressure from his brothers over the Korvettes' acquisition but he appeared calm and assured during the discussion. His remarks during the one-hour interview ranged widely and were for the most part very candid:

"Our business in Agache-Willot is very profitable . . . What is our attitude about Korvettes after we have owned it a year? We bought it because it is in New York and it is the capital of the world. We knew very well that the company has problems and these couldn't be corrected in a year. But we are not disappointed. Its biggest problem—at first glance, one must stop the cost it is incurring, there must be some necessary in-house cleaning. I see increased sales later. But I am not pleased with Korvettes' sales or its continuing losses. It is still losing money but less. There is a $1 million loss less each month and $2 million a month less operating expenses.

"I believe that the company can be made profitable. In Europe, we had a lot of unprofitable companies and made them profitable . . . We are working with our bankers to reach an understanding with them . . . We feel we have made a substantial productivity improvement in Korvettes —there is 2.5 times better productivity in the home office and 2.4 times increase in the warehouse. In the stores, there is a 30 percent improvement in sales by man-hour. There may be some other cost reductions.

"As of now, my first priority is to turn around Korvettes. But due to my interest in this country, as well as the industrial progress of Agache-Willot, nothing is excluded here from our interest. I am impressed by U.S. management efforts. We are right now in retailing and interested in it but how much funds we would use to buy another company depends on the situation. In this country, there is the freedom to act and to move. If one would compare the freedom to act in business between the 'Old Europe' and the 'Young America,' this offers a challenge and a stimulation.

"Why do we have troubles with the French securities laws? In the U.S., you know all the laws because they are on the books. In France, there is no set of laws for holding companies and what there is there and in Europe generally is not as yet well defined. The stock exchange commission has asked some questions about Agache-Willot and we have replied . . .

"One of the problems in operating a business in the U.S. is the high prime rate. One can be preoccupied and concerned by it. In France, there exists price controls and credit controls for many years but fortunately the prime rate is not so high as 20 percent, it is more like 12 percent . . .

"Yes, in the 60's and 70's, Korvettes enjoyed a great expansion to fifty-eight stores but at the same time the company has been losing a lot of money . . . I still believe that this is a good company and can be turned around and I have a complete faith in its future. It should take three years to do it. The first year to clean it up. The second year to relaunch the sales activity and the third year to make it profitable. This is our experience in Europe. Sometimes, profits come in the second year . . ."

J-P Jr.'s efforts to translate left something to be desired and the slack was picked up by Joseph Ris who sat at the opposite end of the room. Mathieu remained silent during the entire interview. J-P Sr. appeared to defer to Ris not only in the effort to translate his remarks into English but to suggestions in French made by Ris. As an aide, Ris appeared self-assured and that recalled rumors the press had picked up that he might succeed Mathieu. But Mathieu was very much in evidence, however silently.

Known around Korvettes and Arlen as "The Old Man," J-P Sr. left a trail of concern and even fear. When one of the senior Arlen executives asked the Frenchman how he planned to improve matters at Korvettes, he recalled that J-P Sr. simply drew a finger across his throat. "I used to stare at 'The Old Man' with horror and fascination," said a senior Korvettes executive. "He would sit in front of our executive committee and rant and rave at the top of his voice even though we couldn't understand a word of his French. And the kid would look around at the rest of us with a sheepish smile and translate, "My fahzair, he saiz 'too much expenses,' he saiz 'too much people . . .' "

The young man would irritate some of the Korvettes executives. When they would complain to Mathieu or J-P Sr. on one of his regular visits, they would get little satisfaction. After a visit home, J-P Jr. returned to New York with the message that he delivered to a number of the American executives: "My fahzair, he saiz I am young. He saiz I have much to learn. And Mathieu is the boss."

Shirley Young, of Grey Advertising, said that shortly after the French took over she met Mathieu and J-P Jr. in

Arthur Cohen's house on Long Island. The new Korvettes' chairman said that he was concerned with the chain's basic structure and expenses combined with the lack of financial controls. He told her, "We need more basic merchandise, better stocking, and to sell more basics." She replied, "You might sell more basics but you must have enough of the more interesting stuff or your customers won't buy the basics."

He shrugged. "Yes, we need to have some of that," Mathieu said. "But we must make the operation more productive. It is too sick."

The result of the conversation was that soon after the budget for "The Other Korvettes" was drastically reduced. But by that time, it didn't matter. Brous, Warner, and Kaplan, who had been its greatest supporters, were already gone and it languished for a few more months before it was dropped entirely.

In Mrs. Young's view, "The French thought that they could strip down everything and do well but you can't run a retail business with financial controls without having a merchandising concept, too. Now, more than a year later, we feel that continuing 'The Other Korvettes' would have made a big difference."

Could it have saved Korvettes or was Mathieu right that better productivity and controls were the answer?

A retailing marketing expert who has worked for years with some of the nation's largest chains, she responded, "He was not right. The program was a strategy, not just a campaign. It could have saved Korvettes if executed well. It needed further improvements and refining. How long would that have taken? Time and money are two interrelated dimensions. If there is more money available, less time is needed. If less money, more time is needed. The hardest thing in retailing is to find a strategy which has viability and can be converted to sales. We had demonstrated that 'The Other

Korvettes' was just that. Arlen was for it but just didn't have the money. But I was glad we had the experience, even though the fees we received were modest. We had a good client and had the satisfaction of seeing something good happen but ultimately we were disappointed by its discontinuance. The French thought that the customers just want cheap goods and they thought they knew that without asking the customers. Well, besides the fact that the customer is always right, the customer knows what she wants so that the thing to do is to ask her. That's what we did. The trick in retailing and I believe in any business is to go right to the source, find out what's needed, use imagination and creativity to stimulate people, and then get feedback from the customers. The French didn't do that."

To some of the company's executives who had already weathered several regimes, Mathieu's advent on the scene represented the worst episode in the company's fading saga. "It was understandable that he should cut some people considering Korvettes' problems," said David Rothfeld, the records-tapes-audio expert. "But he lost sight of the fact that you had to buy and sell goods in order to do any business. And then he raised the markup while cutting the help. You have to maintain your reputation in a competitive climate.

"And yet, a month before his tenure ended, he said, 'Let's go back to being a discounter.' It was as if you turn on the faucet and suddenly the dollars flow out. The professional retailer knows it doesn't work that way," Rothfeld said.

An Arlen's top executive who worked closely with Korvettes and for a while with the Agache-Willot regime commented, "When they brought in Mathieu, the new owners had little recognition of U.S. business characteristics. He was very austere and difficult. He angered the vendors, fired the buyers or most of them, and cut advertising. One of his biggest problems was his difficulty with the language.

Nuances in language and in business mean a great deal. Berlitz English isn't good enough to run a company with 10,000 employees."

The French made "a horrible mistake," in the view of another Arlen man. "They didn't understand that profits begin at the top, not at the bottom—by selling merchandise in other words. You've got to have something that people want, otherwise they go up the street. But one of the worst things that they did was to fire Phil Kaplan, whom the banks trusted. So there was a crunch against them in the credit market."

Lewis L. Salton, chairman and founder of Salton Inc., Bronx, N.Y., famous for its "Salton Hot-Tray," had long been a housewares supplier to Korvettes. Summing up that thirty-year relationship, he declared, "In my opinion, Korvettes had it all to itself until there simply got to be too many mass merchandisers which robbed it of its uniqueness. And when it had to cope with at that competition, Korvettes' management made a fatal move to take the Bloomingdale's route of a class department store. That required solving new problems of sales promotion, advertising, and merchandising.

"Even the Fifth Avenue store was a move in that route," he said, "but it didn't work out, any more than Alexander's going to Lexington Avenue made any real inroads into Bloomingdale's. The plain fact is that a mass merchandiser, a discounter, shouldn't try to create an image above and beyond its capacity to back up. And then, of course, when it was sold to the French company with its absentee management, it was the worst thing of all. For us at Salton, it was the end of a rewarding and a long and pleasant relationship."

On May 21, 1980, Alain Mathieu resigned as Korvettes' chairman under pressure from the company's board. Jean-Pierre Willot, Sr., who also had the additional title of president of Agache-Willot's executive board, attended the Korvettes' board meeting as a director. A spokesman for the company said that Mathieu left "because the board made a preliminary appraisal of the results of the past fiscal year and was disappointed by the performance." But it's safe to say that J-P Sr. took the lead in asking for Mathieu's departure. However, based on information obtained later, Mathieu had offered to resign months earlier but his superiors had refused to accept his resignation.

The new chairman of Korvettes, as expected, was Joseph A. Ris. The third chief executive of the company in only thirteen months, Ris was born in France and had been an American citizen since the early 1960's. He had been a vice president of Chrysler Motors International in Paris and had more recently been associated with Agache-Willot as a consultant for several years. In a prepared statement, the forty-three-year-old Ris promised that the chain "will respond to today's economic realities and attract a greater share of the price-conscious customer market by rededicating the company to its origins as a full-line discount retailer."

The board took a further step. It elevated Jean-Pierre Willot, Jr., to the new post of vice chairman. The younger Willot, who had been assistant to Mathieu, would now report to Ris. If there were groans among some of the Korvettes' executives, it presumably did not reach into the board room.

At the end of May, reports surfaced that Korvettes was planning to terminate the jobs of another 2,000 employees. Ris, bluff, hearty, and quickly liked by the staff people more than Mathieu, apparently was concerned in those early weeks of his tenure how much freedom he had under J-P Sr. He denied the discharge rumors even though it was known that the layoffs were already under way. But Ris said he and his top associates were preparing to meet with the bankers to present a plan for marketing and operational changes. The prime rate in mid-1980 was 14 percent. Agache-Willot not only wanted new short-term funds from the American banks but also a restructuring of long-term financing at interest rates under the current prime. It was for that purpose that Edwin Markowitz, Korvettes' vice president and treasurer, agreed to delay his planned resignation.

Under pressure, reacting to an entirely new team (Pahlinich left soon after Mathieu) and running up against uncertain supplier shipments, Korvettes was in dire straits. A week rarely passed without another new development, some negative, some promising. On June 18, the company confirmed the reports that it would lay off 2,000 employees, about one-third of its total staff, over the next two or three months. On June 26, the chain announced that it had negotiated the restructuring of about $55 million in debt and a new arrangement allowing the company to continue the use of its credit card. The debt restructuring would satisfy obligations to two insurance companies and three banks. The latter would have the right to share in certain of Korvettes' income and profits through 1987.

And on July 9, there was a dramatic and perhaps symbolic development. Eager to raise cash to stave off growing trade debt, the company agreed to sell the lease on its Fifth Avenue store to Sterling Equities Inc., Manhasset, Long Island, which planned to reconstruct the building into a diamond dealer's showroom and office building. The sale would give Korvettes $18 million. But the move left many with mixed feelings. The 180,000 square foot store, opened in 1962, had represented Korvettes' coming of age, its entry into the golden tier of retailing on Fifth Avenue.

By giving up a lease on which there was another twenty years to run, the new Korvettes' management was patently admitting that the sands of time were running out unless it could scale the company down to a small core. Yielding its most important store property from a prestige standpoint was a watershed move. Not only did it involve sacrificing some $29 million in annual sales and a profitable business but it signified that the French might be close to the edge of folding the entire business unless things improved.

By then, however, with fifty-eight stores reduced to thirty-five, with some 7,000 employees already discharged, with sales reduced from a peak $850 million to about $330 million, few people except possibly for those nostalgically inclined seemed to shed any tears over Korvettes' latest, desperate move.

Ris, the new chairman, though, seemed to consider it not a negative but a constructive step. He was deeply involved in continuing negotiations with lenders, holding a series of meetings with trade creditors and attempting to sell additional store leases and properties. He was under strict orders to cut expenses, reduce the number of stores, and negotiate viable deals with creditors. Frequently admitting to the unpleasant nature of his assignment, Ris nonetheless earned plaudits for his good-natured ways and harsh criticisms from those adversely affected by his decisions.

A week later came even more dramatic revelations, jarring those already rocked by the previous actions. Ris announced that Korvettes would close half of its remaining stores, leaving only eighteen stores in a strictly metropolitan New York area group, by August 1. He also said that as part of the survival plan 25 percent of the chain's earnings through 1987 would be turned over to three banks and an insurance company. This was a refinement of an earlier agreement. By accepting the share in the profits, the financial lenders would "forgive" about 55 percent of the chain's $57.2 million in outstanding debt. The four creditors would also waive interest on the retail chain's debt through the end of 1981.

In what appeared to be a state of combined exhaustion and exhilaration, Ris said the store reduction program called for the closing of all the remaining fourteen out-of-town stores, including five in Detroit, four in the Maryland-Virginia suburbs, four in the New York area, and the Wayne, N.J., store. He termed the lending arrangement "very unusual but satisfying because it indicates that the banks believe we can return to a profitable path." The lenders involved were the Chase Manhattan Bank, Manufacturers Hanover Trust Company, the Bankers Trust Company, and the Prudential Insurance Company.

He said that Korvettes would pay the banks and the insurance company $11.4 million in cash 30 days after the settlement agreement was ratified, $3.7 million by December 31, 1981 and $8.6 million with interest by January 31, 1985. Korvettes also arranged to maintain its own credit card by making certain payments on debt to the Citicorp Financial Company, a Citibank subsidiary.

Leaning back wearily at the same huge desk that had held his predecessors, Ris said that he regretted the additional employee dismissals that would result from the store closings. "But," he added with a sigh, "we cannot keep any store that doesn't contribute to the company's profitability."

On August 6, irked by the plan to turn over potential profits in Korvettes to the lenders, Agache-Willot announced that it had repudiated the arrangement with them which had been made to relieve the retail chain's heavy burden of debt.

After less than three months, Ris resigned.

16.
The Final Irony

All during that weekend of August 8, 9, and 10 of 1980, Joseph Ris sat around his Riverdale, New York, house and swimming pool, brooding and recapitulating. The mid-summer heat was oppressive yet he felt a sense of relief. Eleven weeks of difficult negotiations, of hard-sell, of sitting on a turbulent volcano were behind him. But he also felt disappointed and frustrated.

The uneasy state of his mind also contained some stabs of self-annoyance.

True, he felt violated by the unexpected disapproval of the financing arrangements by the "shareholder," as he called Agache-Willot, after its board, as well as Korvettes, had agreed to the principle of the lenders' sharing in the profits. But there was a sullen core of self-disappointment in his unsuspecting blindness to the mercurial nature of the Willot *frères*, particularly of Jean-Pierre, Sr. He had seen it at work before. And he had always prided himself in sensing the unexpected directions that it might take or at least in permitting himself enough cushion so that he wasn't crushed by the sudden reversal or new tangents.

Perhaps the most difficult thing to swallow was that J-P Sr. didn't explain his abrupt changes of heart. He didn't furnish a reason for his repudiation of the bank deal. In the three years in which he had served as consultant for Agache-Willot, Ris had concluded that J-P Sr.'s introversion and inability to articulate why he did certain things stemmed in part from his difficulties with his three brothers. He was the only one who put his full time into the top management. Not long ago, Régis Willot had written to Ris instructing him that he no longer wanted to be kept informed about Korvettes' activities. Antoine Willot, head of Boussac-Saint Frères, similarly wrote to Ris advising him that he declined henceforth to see any more documents about Korvettes. And Bernard had requested to leave the Agache-Willot board. So perhaps, Ris reasoned, J-P Sr. simply made the decisions, reversed them, and promulgated new ones because the others weren't willing to exercise any corporate authority.

So Ris lounged through the weekend, relieved, annoyed, disappointed but in general relaxed. He received occasional phone calls from former colleagues at Korvettes and he was kept apprised of what was happening. His wife, an American, largely left him alone, as did his two teen-age children, accurately sensing that he wanted to think and to let his built-up tension dissipate.

On Monday, August 11, his strange, mixed mood continued. So did the heat. He sat around the pool again. At noon, he found himself alone, the rest of his family out on errands. Caught in his train of retrospection, he vaguely heard the telephone ringing in the house but ignored it. The events of the last few weeks retraced themselves in his head . . .

It was early in August, not quite a month after the lenders and he and his team had reached agreement on the refinancing terms, and he studied the final documents at his desk. He told his secretary, Gloria Rosen, to place a call to J-P Sr. in Lille. J-P Sr. wasn't in but he left a message for him requesting that Agache-Willot dispatch Jacques Borel, its outside counsel, to come to New York to study the documents from a French standpoint so that there might not be a hitch later. Borel flew in on Wednesday, August 6, on the Concorde on the morning of the day that Ris and his staff were to meet and seal the final documents with the lenders in attendance. Borel, a matter-of-fact, hardened corporation attorney, came to the point immediately.

"There is no point in looking over the papers," he told Ris. "Jean-Pierre, Sr., has decided that he does not want to enter into this arrangement."

Ris paled. "You must be joking . . ."

"No, I am altogether serious."

"But why?"

"I do not know. He simply doesn't want to go ahead."

"You don't know what this means," Ris said, angrily. "What we will be faced with if we do not go through with this arrangement."

Borel shrugged. Feverishly, Ris turned to the telephone and after a short period managed to get through to J-P Sr. They spoke for more than two hours but the board president was adamant. What Ris understood from it was that Willot did not want to share any of the profits with the American lenders.

That afternoon, with Borel in tow along with several of

his staff, Ris entered the meeting room of Manufacturers Hanover Trust Company in the Empire State Building. Somberly, he stared at the assemblage of smiling, expectant faces. Besides the "Manny-Hanny" representative, there were others from the Chase Manhattan Bank, the Bankers Trust Company, Citibank, Prudential Insurance Company, Massachusetts Mutual Insurance Company, and other lenders. "Gentlemen," Ris told them in a hoarse voice, "Jean-Pierre Willot, Sr., has decided that he does not wish to join in a profit-sharing arrangement. He prefers an all-cash settlement. I'm sorry. As for myself, I resign immediately."

The dismay on the faces in the room quickly shifted to anger and impatience. "When is J-P Sr. planning to come here?" one of the bankers asked. "We're not going to wait and let him do everything that he wants." "Absolutely not," said another. "We want another meeting." "Monday! No later!" said a third man. There was a murmur of resentful assent. "Monday!" several repeated.

Ris got up to leave. "Wait!" someone said. "If you're quitting, who is in charge of Korvettes?" The bankers stared around at the Korvettes' contingent. No one spoke until Ris, standing in the half-open doorway, said, "Jean-Pierre Willot, Jr." The young man, sitting with the three other Korvettes people, blanched. But he rallied, sat up straighter, and glared at the obvious consternation directed at him. "Yes," he said, "I will be in charge."

There was no response or encouragement around the table. "Yes," he repeated, "I will be in charge. I am zee vice chairman of Korvettes. And *mon père*, my fahzair, he is zee president of zee board of Agache-Willot."

After some silence, the bankers demanded another meeting on Friday. On Thursday, Ris returned to his office and cleaned out his desk. On Friday, as they assembled again at the Empire State Building, J-P Jr. was asked, "Tell us your plan, please."

"We have no plan at zis time," said the young man, "but my fahzair, he will come here next week or zee week aftair."

Two of the lender representatives almost exploded with rage. They turned to consult heatedly with each other as J-P Jr. and the three Korvettes' executives sat stony-faced. Five minutes later, a banker who acted as spokesman declared, "That won't do, Mr. Willot. If he is not here on Monday, we will appoint a trustee for Korvettes. Or, as an alternative, we want Joe Ris back to operate the company."

"I will have to speak to my fahzair."

The banks' spokesman nodded. "Of course. But we want a meeting again at the same time on Monday."

Jean-Pierre phoned his father that afternoon. He told the older man, "They said that they want to put a trustee in charge."

"Never!"

"Or they want Joe Ris back."

"Over my dead body!"

Later that afternoon, on the advice of Steven Mann, Korvettes' outside attorney, the son phoned Lille again and told his father that the best alternative that the American lawyers suggested was that Korvettes file for court protection under the Chapter XI provisions of the United States Code. This would allow the retail chain to stave off any suits from creditors while it continued to operate and prepare a schedule of payment of its debts.

J-P Sr. agreed. That weekend, Mann and Harris Levin of Levin and Weintraub, the law firm in New York long identified with bankruptcy proceedings, worked deep into each morning to complete all the detailed documents necessary for the XI filing. Just about when they were ready, J-P Jr., who had been up late, received a phone call from his father. "I have changed my mind," J-P Sr. said. "I do not want an XI. I am afraid that if we have it in Korvettes, the obligations will be such that the whole company will have to be bank-rupted."

The son was stunned. "Then the bankers will want to have a trustee," he said.

"We cannot deal with him."

"Then—?"

"That is what I have been thinking."

It was almost 12:30 and the phone, Ris noticed vaguely, was still ringing. He guessed that it had been ringing for about a half-hour, off and on. He stretched. It was a great luxury, being able to laze about from Thursday through Monday, after the toughest three months or so of his life. He got up and went to the phone.

"Joe?"

"Yes."

"It is me," said J-P Jr.

"How are you, Jean-Pierre?"

"Fine. Joe—?"

"Yes?"

"We want you to come back. I am terribly sorry what happened. But you are zee the only one who can pull it together. Please—"

"Thank you. That makes me feel good. But is it just your idea or is your father in agreement, too?"

"He wants you to come back as soon as possible," J-P Jr. said. "If you agree, he plans to send someone from Lille to make his apologies. And to sweeten your return."

The next morning, Tuesday, Ris received a visit in River-dale from Robert Maze-Sencier, the assistant to J-P Sr., and soon to become director of Christian Dior. Maze-Sencier

was very gracious, apologized profusely for the embarrassment the company had caused Ris and, as Ris put it, "put
some money on the table."

He returned to his desk that same afternoon. But J-P Sr.
didn't come to New York until ten days later.

In the meantime, the situation was dire. Immediately
after the parent company had spurned the offer Ris had
arranged with them, the banks had seized $6 million in
deposits that the retail chain had with them. The day Ris
returned, on August 12, Korvettes suspended all consumer
credit transactions, not only on bank credit cards but on its
own card. This was done, according to Ris, to keep the
company's revenues out of the hands of the banks. Credit
sales normally involve cash reimbursement from banks for
each sale. But Korvettes' banks were taking money ear-
marked for the chain and using it instead to retire debt. In
addition, the banks had accelerated the repayment schedule
for the $57 million in loans that Korvettes held with them.

At Bankers Trust Company, a spokesman said that the
bank and two others which had taken over Korvettes' deposits planned no further immediate action. "We are awaiting
the new proposal on the debt repayment from Korvettes'
French owners in a day or two." But the talk of a voluntary
bankruptcy action in the form of a Chapter XI or even the
enforced Chapter X hovered over the company. Few suppliers were shipping to the company and Ris worked on the
strong contacts he had made with the vendors. During those
earlier months, he and Michael Sherman, the new vice
president and treasurer, had held a constant series of meetings with about 1,000 suppliers, 20 to 50 at a time, to tell
them about the "attractive" financial restructing that they
had worked out with the main lenders. Agache-Willot
planned to put in another $15 million, the vendors were told,
while the banks were foregoing 55 percent of the debt in order

to obtain a share in the profits. That would mean not only a stronger line of financing—both the banks and Agache-Willot's—but much less debt service or interest on a lower amount of debt and a lower cost of servicing credit cards arranged with Citibank Financial Corporation.

The suppliers had been responsive, some even enthusiastic, in meetings in New York and Chicago. As Burt Sloane, an independent sales agent who sold housewares and related items to Korvettes and who had been at a Chicago meeting said, "There was some real hope among the producers. Ris made a good impression and a strong presentation. Still, there was skepticism about whether Korvettes would make it. But almost everyone seemed willing to go along."

But events over that long weekend with the banks' seizure of assets and Ris's resignation had taken the heart out of the suppliers. "Those first days that I came back," Ris recalled, "were quite discouraging. We had, by arousing vendor cooperation, raised their daily shipments to Korvettes from a mere $2 million a week cash-on-delivery, to $10 million by the end of July, pay in 30 days. But after I was back, few of the vendors were shipping us. We still had thirty stores and very little fresh merchandise."

Awaiting the arrival of J-P Sr., Ris huddled day after day with his "trade cabinet," as well as the other executives in his dwindling crew. The total corporate staff had been cut by more than half to about 130. Early in his tenure, he had closed the lavish offices and suites on West 33rd Street and transferred the corporate offices to the top floors of the Korvettes' store at Herald Square. There, he carried on the business of the company, still maintaining the huge chief executive's desk that Bassine, Brous, and Mathieu had used. His "trade cabinet," an unusual device perhaps emblematic of his admitted lack of knowledge about retailing and the supplying industries, consisted of a four-man task force of consultants. They were Al Cohen, Al Vogel, Jim Lynch, and Pierre Cort. All knew the various industries that supplied Korvettes and acted as a liaison between the chain and its vendors. Ed Doyle, another consultant who worked independently with Ris, was another matter. He and Ris had worked well together in the past when the Korvettes' chairman had been associated with Chrysler Motors in Detroit and later with Chrysler International in Paris. There, Ris had been instrumental in helping to forge the large, life-saving investment Renault Motors made in Chrysler. Doyle, according to Ris, was an astute negotiator and creative consultant who helped him to "strategize" the campaign with the vendors.

The consultant-cabinet, though consisting of generally unprepossessing, short, dour men smoking big cigars, became helpful in making Korvettes credible to the supplying trades. In effect, it proved to be an innovative concept since he trusted them, listened to them, and found their efforts productive.

But now, they were as frustrated as Ris was and found it difficult not to feel helpless.

Hopelessness, however, was a luxury that they, as well as anyone in a nutcracker situation such as their's, could not afford. Ris continued to exhort the creditors, the banks for forebearance, while keeping in constant touch with Agache-Willot. Three days after he had returned to Korvettes, Ris announced that a framework for a new agreement had been put together with the three lead banks and Prudential Insurance. Under the terms tentatively reached, the lenders offered to repay to Korvettes the funds that they had frozen the week before and Agache-Willot agreed to make a "substantial" cash contribution to Korvettes.

The arrangement also called for the $57.2 million outstanding debt of Korvettes to be acquired by an affiliate of the French company. Agache-Willot will then give the lenders an immediate partial payment with the balance due January 2, 1981. The agreement was subject to the approval of Agache-Willot's board and the French securities authority.

Ris, much encouraged by the willingness of J-P Sr. to make a further investment in Korvettes, said that the cash contribution was of a sufficient amount that "will fully restore trade confidence in the company." Korvettes also resumed the acceptance of credit cards and resumed accepting shipments from suppliers at its Bayonne, N.J., distribution center. During the disastrous long weekend, Korvettes lawyers had advised the action so as not to run the risk of accepting goods when the company's financial position was so uncertain.

As always, Ris and his men went from the emotional depths to euphoria with each of Agache-Willot's positive decisions. But the banks and especially the creditors remained skeptical. Even two days later when Agache-Willot notified Korvettes that it had received final approval from the French authorities to transfer funds, amounting to between $26 million and $28 million, to repay the lenders in cash, the skepticism lingered. Vendors continued to hold back on most shipments and it began to appear that Korvettes had already missed out on most of the important back-to-school selling season.

But while the doubt and tight faces persisted outside, within Korvettes' corporate offices on the eighth floor of the Herald Square store hope and some smiles were evident. Ris and Michael Sherman, the thirty-three-year-old vice president-treasurer who had been an audit manager at Coopers and Lybrand, the certified public accountants, showed their pride by noting that Korvettes ability to avoid a Chapter XI filing, however close it came to it on the long weekend, was unprecedented for a large company in such a difficult situation. It was entirely reasonable, Ris insisted, that Korvettes could yet become a viable retailer by operating as a sixteen-store cluster in the New York metropolitan area and by returning to its discount roots. True, the sale of many of the leases of the closed thirty-two stores lagged but that was simply a matter of time and no doubt of the advent of more confidence about Korvettes in general.

On August 27, the day after the announcement of the approved transfer of funds, J-P Jr. resigned his post as Korvettes' vice chairman but would remain in New York as a representative of Agache-Willot which also operated the Ted Lapidus boutique and the Christian Dior wholesale operation in the city. No reason was given for the move. But several sources inside Korvettes indicated that the young scion had ruffled too many feathers there, including Ris's, and his father had agreed that the son would give up his official capacity at Korvettes.

Six days later—September 2, 1980—the biggest bombshell and most dramatic reversal by Agache-Willot were delivered in a single announcement in Paris. Much afflicted by reverses at its Boussac-Saint Frères textile subsidiary, Agache-Willot said that it was seeking to sell Korvettes. The company said that it had decided that the American retailer was "a bad investment, made worse by the American recession and high interest rates." Plans were being made "to find a way of disposing of Korvettes in the most advantageous manner possible," added a French spokesman.

The announcement clashed directly with a statement made only a few months earlier by Jean-Pierre Willot, Sr., when he had stated that Agache-Willot planned to make Korvettes profitable within three years. The parent company spokesman also said in Paris on September 2 that Agache-Willot planned to dismiss 1,000 workers at Boussac and to sell real estate in a further effort to resolve its financial difficulties. Two years earlier, the French company had acquired the bankrupt empire of Marcel Boussac, but had managed only to increase the red ink which that textile-and-apparel maker was spewing forth.

In New York, Ris, Sherman, and the others reacted with shock. That same day, they continued to meet into the early evening with the three main banks. The meeting had been scheduled for Korvettes to make the promised cash payment. Some close to the negotiations conjectured that Agache-Willot may have decided to time its announcement that particular day in order to gain some bargaining power with the American bankers by taking decisive action on its financial situation.

But even the next day, September 3, when Korvettes formally announced the agreement with the lenders in which it would repay $28 million of the $57.2 million debt—the rest to be forgiven—it appeared to be an anticlimax. A check for $10 million from Agache was turned over to the lenders at the end of the day. The French also agreed to pay an additional $5 million on October 15, $5 million on November 15, and $2 million on January 2, 1981. In addition, it was agreed that the banks would retain the $6 million they had appropriated in deposits.

The damage, however, had been done. Shipments still came in only at a trickle. Most suppliers had reverted to shipping what goods they elected to only on a cash-on-delivery basis. Estimates were that Korvettes owed its suppliers about $28 million. As to performance, the chain was in a deep trough. It was estimated that it had an operating loss of about $35 million in the first half of 1980 and a loss of about $18 million in the last ten months of 1979. And current cash flow was at a minimum.

On September 8, after a series of back-and-forth tele-

phone calls from New York to Lille, Ris called a press conference to announce that Korvettes would reduce its number
of stores and staff by 50 percent. There were still thirty-one
generally functioning stores, so that only about sixteen
would remain open, mostly in the metropolitan area, while
1,800 employees would be discharged, mostly those working
in the stores to be closed and about 100 employees in the
corporate office.

The remaining stores would continue to operate "at
least" through the rest of the year. In the meantime, Korvettes had appointed the Schottenstein Brothers of Colum-
bus, professional liquidators, to help it sell the goods in all
thirty-one stores. All the stores would close the next day,
Tuesday, September 9, for inventory-taking and then reopen
for a mass, public sale.

Under the arrangement with Schottenstein, the liquidator would immediately pay Korvettes a portion of the guaranteed proceeds and the remainder from the sale's proceeds. Ris said that Schottenstein will buy goods of Korvettes valued at $60 million at retail for $25 million and sell it
to the public. After that, both Korvettes and Schottenstein
will buy new merchandise to restock the stores totaling
about half of Korvettes' normal weekly needs.

Korvettes plans to pay its trade creditors "in full," Ris
went on. This would involve payment of 30 to 40 cents on the
dollar within thirty days and the balance over six to twelve
months.

Several retailers, including Allied Stores Corporation,
Caldor Inc., Vornado Inc., and Alexander's Inc., have expressed interest in the Korvette store sites. But, complained
Ris, "They want only to cherry-pick our best ones and leave
us with only the unattractive ones."

The combined moves appeared to everyone at the press
meeting to be a clear prelude to going out of business. Ris

and Sherman were obviously putting on some bravado in the face of disaster. I glanced curiously at John Cook, Korvettes' spokesman, who responded with a shrug. Everyone seemed to be ignoring the corpse, but there was blood, lots of it, on the floor.

It was not long after that point—a matter of a few weeks—that I was asked to do this book. As a newspaper reporter and later as author, I had followed Korvettes since 1962, or for almost two decades. Yet while I had written easily a hundred stories in the New York *Herald Tribune* and later in *The New York Times* about the company and reported on it in depth in one of my books, I felt that the new assignment required much additional reporting, interviewing, and analysis. What was missing in my prior reportage, I decided, were the connecting links, the tissues and ligaments, between the actions, as well as the motivations which compelled the principals to do as they did.

I started then as Korvettes began its final phaseout. The sixteen stores in the New York area and thirteen out-of-town generally reopened within a week to ten days after inventory taking was begun. Schottenstein engaged the Sam Nassi Company, of Beverly Hills, a well-known liquidator as subcontractor, for the sales in the twenty-nine Korvettes' stores. Customer response for the first week or so was strong but it quickly fell into a plateau. After two weeks, eleven of the stores closed permanently and eighteen units, mostly in the New York area, continued to operate through December 24, 1980. None of the stores reopened in 1981, with the exception of the Herald Square store which under the Schottenstein aegis continued business there as "Vet City," a socalled bargain outlet.

In pursuing my reporting and interviewing starting in

late fall of 1980, I found that psychologically all the principals I spoke to had for months already regarded Korvettes' demise as an operating retailer a foregone conclusion. To some, like Ferkauf, the connection had ceased fourteen years earlier. Dave Brous, then in litigation with Korvettes and Arlen to reclaim remuneration due him, still felt the wounds of being superseded by an executive of a company that had bought out Korvettes from under him. Arthur Cohen tried not to be critical of the French but it was obvious that he was when he insisted that "they bought a healthy company." Others, such as Bob Warner, Mel Friedman, Leo Cohen, Dave Rothfeld, Herb Ricklin, as well as still others who asked not be identified, sadly took the posture that mistakes compounded had simply doomed a company that in its formative years appeared to be headed for the stars. Hence, much of the tracking back, or interviewing after the fact, drew out a combination of the negative, the nostalgic, and the regretful.

"It comes back to me from different directions, K mart is one, that we were the precursors at Korvettes," observed Eugene Ferkauf. "We showed the way, maybe, and that's good to know. When I sold out to Charley Bassine, that was the end. Was it the right move in retrospect? You can't look back. It was a judgment of the time.

"The one complaint I have about 'E. J'," he went on, referring to the designation of the company as he had known it, "was that they never called me, even in the midst of all their troubles. Retailing is a people business, not a science, but a love of work by people in it. When I left 'E. J', I was tired mentally and physically. I never took a vacation in eighteen years. But later, I was back in good shape and available."

That aside, the sixty-year-old Ferkauf, who after leaving the company had four unsuccessful retail businesses, in what many consider a quest to demonstrate that "he can do it all over again," has another deep regret. "Our first big store was in Carle Place," he said, "and it had a separate 10,000-square-foot toy store. Why didn't we go into a separate chain like Toys R Us? We didn't realize the significance and potential of the specialty department store—toys, clothes, sporting goods, records, and books—and the catalogue showrooms. What a tragedy that was. How could we have failed to exploit the catalogue showroom—we had so many of its attributes right in our basic operation. At its inception, 'E. J.' was a catalogue showroom.

"In the 1950's, there was a retailing phenomenon—the arrival of the suburban malls. A couple of struggling merchants here and there opened a little specialty store selling budget clothes in between the big department stores at each end of the center. That was 'E. J.'s merchandise? Where were we? So there they are now—the big specialty chains, Petrie, Lerner, Brooks Fashions—these became great businesses that came from things they saw at 'E. J.'

"Amazingly, people looking in at us from the outside saw the opportunities we missed," Ferkauf said. "I feel it was a failing on my part, my biggest mistake. It was unfortunate that others in my organization didn't see it, either. Who knows where 'E. J.' could be today instead of where it is now?"

Ferkauf in 1981 has two separate businesses. One is Penfield Stores, a retail consulting and management company in New York. The other is a chain of apparel stores in the South, also known as Penfield corporately but operating under different, local names. He is a busy, at least outwardly happy man, perhaps as restless as ever but apparently more restrained with it. He is still recognized by strangers on the streets of New York, although that is certain to fade with time but he will probably remain something of a lasting legend in American retailing.

Dave Brous said he was convinced that the French floundered at Korvettes because "they had no merchandising philosophy. The good management had left or been asked to leave," he said. "They let all the good help go in the stores and allowed stocks to run down." He was asked, perhaps simplistically, who were the principal villains and heroes in the unhappy Korvettes saga. "I consider Jean-Pierre Willot, Sr., the villain," he replied. "And I think Gene Ferkauf was the hero. There were a lot of guys between Ferkauf and Willot who were something of both. But I like to think that Dave Brous tried his damndest to turn Korvettes into a real professional business that could have survived."

Brous, who, at this writing, was seeking a retail business that he could buy and run, received $200,000 as a "finder's fee" from Arlen Realty & Development for helping in the sale of Korvettes to Agache-Willot. That action to reward Korvettes' president was later defended by Arthur Cohen as "something we thought Dave deserved because of all the work he put in to make the sale." After leaving Korvettes, Brous sued Korvettes and Arlen for unpaid future remuneration under his contract and received a relatively small, court-ordered settlement of $320,000.

After a number of requests and a delayed response, Arthur Cohen agreed to an interview on March 30, 1981. It was to this writer a relatively surprising discussion since his manner was so remote from the actual dire situation in which Korvettes was involved.

"I ran a private real-estate company and had to make a decision as to whether to remain private, go public, be acquired by a major corporation like I.T.T. acquired Levitt & Sons, or acquire a retail company and go public," Cohen said. "With our depreciation and carryforward of interest, there was synergism in that we could shelter a retailer's taxes and profits. That was one aspect of merging with Korvettes. And as a shopping-center developer and with Korvettes in a heavy expansion program, that would help us, too. We had built twenty-five of the stores that they occupied so we knew something about Korvettes. And Korvettes' management felt that the additional cash flow from real estate would benefit their cash flow and help their expansion.

"It made a lot of sense then for us to merge with Spartans and Korvettes," he continued. "The charges of nepotism didn't bother me. My record stood for itself.

"We made Korvettes a separate corporation so it could not be branded with our troubles. The retail stores started showing some good progress. Korvettes was a solid, viable chain up to the time it was sold. We had to sell it because the capital requirements to bring it to its potential required more than we were prepared to put into it. The question was how big you wanted to make it, to get it to its maximum, but it was obvious that new funds were needed.

"Agache-Willot had a desire to be in the U.S. They had turned several European chains around and made them very viable," Cohen added. "We came close to a deal with W. R. Grace but the French were ready to close. And when Agache-Willot bought Korvettes, it was trending very well. But, unfortunately, it got caught up with a tough retail environment, the gas crunch, and a historically high prime rate of 20 percent. Credit business was badly affected. And then Agache-Willot put in new management and got rid of some really fine people who knew the business. It was a good company that, in my opinion, should have been able to keep afloat in good or bad times."

The failure of the Korvettes stores to reopen after Christmas 1980 was not the final chapter in the company's amazing story. A further irony was yet to come.

Concerned by the continuing problems of Boussac-Saint-Frères, and Agache-Willot's apparent inability to solve them by allowing Boussac to file for bankruptcy in Lille, that city's Tribunal of Commerce appointed an independent administrator to head Agache-Willot. Beginning June 28, 1981, Albert Chassagnon assumed control of the Group's assets and funds. The implication was that Agache-Willot was so strapped—Boussac alone said it needed $70 million a month in order to remain in business—that it would be forced to sell some of its key divisions, including Au Bon Marché, the Paris department store, and Conforama, the home-furnishings chain.

On July 6, the French Labor Minister announced in Paris that the financial problems of Agache-Willot were of such dimensions that the new Socialist government of François Mitterand might make funds available to bail out both Boussac and Agache-Willot.

In the meantime, Administrator Chassagnon moved to arrange a sweeping reorganization that would involve not only unprofitable but profitable arms of the Agache-Willot empire. And in the process, he froze the transfer of any funds outside of France.

For Joseph Ris, the financial debacle was academic at that point. He had left the company a month before and had been succeeded by Charles Herlin, a career Agache-Willot executive.

On July 16, 1981, squeezed by the turning off of the money faucet from Paris so that it could not pay $7.3 million in trade debt, $6.8 million in expenses and taxes, and other obligations, Korvettes, Inc., finally filed for Chapter XI proceedings. After four mergers, the discharge of more than 11,000 employees, and the closing of all its fifty-eight stores,

Korvettes said it was insolvent to the tune of $113.4 million in debts with only $27 million in assets.

The final irony was that it was Agache-Willot which pushed Korvettes into bankruptcy, not the reverse as the French company had feared.

But by then, the action was only the anticlimax to an anticlimax. Korvettes had already passed into legend.

INDEX

Index